The publisher gratefully acknowledges the generous support
of the Authors Imprint Endowment Fund
of the University of California Press Foundation,
which was established to support exceptional scholarship
by first-time authors.

Savage Frontier

Savage Frontier

Making News and Security
on the Argentine Border

Ieva Jusionyte

UNIVERSITY OF CALIFORNIA PRESS

University of California Press, one of the most
distinguished university presses in the United States,
enriches lives around the world by advancing scholarship
in the humanities, social sciences, and natural sciences.
Its activities are supported by the UC Press Foundation
and by philanthropic contributions from individuals
and institutions. For more information, visit www
.ucpress.edu.

University of California Press
Oakland, California

Library of Congress Cataloging-in-Publication Data

Jusionyte, Ieva, 1983– author.
    Savage frontier : making news and security on the
Argentine border / Ieva Jusionyte.
        pages cm
    Includes bibliographical references and index.
    ISBN 978-0-520-28351-0 (cloth)
    ISBN 978-0-520-28647-4 (pbk.)
    ISBN 978-0-520-95937-8 (ebook)
    1. Crime—Tri-Border Area (Argentina, Brazil, and
Paraguay)   2. Crime—Press coverage—Tri-Border
Area (Argentina, Brazil, and Paraguay)   3. Security,
International—Tri-Border Area (Argentina, Brazil, and
Paraguay)   4. Border security—Tri-Border Area
(Argentina, Brazil, and Paraguay)   I. Title.
    HV6878.5.J87 2015
    364.1098—dc23

                                        2014048461

24 23 22 21 20 19 18 17 16 15
10 9 8 7 6 5 4 3 2 1

To my family

Contents

Acknowledgments

I did not write this book alone. Writing it has led to unexpected encounters, thrived on mentorship, forged friendships. Many people helped me along the way. Although I cannot name here everyone who has contributed, I would like to thank those without whom this book would not have been possible.

First and foremost, I am grateful to the Argentine and Paraguayan journalists who accepted me into their ranks—as a researcher, a colleague. and a friend. This book is *for* them as much as it is *about* them. Kelly Ferreyra, the editor-in-chief of *La Voz de Cataratas,* was the one who introduced me to Puerto Iguazú and welcomed me into her family. Proudly, she showed me the beauty of the town by the waterfalls, and she guided me through the intricacies of making news on the margins of the state. Throughout the years we have known each other, she criticized me and she tried to protect me from dangers, which—as I soon learned—came in forms I would have least expected. Yet she cared for me even when I ignored her warnings and when, scarred and scared, I would come back to her for advice. She was patient and understanding. She was passionate and critical. She was the best and the worst research participant. She is a good friend now. Silvia Martínez was learning how to be a journalist at the same time that I was acquiring the skills of an ethnographer. With her, we crisscrossed Iguazú in search of news. Often, we left home early in the morning, when the barrios were still covered in cold mist, sipping *mate* to keep us warm and eating *chipas* sold on street corners. Hopeful to get information, we waited for hours at the doors of government offices, bonding over discoveries and frustrations of media work in a small border town. She became a *compañera* with whom I shared the most unlikely experiences. Javier Rotela was my partner in *Proximidad,* an independent television program that we made together and that taught me more about the backstage of journalism than I could have ever learned as an outsider. Javier had a critical stance toward local issues and local media, and his commitment to do better inspired and motivated me. Javier Villegas, Hugo López, Yanina Faria, Pablo Longo, Andrés Colmán Gutiérrez, Mariquita Torres, Jorgelina Bonetto, Ernesto Azarkevich, Horacio Valdés, Darío Chamorro, Jorge Taglioli, Viviana Villar, Mario Antonowicz, Oscar Perrone, and others invited me to take part in their routines of making news on the border, and I am grateful to every one of them for sharing with me their knowledge and their time. I would also like to thank people who were not journalists yet whose backing and friendship was invaluable while I lived in Argentina: Melina Astroza, Germán Montalvo, Diego Riquelme and the Riquelme family in Iguazú and in Santa Ana.

This book has benefited immensely from the feedback and critical commentary offered by my academic mentors and colleagues. Above all, I'd like to thank Elizabeth E. Ferry, who, as a good advisor, often understood my ideas before I could articulate them. She showed me how to grasp the theoretical implications of my work, pushing me to rethink the relationship between violence, media, and the state. More than that, as an attentive mentor, she went far beyond her obligations to help me out in times of crisis. Other fellow anthropologists have generously supported me in different stages of this work. I am particularly grateful to Kay B. Warren, who in 2008 invited me to attend her weekly seminar on violence, governance, and transnationalism at Brown University, where many of the ideas for this book took shape, and who has encouraged me ever since. I also want to thank Joe Heyman, M. Gabriela Torres, Daniel M. Goldstein, Catherine Lutz, Dominic Boyer, Rebecca Galemba, Kedron Thomas, and Amahl Bishara for their constructive insights on parts of this book and for much-needed backing when our paths crossed at conferences and whenever I turned to them for guidance. In Lithuania, I was fortunate to know Gintautas Mažeikis, Algis Mickūnas, and Reid Raud. During college years conversations with them sparked my intellectual curiosity, and they supported my application for the Fulbright Scholarship that would set me off on a journey to become an anthropologist in the U.S. Their help and encouragement have been crucial in my pursuits as a scholar ever since.

I wrote *Savage Frontier* at two academic institutions, both of which I regard as my home. At Brandeis University, discussions with faculty and fellow graduate students at the Department of Anthropology, where I completed my dissertation, helped formulate my interests in borders, violence, and the media. In particular I want to thank Charles Golden, Sarah Lamb, and David Jacobson for their feedback on my initial research proposal and other writings, and Laurel Carpenter for her assistance with so many things. My peers in the anthropology PhD program—Melanie Kingsley, Bryce Davenport, Anna Jaysane-Darr, Rachana Agarwal, Ryo Morimoto, Casey Miller, Mrinalini Tankha, and Casey Golomski—have read pieces of the manuscript and provided helpful comments, but, more importantly, I'm grateful to them for being there for me during the difficult parts of fieldwork and in its aftermath. Anna and Melanie also proofread earlier versions of the manuscript. Bryce drew the maps.

At the University of Florida, the Department of Anthropology and the Center for Latin American Studies have provided me with ideal working conditions, including a course reduction and a faculty research award, which enabled me to finish this book. I am grateful to Philip Williams and Susan deFrance for these opportunities and for their ongoing support. Since I joined the University of Florida as a new faculty member in 2012, I have benefited from the intellectual companionship of my colleagues in anthropology and Latin American Studies, who pushed me to think broader and reach further. Above all, I would like to thank Richard Kernaghan and Charles Wood for discussing my texts in their classrooms and for giving me critical feedback and advice. While I was writing the manuscript, the interdisciplinary Crime, Law, and Governance in the Americas working group was a productive space for engaging with questions of law and order. Our conversations motivated me to work through moments of doubt and uncertainty. Richard Phillips from the Latin American Collection and Jessie Franey, my wonderful research assistant at the Center for Latin American Studies, both helped me find background information for the book. I relied on timely assistance from Karen Jones and Margarita Gandia for travel and administrative matters. Research for the book was funded by the Center for Latin American Studies Faculty Research Award at the University of Florida, the Mellon Dissertation Research Grant, and, at Brandeis University, Jane's Travel Grant for Latin American Studies, the Department of Anthropology's Graduate Travel Research Grant, and the Provost Award.

I am particularly indebted to my editor at the University of California Press, Kate Marshall, for her amazing work at making this manuscript into a book. Her enthusiasm and dedication gave me confidence to finish writing it in a timely manner, and she has been on top of things at every stage of the publishing process. Stacy Eisenstark and Kate Hoffman guided the manuscript through revisions to completion. I am grateful to Sue Carter for her skillful copyediting of the text and to Andy Christenson for preparing the index. The feedback I received from Winifred Tate, Daniel M. Goldstein, and two anonymous reviewers for UC Press has been most helpful in improving the earlier draft.

Finally, I would not have written this book without the unconditional support of my family and friends. Over the years of research and travel they provided me with company and shelter, with compassion and motivation. They patiently listened to my stories and offered much-needed advice. I knew I could rely on them no matter what. A thank you to Henry Rivera, Mary Risner, Rachana and Sachin Agarwal, Arto Suren, Burcu Yücesoy, Jesse Modican, Goda Jurevičiūtė, Aistė Marozaitė, Deividas Šlekys, Vytis Jurkonis, Justinas Dementavičius, Vykintas Pugačiauskas, Stephan Brunner, and Simon Pützstück won't be enough to express my appreciation of our enduring bonds. My parents, my brother, and my grandparents in Lithuania have been supportive of the path I have chosen as a scholar. Even though at times they were concerned about my safety and well-being in places far away from home, it was their love, their sharp criticism, and their honest encouragement that enabled me to get through difficult periods of research and writing. I am grateful for their patience and understanding. Free-minded intellectuals and dedicated civic actors, they have inspired me to pursue my goals in academia as in life. It is to them that I dedicate this book.

Introduction

Hide-and-Seek

Information flows from Puerto Iguazú. It appears in the news because of tourism to the Iguazú Falls, a UNESCO natural heritage site, and because it is a border area where three countries meet. Although many things happen in Ciudad del Este, Paraguay, and in Foz do Iguaçu, Brazil, the media talk about the Triple Frontier as a single news-generating center, enclosing the three cities, confusing them, locating Iguazú in Paraguay; they even make mistakes when publishing photographs. This is what sells. The vast majority of the media edits news stories from their desks and unfortunately never sets foot in this place. There are many other issues that could put us in the news—abandonment of the indigenous people, land scarcity, misuse of government funds, corruption, lack of doctors who all migrate to Brazil—but these problems don't attract the attention of the national media. My work is a constant challenge because I live this reality, I feel this reality, and I suffer or enjoy it more than anyone else. To make news in Puerto Iguazú *es remar contra la corriente* [is paddling upstream]. On the one hand, we care for and protect the tourist destination; on the other hand, the reality often surpasses our own expectations.

—Kelly Ferreyra[1]

UNDER ARREST

Numerous clandestine paths, colloquially known as *piques,* descend down the forested slopes to the clearings on the rivers that separate Argentina from its neighboring countries: Paraguay to the west, and Brazil to the north. Despite being well known to law enforcement—agents have a name for each—piques are widely used by smugglers and traffickers, who avoid identity checks and customs inspection at authorized border posts by using the paths. One of these paths runs off the main road over Tancredo Neves International Bridge, which connects Brazilian Foz do Iguaçu with Argentine Puerto Iguazú. It leads through the jungle, evading the border checkpoint, located a few hundred yards further south on the national highway. It was on this pique that one morning in August 2007 agents of the Argentine National Gendarmerie detained several men. Among them was Ronnie Arias, the host of a popular Argentine investigative television program, and his colleagues from a media company in Buenos Aires. In addition to the journalists, the gendarmerie arrested eight *motoqueros*—bikers who make a living by transporting contraband goods from Brazil to Argentina. The journalists were filming their clandestine ride with the biker-smugglers to document "how a group of people easily crossed the border without being checked at migration control" when they were discovered and detained.[2] The gendarmerie commander told the press, "We are trying to meet people's demands for security."[3] The men were found entering the country through an unauthorized passage, which warranted their arrest, he explained.

The Buenos Aires–based media outlet was furious at the federal security forces, claiming that they had high-handedly treated a respected journalist like a criminal. "Most likely the gendarmes heated up because the guys were showing the permeability of the border," the production company told reporters of a mainstream Argentine paper.[4] The irony, as many in Iguazú pointed out, was that while the journalists from Buenos Aires expected to demonstrate the lawlessness of the border, particularly the failure of the federal forces at protecting it against contraband and their alleged complicity with smugglers, they themselves were captured. The border was not as permeable to illegal crossings as they had anticipated. The chief of the gendarmerie explained the situation in the following terms: "They [the journalists] said they were working. We are also working, and legal work triumphs over illegal trespassing."[5]

Journalists in Iguazú laughed at their *porteño* colleagues, who, they said, had no common sense about the border. In Argentina, the term "porteño" generally refers to a person who comes from Buenos Aires, but in this remote part of the country it is often used as a caricature of the metropolitan character—an ignorant and arrogant urban visitor. Years later, remembering the incident, one Iguazú reporter commented on the fate of the famous television personality: "He should have stayed in jail, *por ser tan canchero* [for being such a smartass]." To Iguazúenses, what happened to the journalists from Buenos Aires was proof that the sensational media representations of the Triple Frontier as a haven of international organized crime—including drug and human trafficking, contraband, money laundering, and terrorism—were unfounded; the coverage of the so-called *frontera caliente* (hot border) was staged.

But the porteño journalists, seeking to expose an alleged alliance between the security forces and the motoqueros, were on to something. Immediately after the incident, in a statement to the media, Ramón "Pájaro" Aranda, the delegate of the biker-smuggler union—the one group of people whose business depended on lax border control—counterintuitively stood up to defend the gendarmerie for their purportedly effective work on the border: "I've been smuggling vegetables for twenty years. There has never been an agreement with gendarmerie to let us pass. But we all know that this [contraband] is out of necessity. It's not that we want to live like this." Hinting at the social consensus that, under conditions of governmental neglect, has been forged between border residents, petty smugglers of food, and the security forces, Aranda said what others were reluctant to admit in public: "The [porteño] journalists came to *embarrar la cancha* [muddy the playing field]."[6] This "cancha," or "the field" that the motoquero invoked, is a highly regulated social playground, though only seasoned players know its unspoken rules. They are what anthropologist Michael Taussig calls "a public secret" (1999:50). Knowing what not to know in Iguazú is a powerful form of local knowledge, protected by deliberately partial exposures in the public sphere.

This confusing event provides an anchor point to explore how the production of news and the making of security on Argentina's northern border with Brazil and Paraguay are based on tactical uses of visibility and invisibility. Iguazúenses share local knowledge about common activities such as food contraband, and, despite their illegalized status, they turn a blind eye to and sometimes engage in these practices. When the television team from Buenos Aires came to "muddy the playing field" by attempting to expose the existence of complicity, local actors—motoqueros, gendarmes, and journalists—mobilized and worked together to protect what was to remain a public secret. The incident condenses several problems that this book addresses: the discrepancy between the legality of the state and legitimacy of informal economies on its margins, the exposure of some events as news stories and the concealment of others, and the underlying ambiguity of the relationship between crime, law enforcement, and the media.

Savage Frontier traces these problems to the lived experiences of people who find themselves at the frontlines of making news and making

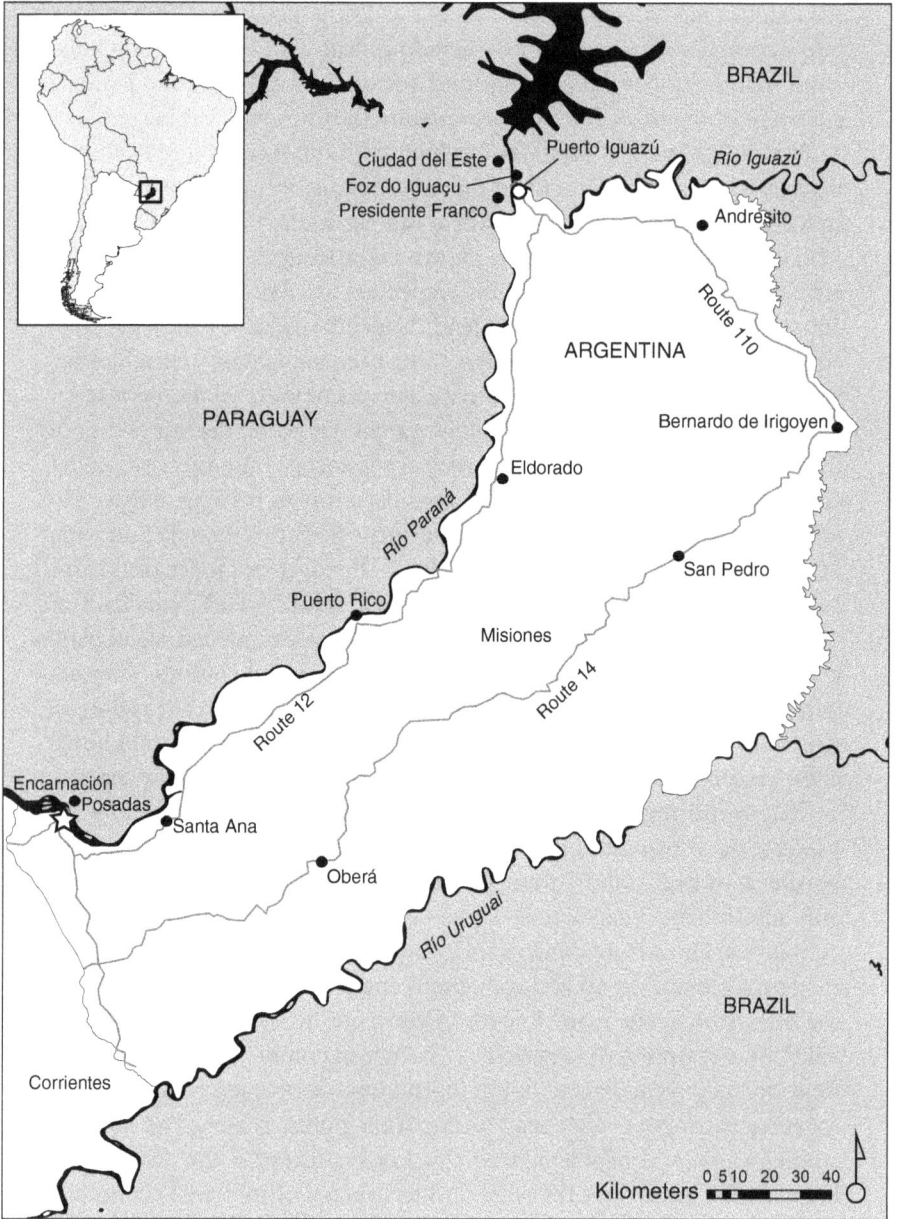

MAP 1. The tri-border region, where Argentina, Brazil, and Paraguay meet. Cartography by Bryce Davenport.

security in the tri-border region. If the construction of social legitimacy is uncoupled from the state-sanctioned dichotomy of legality and illegality, what role do news media play in conveying security as a meaningful issue on the local scale? On an allegedly lawless Argentine border, journalists maneuver between stories *for, on,* and *off the record* to tactically represent some but not other parts of their knowledge about the informal economy and illegal cross-border flows. This ethnography goes beneath the surface of government and mass media narratives that criminalize border residents to untangle the relationships that underlie the intricate knotting between security and news production from the position of those who, as gatekeepers in the circulation of news, play an active part in translating between global, national, and local discourses of security and whose daily lives are simultaneously made possible and potentially undermined by the jagged effects of security buildup.

THE DISCOURSE OF THE FRONTERA CALIENTE

The name "Triple Frontier" is often used to refer to a region that includes adjoining parts of Argentina, Brazil, and Paraguay. As a political definition, it does not apply to a bounded geographical space. Rather, the term designates a vaguely circumscribed area around the merger of two rivers, the Iguazú and the Paraná—the natural boundaries between the three countries—and encompasses the metropolitan areas of Puerto Iguazú in Argentina, Foz do Iguaçu in Brazil, and Ciudad del Este in Paraguay. Puerto Iguazú, located in the northwestern corner of the Argentine Misiones Province, is the smallest of the three neighboring towns. It was excluded from the major regional development scheme between Brazil and Paraguay: the construction of the Itaipú Hydroelectric Dam, which resulted in significant urban growth in Ciudad del Este and Foz do Iguaçu. According to the 2010 national census, Puerto Iguazú, situated eighteen kilometers from the Iguazú Falls, a UNESCO World Heritage site that attracts over a million visitors each year, had 82,227 inhabitants.[7] The waterfalls and the military installations, dating back to the beginning of the twentieth century, have been the two main foci of formal state engagement in the region. Due to the area's convenient position at the crossroads between the low tax haven in Ciudad del Este and the Brazilian and Argentine metropolises on the Atlantic coast, historically, cross-border trade—legal commerce as well as contraband and trafficking—has also played an important role in the development of the regional economy.

The discourse of the frontera caliente opposes the presumed order, or "civilization," of the Argentine state to the criminality, or "savagery," at its remote northeastern edge. Reiterated in global mass media, this narrative script circulates a fear of porous borders, where drug and human trafficking, contraband, and money laundering, allegedly used to finance terrorist operations, proceed unhindered. After the bombings of two Israeli institutions in Buenos Aires in the 1990s, and particularly following 9/11, the presumably ineffective control of Argentina's borders with Paraguay and Brazil became a global security concern. U.S.-based media, including the *New York Times,* the *Los Angeles Times,* the *New Yorker,* CNN, CBS News, and other news outlets began circulating sensationalized narratives, calling the region "a global village of outlaws," "one of the most lawless places in the world," and "a safe haven for terrorists." Evidence notwithstanding, the proliferation of these narratives produced a circular link between causes and effects, giving impetus to revised and expanded security policies. "The essential function of security," argued Michel Foucault in his lectures at the College de France, "is to respond to a reality in such a way that this response cancels out the reality to which it responds—nullifies it, or limits, checks, or regulates it" (2007:47). For Foucault, security is centrifugal, incessantly expanding by incorporating new elements and organizing ever-wider circuits. The discourse of the frontera caliente is exemplary here.

In line with the government's talk about threats, sensationalized media images stigmatizing the place and its residents legitimized the strategic deployment of law enforcement in that area.[8] The strengthening of the security apparatus correlates less with statistics of reported crimes and more with the fear of crime, and the media has been a notoriously effective tool for spreading "moral panics" (Cohen 1972). There is also a stark discrepancy between the types of crimes that are believed to be the most threatening (and thus the most easily politicized) and crimes that may be widespread but that receive little public acknowledgment. In the 1990s and especially in the early 2000s, the concern about drug trafficking and terrorism, rather than the presence of contraband and corruption, led to increased securitization and militarization in the tri-border region. Migration control and customs inspections tightened, surveillance increased, and Argentina, Brazil, and Paraguay started sharing intelligence and participating in joint military operations, supported by the United States. It is less often acknowledged that the security buildup, with its restriction of daily cross-border movements and the suppression of informal local exchanges, further disenfranchised the already marginalized population of this remote area. By negatively affecting the livelihood of local residents, government intervention further intensified their insecurity instead of reducing it.

Security—both discourse and practice—is contested and negotiated between authors and participants in its processes, which are embedded in particular political, social, and institutional settings. Rather than being immutable, the content and methods of security depend on flexible agreements between unequal sets of players, including local and national authorities, foreign governments, private entities, civil society groups, and resident communities. All understand security from the perspective of their position in relation to others. Security politics thus entails realigning multiple answers to questions about the major sources of emergent threats and about legitimate ways of responding to them. Scale, seen as the spatial dimensionality of a particular kind of view, also inflects the meaning of security. Scales are not neutral frames for viewing the world, but, as Anna Tsing wrote, "must be brought into being: proposed, practiced, and evaded, as well as taken for granted" (2005:58). Scale-making and security-making are intertwined as cultural and political projects. Security can be seen in terms of "a particular kind of fact- and scale-making" (Bubandt 2005:277), a political means of managing the ontological issue of uncertainty that produces different scales. News media provide the nexus where scales of security-making—local, national, regional, and global—converge.

Applying the transnational security agenda to the lived reality of a particular community involves mediation. For the U.S.-led global "war on terror" to reach Iguazú, it must be reconfigured against the background of regional political dynamics in Latin America, adjusted to the national agenda of the Argentine state, and reinterpreted within the contours of everyday life in a border town. *Savage Frontier* examines these processes of mediation by juxtaposing the dominant narrative about the presence of worldwide threats and the social and economic precariousness faced by border residents. By translating global and national agendas to make them meaningful in their communities, journalists take part in performing security. Never a mere representation of social reality, the media produces its effects and establishes public truth (Bishara 2012; Boyer 2006; Hasty 2006; Himpele 2008; Goldstein and Castro 2006; Jusionyte 2014; Turner 1992). Production of news is therefore crucial to the politics and practices of security.

In Iguazú, security is wedged in between global and national political agendas and people's everyday experiences of crime, violence, and other forms of social vulnerability. In his foundational text on the anthropology of security, Daniel Goldstein (2010:492; see also 2012:15) wrote about the urgency to understand "the multiple ways in which security is configured and deployed—not only by states and authorized speakers but by communities, groups, and individuals—in their engagements with other local actors and with arms of the state itself." Examining the production of knowledge as a contested process and looking at media's complementary roles in making news and making security, *Savage Frontier* combines an ethnographic study of journalism with a critical anthropology of security. Journalists are positioned at the nexus of scales of security and act as mediators between the government and their community. Focusing on them, this book explores the multifaceted and shifting ways that media production and security-making on the local level intersect.

BETWEEN VOICE AND SILENCE

When in 2008, a year after the reporters from Buenos Aires were arrested while trespassing the border with the motoqueros, I arrived in Iguazú to begin ethnographic fieldwork, people regarded me with the same suspicion that they directed toward investigative journalists. For over a century there have been many of us, outsiders, coming to the region to write about its exotic nature, its savage and illiterate people, its insidious lawlessness, and, most recently, its harboring of terrorists. Scarred by the harmful consequences of these spectacular stories circulating around the world, Iguazúenses were wary. From their experience, narratives of the "savage frontier" elicited deleterious state effects, including strict legal and economic regulations, surveillance, and rigorous border enforcement. In contrast, governmental neglect of the remote town, resulting in infrastructural inadequacies that caused repeated power outages, land scarcity, and corruption, among other palpable results of structural violence, did not have a place in national and global mediascapes. The mainstream press advanced the agenda of the Argentine government on the "savage frontier": instead of improving social and economic conditions that legitimized the persistence of unlawful practices, the state reacted to the popular stories of the frontera caliente by further strengthening its security apparatus. It is not difficult to understand how, to prevent the production of exaggerated stories that rendered the border legible to the national and global publics through the lens of crime, people in Iguazú developed skepticism and mistrust toward outsiders.

Not surprisingly, my initial interest in how journalists managed dangerous assignments in a violent border region was understood as an accusation. Iguazúenses criticized me for taking erroneous media discourses for granted and, defensive about their lives on the border, tried to prove the inaccuracy of my assumptions. My fiercest critic, who later became my dearest friend, was Kelly Ferreyra, the editor of the local paper *La Voz de Cataratas (Voice of the Waterfalls)*. The day that a plane from Buenos Aires brought me to Iguazú for the first time, she met me at a small, centrally located hostel that I had chosen as my temporary home while exploring my future fieldsite. I remember that Kelly took me to a restaurant on the corner down the street, where we sat outdoors watching the slow movement of motor scooters and cars, and I told her my motive for coming to Iguazú. Everything I knew about this place at that time was from the media—mostly adventure and horror stories about the porous borders and rampant lawlessness. The Triple Frontier was nowhere near as prominent in the news headlines as the U.S.-Mexico border, where journalists who reported on the escalating "war on drugs" were risking their lives. Yet, from what I had read about this South American region, organized crime and other illegal activities—from drug trafficking to money laundering to contraband— were flourishing here. Foreign visitors were warned to take precautions, which in the beginning made me question my own safety. This uncertainty was what drew me to this place. I planned to study how concerns about violence and crime in the Triple Frontier affected the daily work of local journalists like Kelly in order to understand, on a larger scale, how security conditioned news production.

By then Kelly had worked in Iguazú media for two decades, her career trajectory winding across the volatile, shifting terrain of border journalism, from radio to television to print. "Soy una periodista todo terreno" (I am an all-terrain journalist), she told me many times. She agreed to show me what being a journalist in the tri-border area was like, and the following evening I had my first Argentine-style *asado,* a barbecue, considered the country's national dish, in her home, which was soon to become my own. Kelly was a passionate and determined instructor about life on the border who taught me to question the terms through which I knew the region. "Triple Frontera?!" she exclaimed, disappointed, when in one of our early conversations I used this phrase to describe my project. The Spanish word "frontera" can be translated both as "border" and "frontier"—two terms with markedly different connotations in English: a border is a formalized boundary line between territorial jurisdictions of

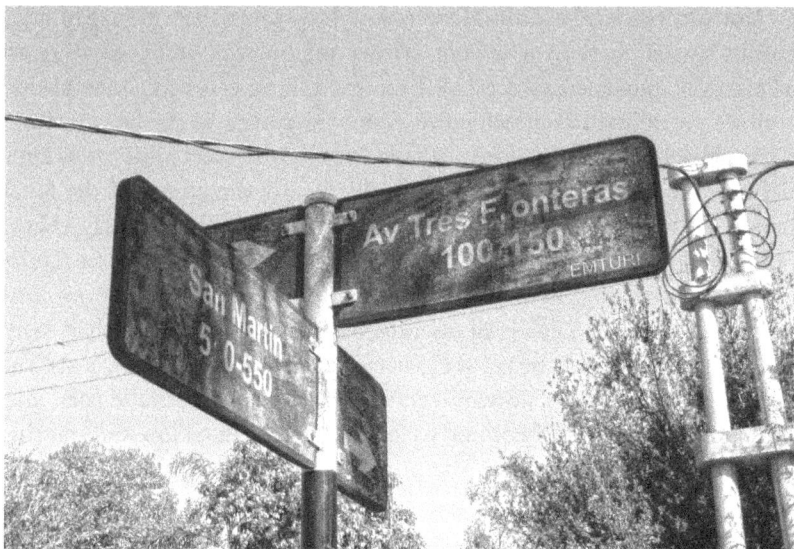

FIGURE 1. Street sign for Tres Fronteras Avenue, Puerto Iguazú, August 2008. All photos by the author unless indicated otherwise.

two states, while a frontier is a more flexible space between domains of strong state control. As a subjective, political definition of geographical space, a frontier is often seen as a zone of disorder (e.g., Donnan and Wilson 1999; Hannerz 1997; Kopytoff 1987; Prescott 1987; Turner 1962 [1893]). When applied to the border area between Argentina, Brazil, and Paraguay, the name "Triple Frontera" invokes the lawlessness of the frontier, accompanied by an invitation of conquest.

Whether she talked or wrote about her home region, like many Iguazúenses, Kelly rejected this ambivalent and discursively loaded phrase. Instead, she preferred to use the more descriptive "Tres Fronteras" (three borders), which is also the name of the street that leads from the town's main plaza to the border landmark at the merger of the Iguazú and Paraná Rivers, where Argentina, Brazil, and Paraguay meet. After Kelly expressed her concern with the term, I never asked people to tell me about the "Triple Frontera" again; instead, I used alternative descriptions of the border zone. But despite my conscious efforts to avoid this charged term, people would mention it in nearly every conversation. It was impossible to talk about crime and security in the tri-border region without referencing the discourse of the frontera caliente. For this reason I could not erase this concept from the book. While I call the loosely delineated geographic region at the junction of the three states the "tri-border area," I use "Triple Frontier" to refer to the object and result of securitization, a space of strategy, which is defined and acted upon by the security apparatus.

In the following years, as I returned to Iguazú and stayed for longer periods of time, I slowly built relationships of trust with local people, which helped to assuage their suspicions about my intentions. Becoming embedded within the community also meant that I had to learn and abide by the unwritten rules that regulated knowledge production. By Kelly's invitation, I occasionally wrote news articles for *La Voz de Cataratas*. Among them was a short piece about the gendarmerie's program for training dogs to detect drugs. Another one, months later, was a critical story about how frequent power outages affected the town's hospital and neighborhood health centers, which, without electricity, were losing their vaccine supplies. These two articles were different in tone: the first was an affirmation of effective security-making, while the second criticized the incompetence of municipal and provincial authorities. But both of these stories fell within the boundaries of the permissible in the local news discourse. Although an outsider, I soon became aware of public secrets that existed in the community, and I respected the public silence surrounding them.

The public secret that the team of journalists from Buenos Aires sought, but failed, to uncover in Iguazú was the alliance between the town's residents, smugglers, and the security forces, in which local journalists were also implicated. From the point of view of Iguazúenses, outsiders who wanted to expose their social pact were coming to "embarrar la cancha." Unlike porteño journalists, I did not intend to publish a sensational story about border crime in Iguazú. Yet I was alert to the fact that an ethnographic book could also violate the unwritten law of silence and, thus, might be equally unwelcome to the community. As Philippe Bourgois and Jeffrey Schonberg (2009) have noted, ethnography is an artisanal practice that involves both interpretive and political choices. In the conclusion I address the politics and ethics of my work, weighing the risk that this book may contribute to the global discourse of the frontera caliente, further criminalizing the people who shared their lives with me in hopes that I would tell their version of events. There, I juxtapose this risk of exposing public secrets against its worse alternative—engaging in complicity with powerful actors, from government institutions to private businesses to corrupt border officials, who profit from breaking the law, while their impunity is guaranteed by the code of silence.[9]

PLAYING HIDE-AND-SEEK

When for months in 2008 and 2009 and for a year between 2010 and 2011 I lived in Iguazú, I regularly interacted with the federal security forces stationed there. Together with other journalists I attended civic-military parades on national holidays, documented training exercises and routine enforcement activities, and interviewed high-ranking officers. During their conversations with me, news reporters often expressed their appreciation for the national gendarmerie, the naval prefecture, the army, and the federal police. There was a symbiotic relationship between them: *las fuerzas* (the forces), as the assemblage of military and law enforcement agencies in this border town were commonly called, invited journalists to their ceremonies and notified them about their operations; the media, in turn, reported that the fuerzas performed effective border control. My experiences with the security forces were similar. Most chief officers agreed to be interviewed and some even took me behind the scenes, where I could observe how they patrolled the border.

Considering these gracious and seemingly transparent relationships between the fuerzas and the media, it came as a surprise to me when the boundary between the security forces and the journalists was suddenly reinforced. On one such occasion a local photographer alerted me that gendarmerie and customs authorities were carrying out a joint raid on a variety store downtown. I knew the place well: by then, I was involved in the production of an independent television program and I used to go there to buy cassettes for my video camera. According to the rumors, the store sold contraband electronics from Paraguay, prompting the gendarmerie and customs to shut it down. I arrived on scene and began recording the operation, but a few moments later the gendarme in charge ordered me to put the camera away. He said I needed a signed permission from a federal judge to film the action and demanded that I rewind the tape and erase its content. I protested, telling the officer that the street was a public place, where no special permits were required for video recording, but my objection had no effect. The officer threatened to confiscate my camera if I refused to comply with his order and retreat. He said he had already warned other journalists. It was only then that I noticed there were no other reporters at the scene. When I told a senior journalist about my bitter experience the following day, he hinted that the fuerzas might have been opposed to the presence of the media because of a secret arrangement between the gendarmes and the business owner. Whether he was right or not, the following week the store was open again and there was no public record to show that the raid had ever happened.

This was only one in a series of incidents in which the security forces marked the boundary that the local media was not allowed to trespass. Compared to my confrontation with the gendarme, such situations were usually less dramatic. When their performances were not intentionally staged for the public, officers in the gendarmerie, the prefecture, and other federal institutions felt unease at the mere presence of reporters with cameras and, despite their activities taking place where anybody could watch, invoked their authority to intimidate the press. During my fieldwork in Iguazú I learned that the federal forces and the local media shared the same agenda: both sought security, even though what it meant was contingent on the circumstances. But I also saw how at other times their aims and methods were at odds. It appeared as if the *fuerzas* and the journalists were playing hide-and-seek, a game between visibility and invisibility. *Savage Frontier* traces these ambiguous optics and politics of obscurity in order to loosen the tangled bind between security and news-making.

HISTORY OF SECURITIZATIONS

Beginning with the earliest journalistic accounts of the region in the nineteenth century, northeastern Argentina has been portrayed as an unruly and dangerous periphery where the federal government was called to take on a civilizing role and establish order. Frontier narratives, which contrast the civilization of the state with the barbarity of the margins, are a common feature throughout Latin America, where they have been used to legitimate economic development schemes and military interventions in border zones. But in the Triple Frontier the nexus between security politics and practices and media production has a global dimension, which was highlighted following two terrorist attacks in Buenos Aires. In 1992 a suicide bomber drove a pickup truck into the Israeli embassy, detonating explosives that killed twenty-nine people and wounded over two hundred others. The Islamic Jihad Organization assumed responsibility for this terror act and soon investigations led to the tri-border area, where the bombers had allegedly planned the attack. Brazilian Foz do Iguaçu and Paraguayan Ciudad del Este have a commercially active Muslim community, largely comprised of migrants from Syria and Lebanon, many of whom fled civil wars and unrest in their home region. Although their main business is in "re-export" trade, as early as the 1970s Paraguayan and Brazilian authorities and news reporters were spreading accusations that Arabs in the Triple Frontier had connections to terrorists (Karam 2011:254).[10] With the attack on the Israeli embassy the discourse of Islamist terror threat was also adopted in Argentina. In 1994, two years after the first raid, a van bomb was detonated in front of the Asociación Mutual Israelí-Argentina (AMIA, Mutual Israeli-Argentine Association), resulting in eighty-five casualties and causing injuries to more than three hundred people. To date, the AMIA bombing in Buenos Aires has been the largest terrorist strike in Latin American history. Investigation into this incident also referenced the Triple Frontier, where the perpetrators of the bombings were thought to have crossed the border from Brazil. Argentine authorities maintain that Hezbollah, with backing from Iran, was behind the AMIA attack, but, marked by accusations of cover-ups and incompetence, the case remains unresolved. Because Iguazú, unlike its Paraguayan and Brazilian neighbors, had no Muslim residents, the primary effect of the discourse of terrorism threat in Argentina was strengthened control of its northern border, protecting the country from threats seeping in from abroad.

After the 9/11 attacks against the U.S., talk of lawlessness in the Triple Frontier further intensified. Security experts suspected that the region served as a hideout for jihadists (Folch 2013), and this vulnerability made it into a target of the "war on terror." The U.S. media echoed worries about an insecure border. "Terrorists Are Sought in Latin Smugglers' Haven," announced a headline in the *New York Times* a few weeks after September 11, 2001.[11] Using alarmist media coverage as evidence that the region was a safe haven for violent extremists, the U.S. government funded research that not surprisingly confirmed the vulnerability of the area (see, for example, Hudson 2003). These open-source reports established the tri-border region as "highly conducive for allowing organized crime," where various Islamic terrorist groups reportedly engaged in "fund-raising, drug trafficking, money laundering, plotting, and other activities in support of their organizations" (Hudson 2003:1, 2; see also Ferreira 2010; Shelley and Picarelli 2005). Media and government discourses served as a tool for legitimizing the deployment of security on the border. As a result, it was subjected to stricter customs and migration regulations, intensified surveillance, and crisscrossing by global and regional law enforcement networks. When in 2002 the U.S. joined the Tripartite Command, originally created by the Argentine, Brazilian, and Paraguayan governments to address the issues of organized crime, the 3+1 mechanism became the main framework of international military cooperation in the region, and its focus shifted to an almost exclusive concern with terrorism.

In the aftermath of 9/11, when the U.S. declared the "war on terror," security came to the forefront as the fundamental paradigm organizing global and domestic affairs. However, as a problem of governance, security was not new. Political thinkers from Thomas Hobbes and John Locke to Max Weber theorized it as a function of the modern state, tying security to the legitimacy of government and to the justification of the use of force. Thus, in political theory, security has long been inseparable from the state, even though, as Foucault (1991) argues, its rise to prominence is fairly recent and can be attributed to the essential role it plays in the logic of governmentality.[12] Concerns with global security were central during the Cold War period, when the U.S. government first produced and then acted to mitigate fears of communist uprisings and nuclear extermination (e.g., Gusterson 1996, 2004; Masco 2006). During the same period, military regimes in Latin America adopted "national security doctrines" to maximize control over their own citizens and validate persecution of anyone alleged to be "subversive"— student activists, trade unionists, journalists, leftist organizers. In Argentina, the generals who engaged in the Proceso de Reorganización Nacional (Process of National Reorganization), also known as the "Dirty War," presented the effort as a mechanism to manage internal threats to the state. Between 1976 and 1983, during "el proceso," tens of thousands of Argentines were "disappeared"—abducted from their homes, tortured in clandestine police stations, drugged and dropped from airplanes into the ocean, never to be found (see Feitlowitz 1998; Robben 2000, 2005). Embracing the national security doctrine, the military regime considered Argentina's remote northeastern border with Brazil as potentially vulnerable. These concerns led the junta to monitor everyday cross-border movements of local residents and to check the background of people buying property in the proximity of neighboring countries to separate the "trustworthy" Argentine nationals from "suspect" foreigners (Ferradás 2004). Calling the area a "buffer zone" against possible invasion from Brazil, the national security state deliberately kept its strategic infrastructure "thin" here. Withholding development of communication and transportation systems in the eastern flank of the Misiones Province was a preventative move: if war broke out between the two countries, Brazil would not be able to take over and use these structures to its advantage.

After the collapse of the military dictatorships throughout Latin America and the end of the Cold War on the global scale, anxieties over external and internal threats to the state did not disappear. The U.S. has continued to justify militarization through its engagements abroad (e.g., Lutz 2001, 2009; Sluka 2013) and constructed an extensive apparatus of homeland security and enhanced domestic preparedness (see, e.g., Fosher 2009; Lakoff 2007; Masco 2014). Furthermore, concerns with security spread from the military and civil defense to other domains of political and social life (for immigration, see Bigo 2002; Bourbeau 2011; Chacón 2008; Coleman 2012; Doty 2009; Stuesse and Coleman 2014; for biosecurity and public health, see Caduff 2012, 2014; Lakoff 2008; Lakoff and Collier 2012). This expansion of the security logic is often called "securitization." According to scholars associated with the Copenhagen School of international relations, securitization occurs when a particular issue is authoritatively labeled as a security concern and is accepted as such by the public (Buzan, Waever, and de Wilde 1998). This process has transformative effects on politics. Security concerns are equated with existential threats to the political community and its way of life, thereby justifying emergency measures and exceptions to ordinary legal procedures (Holbraad and Pedersen 2013). The "state of exception" concept, first formulated by Carl Schmitt (1985 [1922]) and later critiqued by Walter Benjamin (2009 [1940]), has recently been revisited by Giorgio Agamben, who writes that "insofar as it is a suspension of the juridical order itself, it defines law's threshold" (2005:4). In this context, the concept of "securitization" refers to "the deliberate ontological fusion" between ordinary politics and the realm of emergency (Holbraad and Pedersen 2012).[13] In contrast, the so-called Paris School, influenced by the work of Michel Foucault and Pierre Bourdieu, sees securitization as a series of routinized and patterned practices (Bigo 2002). From this point of view, securitization of an issue is not the cause but the result of the development of techniques and technologies of control and surveillance. Didier Bigo, the most vocal representative of this approach, has argued that the security process involves the imposition of a claim about security, relayed by the practical know-how of security bureaucracies and professionals and supported by prevailing discourses in the media (2002:76). Despite differences that define the two schools of thought, scholars acknowledge that the logics of exception and routine are complementary (Bourbeau 2011:2).

The rise of neoliberalism had significant effects on contemporary security discourse and practice. By the end of the twentieth century, governments had retreated from obligations toward their citizens, who live in increasingly precarious social and economic conditions, and at the same time vowed to protect private enterprises by offering them guarantees of economic and political stability (Goldstein 2010, 2012; Gusterson and Besteman 2009; Wacquant 2008). Throughout Latin America, due to shrinking social welfare and other governmental programs, people facing unemployment and poverty complain about being neglected by the state. The state has not "failed"—conditions of a sovereign government continue to exist—but the current peculiar patchwork of order and disorder is more accurately characterized as "the phantom state," which is present through its absence (Goldstein 2012), or a deliberately created "state of (in)security" (Penglase 2009). Increased militarization, policing, and surveillance go hand in hand with denial of access to justice, social services, health care, education, and public space. In Argentina, a decade of President Carlos Menem's neoliberal reforms, austerity measures, and extensive privatization in the 1990s caused broad discontent among residents (Auyero 2003) and led to the collapse of the country's economy in 2001. Since then, the administrations of Néstor Kirchner and Cristina Fernández de Kirchner have implemented important public welfare programs such as the universal child aid plan, which has reduced extreme poverty. Nevertheless, government failures to control inflation, manage unemployment, prevent commodity shortages, and deal with widespread corruption have led to erosions of its legitimacy (Auyero 2007; Ferradás 2013).

Concerns about distorted state effects are also expressed in the transnational discourses of "human security" and "citizen security" (Goldstein 2010, 2012). First and foremost, citizen security is understood as protection from crime and violence. Worried about the erosion of public safety, personal experiences notwithstanding, people advocate for more order, justify harsher law enforcement measures, resort to vigilantism, and embrace alternative—illegal and sometimes violent—power structures (see Comaroff and Comaroff 2006; Dammert and Malone 2006; Fassin 2013a; Goldstein 2004, 2012; Penglase 2009, 2014; Sieder 2011). Surveys, opinion polls, and media reports show that since the early 2000s Argentines have become increasingly concerned with insecurity in urban neighborhoods and, fearing violent attacks and robbery, have become more supportive of *mano dura* (iron fist) policies of crime control (Seri 2012). Initially limited to metropolitan areas, recently this fear of crime has spread to the further reaches of the country. When by early 2011 Iguazúenses began talking about the problem of urban insecurity in their town, they first explained that it was an import, brought by migrants from the poorest neighborhoods of Buenos Aires. Commenting on a series of incidents that the local press reported on, from petty thefts to violent assaults, residents not only criticized police for their incompetence and rampant corruption, but also called for taking law enforcement into their own hands. These struggles for physical security merge with broader demands for a spectrum of economic, social, and political rights, which democratic governments in Argentina and other Latin American countries should guarantee, but which have been battered by states' surrender to neoliberal reforms.

Therefore, although 9/11 was a critical point after which the U.S. and its allies, and consequently the entire world, entered into a new phase of increased alertness about potential global threats, concerns about security and its status as the master trope of contemporary politics were an extension of already existing tendencies, some as old as the modern state, others much more recent. In their work as news reporters and editors, Iguazúenses navigate these different scales, ideologies, and genealogies of security-making—from global threats and "the war on terror" to legacies of state violence under the national security doctrine, from neoliberal restructuring of the economy to the precariousness of everyday life and the new geographies of urban crime that it brought about. As this book shows, these narratives were tactically deployed by the media on the border to the advantage of the community.

MEDIA AS STAGE AND THREAT TO SECURITY

Security is performative. When a claim is made, declaring an issue to be a security concern, and the public recognizes the validity of this "speech act" (Austin 1962), the announcement brings about tangible political and social consequences. Securitization, to borrow the words of Judith Butler, is "a performative accomplishment which the mundane social audience, including the actors themselves, come to believe and to perform in the mode of belief" (1988:520). It makes sense to see journalists as important securitizing agents (e.g., Bourbeau 2014). In the most direct way, news media perform security by providing the stage for delivering speech acts and, thus, legitimizing their effects. The mainstream press in particular is deeply implicated in efforts to bestow authority upon the national community (e.g., Abu Lughod 2005; Hasty 2005; Mankekar 1999; Spitulnik 1998). In what they call "the propaganda model," Edward Herman and Noam Chomsky (1988) explain that mass media adhere to the political agenda of the state by framing events and proc-esses in a broader socioeconomic context in such a way that it serves the powerful interests that finance and control it. But the role of the media does not end here. Messages can go awry and cause inadvertent conse-quences (see Briggs and Mantini-Briggs 2003; Himpele 2008; Larkin 2008). In Brian Larkin's (2008) terminology, media stories get dislodged from the state projects that give rise to them and, as they are taken up and used in everyday life, they spin off in unexpected directions, creating both "signal" and "noise," that is, intended and unintended outcomes.

Residents of Iguazú do not accept the criminalizing discourse of the frontera caliente, delivered to them by both foreign and national mass media, uncritically. Instead of gathering legitimacy for the state's security agenda, the narrative about alleged threats on the border provokes the opposite reaction: the community rejects it as a false accusation, which further erodes their trust in the federal government. Stuart Hall (1980) has argued that news stories are encoded and decoded by publics embed-ded in particular social contexts. Each of these publics, implicated in the performative circulation of discourse (Warner 2002; Lee and LiPuma 2002), reinterprets the meaning of security. In contrast to their colleagues who come for short visits from Buenos Aires and abroad, journalists in Iguazú reconstitute security on local terms: they situate the global dis-course of terror threat and national concerns with rising crime rates within the circumstances of their life on the border. Nils Bubandt (2005:276) introduced the concept of "vernacular security" to address the contradictory outcomes of accommodation, rejection, and reformu-lation that the problem of security undergoes in the interstices between its global, national, and local representations. For Bubandt, securitiza-tion can be a discursive device for community-building. Vernacular secu-rity results from socially specific speech acts, based on configurations of fears and notions of order at a particular scale, and thus establishes different imagined communities on global, national, and local levels (Bubandt 2005:291). In addition to looking for breaking news stories, Iguazú journalists share responsibility to protect pragmatic alliances forged within the community. They act as gatekeepers in the circulation of news and maneuver between stories *for, on,* and *off the record;* they thus play an active part in renegotiating the significance of security.

For the media, security concerns are a double-edged sword. The work of journalists is premised on making things visible; their aim is to draw public attention to issues that have been unknown or obscured. In contrast, national security operates on conditions of secrecy and under the guise of invisibility, where state power rests on the ability of officials to manage the public/secret divide through the mobilization of threats. The U.S. provides a good example of how the scope of media reporting on issues, defined as matters of homeland security, such as the NSA spying scandal, which dominated the news at the time this book was being written, is curtailed, and how people's rights to public knowledge are limited.[14] According to Joseph Masco (2010:449), an information strategy, which combines increased classification, noncirculation, and censorship of public records, has been a key part of the conversion of the U.S. national security state from its earlier anticommunist to the present counterterrorist form. Because of this contradiction between media's mandate of exposure and secrecy as the technology of a new kind of state power, journalists themselves are increasingly labeled as potential threats.[15] The danger they pose to state security is not limited to what they say, but—as Amahl Bishara (2013:26) shows for Palestinian journalists framed as constituting threats to the Israeli government—also includes what they could conceivably do.

In Argentina, at the time of my fieldwork, there was no national law ensuring public access to information held by government bodies. In fact, relations between the federal authorities and journalists have been strained to such an extent that the Human Rights Watch *World Report 2014* cites the country's president, Cristina Fernández de Kirchner, accusing the media of deploying "bullets of ink" to "overthrow elected governments."[16] This particular confrontation can be traced to 2008, when disagreements about the questionable effects of the country's new media law on freedom of expression provoked a well-publicized conflict between the Kirchner administration and the major media conglomerate Grupo Clarín. But in the beginning of the twenty-first century, the broader trend of states using security talk to control free speech is notable far beyond this specifically Argentine scenario.

Straddling their roles of making news and making security on the local level, Iguazú media have been tactically maneuvering between visibility and invisibility. Journalists who live and work in the tri-border region are acutely aware of the political, economic, and social effects of news production. They understand that the media is a powerful loudspeaker for spreading a sense of danger and uncertainty. Sensational coverage of crime and violence may lead to securitization that is constructive of communities and at the same time legitimizing of destructive forms of government intervention as two complementary scale-making projects. In Iguazú I witnessed how journalists navigated the coordinates of security politics practically and how they used the news to tell more nuanced stories that challenged some official state policies while justifying others. At the center of their efforts as knowledge producers was the need to challenge the dominant definitions of violence and crime and renegotiate their meanings.

REPRESENTING VIOLENCE AND CRIME

How can we "capture"—classify, quantify, explain—violence in complex and ambiguous situations? What are the problems associated with transferring violence into media discourse and circulating these narratives in the public sphere? The relationship between violence and representation has been an important subject in anthropological research. One way that scholars have explored it has been by focusing on the narrative forms of violent experiences (e.g., Kernaghan 2009; Tate 2013; Taussig 1987, 2003). Stories can create a culture of terror, where, Taussig wrote, "the signifiers are strategically out of joint with what they signify" (1987:5). But narration not only spreads the culture of terror: it also serves in healing the wounds that terror produces. In the aftermath of violent struggles in Peru, Colombia, and elsewhere, storytelling has become the principal means through which the past is rendered legible, though never transparent (Kernaghan 2009:5). Violent events leave their mark on the form and content of representation and affect storytelling practices. In this context, news media, too, can be used to share the lived experience of violence, thereby acting as a tool to help communities restore social bonds, reconstitute symbolic universes, and survive conflict (e.g., Rodríguez 2011). However, from an anthropological perspective, it is important to go beyond the effects that media has on communal healing and critically engage with the processes involved in representing violence in the media. In her work with Guatemalan photojournalists, M. Gabriela Torres (2014) suggests we analyze how reporters stage and orient their images to tell particular stories and how they consciously produce aesthetic narratives of atrocities.

This book contends that experiences and practices of violence take many shapes, located along the continuum from direct assault to routinized oppression, from its intimate dimensions to "symbolic" (Bourdieu 2006 [1977]) and "structural" (Galtung 1969; Farmer 1992, 2003, 2004) forms of violence (see also Scheper-Hughes and Bourgois 2004; Bourgois and Schonberg 2009). Julie Skurski and Fernando Coronil have noted that violence is not a given empirical object, but is always mediated: it has to be "named, recognized, and experienced in terms of authorizing concepts and relations of power" (2006:4). Violence often presents to people indirectly, through narration, which includes rumors, newspaper reports, and statistics. This means that journalists are important producers of society's knowledge about it. Their definitions and interpretations circulating in the news media, if taken for granted, may have serious consequences. As Winifred Tate (2007, 2013) has demonstrated in her work on human rights advocacy, producing knowledge about violence is a contentious practice that creates both cultural meaning and material rewards for those who can impose their interpretations on violent acts.

From Buenos Aires, the Argentine Northeast has been seen as an area where, first, savagery and, later, poverty and illiteracy of the population, led local people to engage in cruel or obscene behavior that shocked news publics nationwide. Stories about "bad" parents who sell their newborns in exchange for cash or home appliances or send their adolescent daughters off to work as prostitutes are recurrent features in sensational mass media coverage of the region. In contrast, from my experience, Iguazúenses were more likely to understand violence as a function of the state turned against its citizens. For them, talking about violence invoked public memories of abductions, torture, and disappearances during the military dictatorship; governmental neglect, increasing the ranks of the socially vulnerable; pervasive injustice, police brutality, and impunity; and unfair vilification of border residents, who were all lumped together as violent or criminal actors.

As with violence, there is nothing straightforward about the definition and representation of crime. Traced to the Latin word *crimen* (accusation, charge, or guilt), crime is a matter of judgment. In Argentina, *delito,* a Spanish word that originates from Latin *delinquere* (offend, do wrong), is used interchangeably with *crimen.* Because it is determined from a moral-legal position of authority, crime is relative to it. Oxford Dictionaries provides the following commonly used definition: crime is "an action or omission which constitutes an offence and is punishable by law."[17] It encompasses activities that are characterized as "illegal" or "evil," "shameful," and "wrong." The boundary between law and crime is set from the perspective of authority, which is skewed in favor of those wielding political and economic power at supranational, national, regional, or local levels. Because laws differ by states and change with time, categories of crime and their contents are unstable. This makes it especially difficult, if not impossible, to reach consensus on a global scale. The fact that the United Nations Convention against Transnational Organized Crime does not contain a precise definition of "transnational organized crime" or list the kinds of crimes that constitute it is a case in point.[18] In this book, concepts like "organized crime," "border crime," or "urban crime" do not conform to fixed legal definitions, but are applied according to their standard, commonsense usage in public discourse. Rather than drawing boundaries between these categories, my goal is to show how both the categories and the boundaries around them are legitimized and contested through the media. This falls within the broader scope of the book: to document how crime, violence, and security connect, resulting in the production of particular types of news stories and not others.

Anthropological inquiry into crime has included investigating the processes through which governments and the media define certain groups and practices as "criminal" (Schneider and Schneider 2008).[19] Journalists perpetuate the talk of crime, extending and fueling everyday conversations, stories, and jokes. The circulation of fear, Teresa Caldeira (2001:37–38) has shown, promotes discrimination and criminalization, delegitimizes institutions of order, and provides justification for the use of private, violent, and illegal means of protection. The discourse of urban crime leads to increasing anxiety, which results in radical security-making practices and forms of justice. Charles Briggs (2007) introduced the concept of "communicative cartographies" to show that media discourse about violence and crime generates standardized scripts and creates a very limited range of subject positions. Newspaper stories treat crime as separate from history and political economy, depicting it instead as a product of "pathological subjectivities and defective domesticities," thus naturalizing representations of class, gender, space, state, and nation (Briggs 2007:331; see also Penglase 2007; Reyes-Foster 2013). In Argentine mediascapes, Iguazúenses, together with all Misioneros, may not be violent drug traffickers and terrorists, like their Paraguayan and Brazilian neighbors across the border are alleged to be, but they are portrayed as entrepreneurs of the illegal, tampering with the laws and twisting them to their economic advantage. In Iguazú, when people talk about border crime, they rarely associate it with direct bodily harm—contraband and corruption are essentially nonviolent, "victimless" crimes. But here, instead of being the fault of local residents, crime is generally considered secondary to national and global economic policies and the structural violence of the state.

Some of the region's most dire social and infrastructural problems, including poverty, scarcity of drinking water, frequent power outages, landlessness, lack of employment opportunities, child malnourishment, and human trafficking, among other concerns, relate to faulty policymaking and weigh on the government's shoulders. Such forms of structural violence, or "the violence of everyday life" (Scheper Hughes 1992), have little resemblance to the spectacular lawlessness presented in the frontera caliente narrative. Journalists who are embedded in these everyday realities choose to focus on them as news events. They report on infrastructural collapses, such as blackouts, most often, but they also address poverty, malnourishment, and trafficking of children, which, together with other acute social problems, result from uneven state effects and structural violence.

Prioritizing socially conscious and locally relevant news-making, journalists reject sensationalized stories of global threats as untrue and rarely discuss them. Reporters and common residents alike told me that the heightened attention that the U.S. government and its corporate media gave the region masked a conspiracy. They argued that securitization and militarization of the tri-border area was part of the U.S. plan to establish control over the Guaraní Aquifer, one of the world's largest freshwater deposits, located beneath the surface of Argentina, Brazil, Paraguay, and Uruguay.[20] Besides deploying conspiracy theories, on other occasions local journalists reacted to global criminalization by parodying what they said were ridiculous allegations. In an exemplary case, when the U.S. media reported that Osama bin Laden visited the tri-border area in mid-1990s, spreading suspicions about the presence of terrorist activity in the region, a Brazilian newspaper in Foz do Iguaçu publicly satirized these claims by making Bin Laden into a poster boy for a series of tourist advertisements (Karam 2011). "If Bin Laden risked his neck to visit Foz de Iguazú, it must be worth it," said one of the mocking ads.[21]

Journalists that I met in northeastern Argentina subvert "the geography of blame" (Farmer 1992) by ricocheting incriminating narratives back to Buenos Aires—the main source of sensational border coverage and, according to them, the original location of violent crime. Their claims were based on their individual life trajectories. Reporters told me about assaults they had experienced while living in or visiting urban centers in Argentina and Brazil. In contrast to these metropolitan areas, which they associated with violence and crime, Iguazú, albeit situated in the vilified Triple Frontier, was a safe place for them. I remember a conversation I had with Javier Villegas, a former army soldier who at the time we spoke in 2010 was working for one of the town's radios. It was a quiet afternoon in late spring and we were sitting at an outdoor café overlooking *siete bocas* (seven mouths), an intersection of seven streets at the center of Iguazú. By then I had spent many months living in northern Argentina and I felt safe here. In this allegedly lawless place I was not afraid to walk alone at night, even when I had to go from one end of the town to the other. The crime and violence that I was witnessing in Iguazú was not of the proportions—and often not of the kind—suggested by the mainstream media. When during our talk Javier insisted that local criminals were "less malevolent than in other places" because they would not kill you "for two pesos or for a pair of shoes," his words reflected my own experience:

> Insecurity is everywhere. Now it is getting worse here because people from other places come looking for "virgin lands." Puerto Iguazú is a virgin land for criminals: even the *chorros* [thieves] here are less malevolent than in other places; they steal your shoes or your motor scooter, they break into your house, but that is all. In big cities, for example, Foz do Iguaçu, Ciudad del Este, Buenos Aires, they can kill you for two pesos or for a pair of shoes. True, a crime is still a crime, but if we are looking for a positive side, the criminals here are still rather gentle with the local people.

Comparing Buenos Aires and Iguazú, Javier was one of many local journalists who accused the metropolitan media of "looking for a hair in the milk":

> It is as if they [metropolitan media] were looking for *un pelo en la leche* [a hair in the milk], *la quinta pata al gato* [the fifth paw of a cat]. They are looking for what does not exist. [. . .][22] What annoys me sometimes is that our own national channels come and want to make documentaries, showing that this is the "Mecca" of contraband, when the biggest contraband passes through the customs of Buenos Aires, through Río del Plata. Here only small things get across.[23]

I heard people repeatedly reject the geography of blame that indiscriminately lumps all border residents together with terrorists, traffickers, and smugglers. This is not to say that Iguazúenses deny the presence of organized crime and extensive flows of contraband in the area. As the book shows, intercepted shipments of marijuana and cocaine on the rivers as well as vehicles caught with smuggled goods at the border checkpoint on the bridge make the news nearly every day. But this situation is in no way exclusive to the Triple Frontier. Development of informal markets—where smuggling of legal products such as food and cigarettes intertwines with trafficking in illegalized commodities from narcotics to endangered animal species—is a side effect of regulations imposed on the free movement of people and things. It is not the exception, but the rule in international border zones (for a parallel discussion about the U.S.-Mexico border, see Andreas 2000, 2013; for the Guatemala-Mexico border, see Galemba 2012, 2013; for the Chad Basin in Africa, see Roitman 2004; for Central Asia, see Reeves 2014).

In 2011 Argentine federal forces reported seizing over 87 metric tons (MT) of marijuana, most of it in the tri-border region.[24] The Argentine government also reported to the U.S. capturing approximately 5.8 MT of cocaine. But this data, appearing in the 2012 *International Narcotics Control Strategy Report,* has limited value in determining whether organized crime in the area presents a serious problem. As I discuss in chapters 2 and 4, using statistics to estimate the level of crime in this region and compare it with other borders is fraught with complications because the production of official data on crime and the underground economy is both limited in scope and highly politicized in its application (see also Andreas 2000; Andreas and Greenhill 2010; Merry and Coutin 2014). This book will disappoint those who expect it to deconstruct alarmist mass media representations of the frontera caliente in order to provide a better mapping of actual criminal trajectories. What I know about crime and violence in Iguazú is based on my own experience of living there for periods of time between 2008 and 2011, stories that local people told me, information made public by the security forces and by the police, scarce and unreliable statistics, and conflicting media reports. These pieces complement each other to form my understanding of the situation on the ground, as shared in the pages that follow, but the picture they present is far from conclusive. The purpose of this book is not to verify claims about crime and violence in the Triple Frontier, but to show that the production of knowledge about them is a contested and contradictory process.

LEGALITY AND LEGITIMACY OF THE INFORMAL ECONOMY

Historian E. P. Thompson wrote that crime is problematic "when we simply take over the definitions of those who own property, control the state, and pass the laws which 'name' what shall be crimes" (1975:193–194). Set in accordance with state interests, the boundary between the legal and the illegal is subjective. Willem van Schendel and Itty Abraham (2005:31) suggest focusing on people's perceptions of activities to distinguish between *legality* as political legitimacy and *licitness* as social legitimacy. Alternatively, Joe Heyman (2013) offers a compelling argument for thinking of *legalization* and *illegalization* as processes rather than as states of being. The use of the past participle form of the words—*legalized* versus *illegalized* instead of *legal* versus *illegal*—illuminates the role of the state and other powerful institutions in determining the official status of practices, objects, and people. As I write elsewhere (see Jusionyte 2013), activities are never legal or illegal, legitimate or illicit in and of themselves, but become such through complex processes of labeling that involve multiple authoritative actors, including the government and the media (see also de Genova 2004).

This acknowledgment that the boundary between law and crime is political and contested is grounded in studies that demonstrate continuities between the state and illegal practices. Building on Charles Tilly's famous observation that states are "quintessential protection rackets with the advantage of legitimacy" (1985:169), anthropologists have shown that crime is intricately connected to the operations of the state (e.g., Comaroff and Comaroff 2006; Heyman and Smart 1999; Jaffe 2013; Nordstrom 2007; van Schendel and Abraham 2005; Schneider and Schneider 2003). To use Carolyn Nordstrom's terminology (2007:22), the state is founded on the riddles of il/legality, and these junctures of state laws and prohibited economic practices have given rise to the emergence of alternative moral-legal regimes (e.g., Herzfeld 1997; Flynn 1997; Galemba 2012, 2013; Grimson 2002b; Reeves 2013; Roitman 2004, 2005; Thomas 2012). However, if we uncouple the construction of legitimacy and morality from state-centered dichotomies of legality/illegality (Galemba 2013:275), the role of the media, often seen as a loudspeaker of the government, is put into question. When the official legal coordinates fail to capture the common knowledge of maneuvering the particular social terrain and misrepresent morally justified practices, local journalists need alternative communicative cartographies to make news. They face decisions about *if* and *how* to report on activities that are illegalized yet legitimate on the border. Under these circumstances, their choices in news coverage greatly depend on their interpretation and experience of security in their community.

Proximity to Brazil and especially Paraguay has always been considered a resource for residents of Iguazú. For decades, by crossing international borders they could benefit from a greater variety of goods and significant price differences. Low import tariffs and tax rates for electronics, perfumes, tobacco, alcohol, and luxury commodities such as precious stones, complemented by Paraguay's weak customs enforcement, made Ciudad del Este attractive for both legal and illegal commerce. Seeking to protect their internal markets from cheaper foreign products, in the 1990s the Brazilian and Argentine governments began implementing stricter import regulations. Together with Uruguay, the three countries

FIGURE 2. Three borders: The photograph is taken from Argentina; across Río Paraná, to the left, is Paraguay; across Río Iguazú, in front to the right, is Brazil, March 2014.

also formed MERCOSUR, the Southern common market, which facilitated large-scale international commerce by removing most barriers to free trade, but imposed new constraints on local residents (Ferradás 2004; Grimson 2002b; Jusionyte 2013). The new border trade regime not only prohibited Iguazúenses from going to Ciudad del Este to purchase electronics and luxury items, but also, through its revised public health policies, included bans on cross-border flows of fresh produce and other foodstuffs. This pushed a significant part of local commerce, which for decades had relied on people and goods circulating freely across the borders, underground. As a consequence, the informal economy in the tri-border region soared, with Paraguay becoming the source of illegal flows of everything from electronics and household appliances to contraband cigarettes and alcohol to guns and drugs.

When the circulation of certain types of commodities across the borders was illegalized, the social legitimacy of these informal exchanges among local residents did not automatically change (see chapter 5). Despite increased regulation and more rigorous customs control, Iguazúenses continue to engage in what they consider to be justified economic practices. Most do not regard a few bags of bananas, oranges, or poultry carried across the bridge by motoqueros as contraband. Nor do they consider it a crime to bring untaxed computers, cameras, cell phones, or even flat-screen televisions into the country, as long as they are for personal consumption and remain in local households, regardless of official policies that prohibit it. Rather than adhering to strictly legal definitions, when they make news Iguazú journalists are bound by the local interpretation and classification of practices. Even though they know about widespread law violations, many border residents do not support public exposés of the intricacies of regional trade (see also Ferradás 2004). They are aware of their own dependence, direct or indirect, on illegalized economic exchanges, so media coverage is both unwarranted and undesirable. Since everyone knows about these activities and many engage in them, on the local level they are not newsworthy. If made public on the national and global level, however, stories of food and electronics contraband blend with narratives of trafficking in drugs and guns, potentially harming the community. Reports of widespread smuggling may be mobilized to call for further securitization and militarization of the border, making the life of its residents ever more precarious.

Revenue from tourism, generated by more than a million visitors that come to the Iguazú Falls every year, provides the backbone of the local economy. Most if not all of the journalists I came to know in this northeastern Argentine town understand this dependency and acknowledge their interests and their role in protecting Iguazú as a tourist destination. When stories of trafficking, urban crime, or epidemic disease—as was the case with dengue and yellow fever—threaten to disrupt the constant flow of visitors to the falls, economic considerations triumph over their mission as journalists to report breaking news. Such selective news-making is tactical, in Michel de Certeau's use of the term. De Certeau (1984) suggests that people have invented numerous makeshift practices by which they maneuver the disciplinary regime. Poaching on power, tactics are a "guileful ruse," writes de Certeau (1984:37). This book documents how in situations where they perceive the community's well-being to be at stake, local journalists use news as their tactics. Instead of "blowing up" news stories the way their colleagues from national and foreign mainstream media do, reporters in Iguazú prefer to "cover up" issues that fall in the gray zone between the legal and the illegal.

PIRATE MEDIA IN ARGENTINE STATECRAFT

It is difficult to know how many media organizations there are in Iguazú at any given time. Their number fluctuates: during the same year, radio and television stations open or close, digital dailies go online or become inactive. Since not all of the media work under government licenses, there is no official legal record to consult. Therefore, what follows is a generalized sketch.

By the end of my fieldwork in 2011, local multimedia company C.V.I. held the town's cable monopoly. Their Canal 5 was the area's main television channel, broadcasting local news and regional sports. It was integrated with radio station FM Visión, also owned by C.V.I., and most of the programs were simultaneously aired on television and on the radio. Canal 5 received little competition from two other channels: the newly opened Canal 11 broadcast municipal news and Canal 6 transmitted music. Since 1972 Iguazú has been the regional seat of the Argentine public radio, Radio Nacional Puerto Iguazú LRA 19. The town's second oldest broadcaster and its first private station, Radio Cataratas, went on air in 1985, on the same day that the Tancredo Neves International Bridge between Argentina and Brazil was inaugurated. Other well-known commercial radio stations included Radio Yguazú, Radio Sol, and Radio de Frontera FM NEA. There were two digital dailies: the older and more widely read *La Voz de Cataratas,* which for a period of time also had a print edition, and its new rival, *Iguazú Noticias,* founded by a young, entrepreneurial migrations officer. Several local journalists worked as correspondents for three provincial newspapers, *El Territorio, Primera Edición,* and *Misiones Online,* and one provincial television channel, Canal 12. But the nationwide press, including two major Argentine dailies, *Clarín* and *La Nación,* had its regional bureaus in the Misiones capital, Posadas, and rarely sent correspondents all the way up north to Iguazú.

The present condition and history of the Iguazú media sphere is inseparable from the development of this border town, territorially remote but geopolitically strategic. Throughout the twentieth century the hilly jungle terrain in Misiones created obstructions for national television and radio signals to reach the distant province. However, in contrast to Brazil, which actively implemented policies facilitating cultural expansionism in its border regions, Argentina did not prioritize building communication infrastructure in Misiones. In part, the government's disinterest in developing the Argentine Northeast was secondary to its national security politics, especially its concerns that the area might be usurped in the case of war with Brazil. The only commitment to strengthening the media on the border was the decision, made under the dictatorship of Alejandro Agustín Lanusse in the early 1970s, to establish in Iguazú the regional headquarters of the Argentine national radio. It was a significant historical investment. However, at the end of the twentieth century, during the town's busiest years of rapid urban growth, transmissions of Radio Nacional were discontinued and Iguazúenses turned to news and entertainment broadcasts from across the border in Brazil and Paraguay. Radio and television signals from Foz do Iguaçu and Ciudad del Este were so powerful that, in the words of local historian Carlos Villalba, they "entered like gunshots" and "monopolized the sky."[25] Brazilian media had such a strong cultural influence over Iguazú that many of the town's residents grew up speaking *portuñol,* a colloquial mix of Portuguese and Spanish. "We did not know whether we were living in Argentina or in Brazil," remembers one radio director.[26]

As the edges of state sovereignty, border zones are exceptional spaces in terms of both making security and making journalism. In the tri-border area of Argentina, Brazil, and Paraguay, media and national security were unlikely allies. Except for Radio Nacional and later Radio Cataratas, for decades most of the radio stations in Iguazú were founded without licenses and operated without registration. They have been called *FM truchas* (fake FMs), *radios piratas* (pirate radios) and, more recently, *radios clandestinas* (clandestine radios). Despite their negative connotations, pirate radios were legitimate in the local community. Iguazúenses preferred their programming, which was in Spanish, to the alternatives that were available to them: Brazilian radio and television broadcasts in Portuguese, or the weak and unreliable transmissions of mainstream Argentine media from Buenos Aires. Created in the infrastructural and legal gaps of the state, these clandestine radios were widely justified in nationalist terms (see Jusionyte 2014). Many of them were founded by frontier entrepreneurs who had moved to the remote border region in search of business opportunities. But, according to the mythology of pirate radios that I heard repeatedly during interviews, these entrepreneurs were motivated less by plans to make future profits than by their concerns about the weakness of *argentinidad* (Argentine-ness) among local residents, who lived under foreign cultural influence. Mario Antonowicz, the founder and director of Radio Yguazú, conveyed to me the significance of clandestine media: "If not for these FM truchas, or the cable television system, which was born as pirate television and was legalized years later, today many kids would still be speaking portuñol here."[27] By providing them news in Spanish and about Argentina, pirate radios strengthened national belonging among the Iguazúenses by including them in the "imagined community" (Anderson 1991 [1983]); therefore, despite their outlaw status, they played an active role in performing national security.

FIGURE 3. Mario Antonowicz and Jorgelina Bonetto in the studio of Radio Yguazú, June 2010.

In his ethnography of the media in Posadas, on the border between Argentina and Paraguay, south of Iguazú, Alejandro Grimson (2002a) argues that by literally and metaphorically co-authoring local, regional, and global identities, journalists are important actors in the everyday production of nationality in border zones. In Iguazú, the protection of national identity, and, thus, national security, retroactively justified illegal entrepreneurship. The existence of these makeshift media outside of the law paradoxically allowed them more freedom of expression. Unlicensed radios and television stations in Argentina were not subject to government control of the media, which began when President Juan Perón established the Secretary of the Press in the mid-twentieth century (Romero 2002). Nor did they experience the most severe censorship and persecution of journalists in the 1970s and 1980s during the Dirty War. By the early 2000s the entire northeastern border region, including Iguazú, was fully integrated into Argentina's nationwide media sphere. But the plethora of mainstream and alternative global and local media sources, enabled by daily delivery of regional and national newspapers, reliable cable connection to metropolitan television networks, and internet access to worldwide media, did not undermine the significance of pirate radios.[28] Their contribution to statecraft and their legacy to Argentine identity in this peripheral border area were noted by many I talked to.

Between 2008, when I first came to the tri-border region, and the completion of fieldwork for this book in April 2011, I conducted about fourteen months of ethnographic research with the Argentine media. In anthropology, interest in journalism is still relatively new. It might be odd, as Mark Pedelty put it, to engage in "observing those in the act of observing others, writing about their writings about others" (1995:5). But beyond the unusual degree of reflexivity that news ethnography entails, parallels between anthropological research and media production as two similar arenas of cultural meaning-making also have direct effects on the fieldwork process. Building on Laura Nader's (1972) term "studying up," which she juxtaposed with the common anthropological practice of privileging the subaltern, or "studying down," Ulf Hannerz (2004) called the ethnography of journalism "studying sideways." Most of the reporters I worked with in Iguazú and the surrounding areas were my peers. Though we came from different national, educational, and professional backgrounds and though the objectives we had in knowledge production diverged, these incongruities did not preclude the possibility of creating "epistemic fellowships" (Bishara 2013).

Although I arrived in Iguazú as another suspicious outsider, lured by the thrills and dangers of the frontera caliente, I left it with a new nickname, "Lituanera," which Kelly made up by joining "Lithuanian" with "Misionera," indicating my new belonging to the place and commitment to its people. Fieldwork in the tri-border area did not change just my relation to Iguazú and Iguazúenses. It also destabilized and blended my professional roles, as an anthropologist and as a journalist. I wrote news articles for *La Voz de Cataratas* intermittently from 2009 to 2011. But it was my collaboration in the production of the investigative television program *Proximidad,* broadcast on Canal 5 in 2010, that became the most involved part of my fieldwork. The next chapter of the book addresses in detail my experience of doing ethnographic research and journalistic investigation while I lived in Iguazú. Changing my roles enabled me to see how the law of silence defined the boundaries between public secret and public knowledge, and how these unwritten rules were practiced, enforced, and sometimes circumvented in the interactions between journalists, security forces, and people who engaged in illegalized activities (see chapter 6). Participation in local media production was not only my minor contribution to the community, a form of giving back to Iguazú journalists who welcomed me into their midst, but also critical for writing *Savage Frontier*—an ethnography of news-making practices under conditions of competing discourses and experiences of violence, crime, and security in the tri-border region.

BOOK OVERVIEW

Savage Frontier examines how people who live in an allegedly lawless place, targeted by intensified economic regulation, policing, and surveillance initiatives, understand and experience security, and how they use news media to mitigate their uncertain situation. In the border region between Argentina, Brazil, and Paraguay, which has been defined as the frontera caliente, I follow journalists, exploring how they translate discourses about global threats to make them locally meaningful and legitimate within their own community. Since the "war on terror" began in 2001, concerns about security in the Triple Frontier resulted in increased control of the border, directly affecting the livelihood of its people. Rather than reducing insecurity, such government intervention further intensified it. In this context, local journalists have been working against criminalization and securitization of their hometown. As this book shows, for them, making news has become entangled with making security.

My newswriting and participation in producing *Proximidad,* together with my ethnographic work, formed a dual engagement that allowed me to explore the code of silence that circumscribed knowledge production about security and crime on the border from two parallel yet critically different perspectives. In chapter 1, I use my experiences as an ethnographer and a journalist to tease out the tensions between anthropology and news media as two modes of knowledge production and the particular processes and politics of representation pertinent to each genre.

Chapter 2 provides the historical background of the region and traces its representations in the media. News production relies on thematic, logistical, economic, and political frameworks that reduce the physical and social geography of the state into a legible narrative. In the case of the Argentine Northeast, this standardized news script has been built around the opposition between civilization and savagery, and the order of the center against the violence of the periphery. Since the nineteenth century, both the foreign and the national press have construed the Argentine border with Brazil and Paraguay as a savage and violent frontier where state control and the reach of the law were weak. This chapter traces contemporary security buildup in the Triple Frontier to the particular history of state advancement in the tri-border region, legitimated by the master trope of civilization over barbarism.

Chapter 3 examines the effects that global and regional security policies have had on the everyday lives of residents in the tri-border area. After two terrorist bombings of Israeli institutions in Buenos Aires in the 1990s, the Argentine government blamed the attacks on an Iranian-backed Hezbollah cell operating out of the border region. Since the initial connection with the terror threat was made, and especially after September 11, 2001, the area has been subject to global security talk as an alleged haven of organized crime and a remote hideout for terrorist financiers and sleeper cells. This chapter shows that journalists play an important role in translating security talk across scales and regimes of knowledge: they selectively reject and adapt stories and rewrite global narratives to fit local situations. Examining these processes of translation and negotiation from inside the allegedly insecure border milieu allows us to better understand the role of the media in mitigating securitization of emergent threats. This chapter engages with the paradox that local resistance against the frontera caliente narrative might inadvertently result in perpetuating the same criminalizing discourse about the Triple Frontier that residents of the border region are attempting to change.

Pueblo chico, infierno grande (small town, big hell) is a saying many like to repeat when asked to explain what constraints face those who report on crime in the border town. In chapter 4 I shift the perspective from the broader discourse of threat to the ethnography of individual ways of experiencing violent crime and interpreting insecurity on the border. Security on the local scale is very different from that defined in national and global doctrines. Public memory and the enduring legacy of terror during Argentina's last military dictatorship, journalists' firsthand experiences of crime in urban centers, and the rules of complicity that a small border community abides by all have important effects on news-making. This ethnographic chapter shows that journalists, like many Iguazúenses, often interpret violence as an inherent feature of the state. Local media invert the dominant geography of crime and violence, in which the nationwide press portrays the border as lawless and dangerous, and provide a forum to put the blame for the rising crime in Iguazú on suspected migrants from the shantytowns of Buenos Aires.

Journalists maneuver between stories *for, on,* and *off the record* in compliance with the local understanding of what constitutes illegal yet socially legitimate practices. Chapter 5 illuminates the seemingly contradictory position of reporters in the border community: as residents, they often engage in the informal trade, but as cultural producers, their job is to make news about contraband. Trying to find their way out of this predicament, journalists tactically keep activities that have widespread social legitimacy off the media agenda. By not reporting on some potentially newsworthy illegal exchanges, they indirectly contribute to preserving the informal border economy, which, in the absence of sufficient legal employment and social welfare, supports their community.

My anthropological research on security and my collaborative involvement in media production converged when I made a television program about illegal adoptions and child trafficking. Following the motion video format of consecutive "takes," chapter 6 examines why Iguazú residents treated adoptions as a public secret and refused to talk about them on the record. Scarred by sensational media stories about the trade in babies, residents of the marginalized province were fearful that common practices of informal fosterage could be misinterpreted as child trafficking, resulting in more deleterious legal and socioeconomic effects. Comparing my experience of making the television episode with writing this book, I highlight important differences between methods and ethics of journalistic and ethnographic knowledge production.

In the conclusion, I engage the idea of in/visibility to reflect in more depth on the relationship between security and the media. Security-making and news-making both involve tactical uses of visibility and invisibility. While people invent ingenious ways of remaining invisible to law enforcement and continue to engage in illegalized activities that mitigate their economic insecurities, government agents on the border not only often tolerate such practices, but, through corruption, become part of them. Journalists maneuver between exposure and disguise, working on the murky terrain of in/visibilities and in/security in the border region. Here I also address the politics of ethnographic representation pertinent to the anthropology of security. I argue that an informed discussion of crime and violence should replace tactical silence, which is perpetuated in complicity with powerful actors that benefit from keeping stories of the lived experience of insecurity on the margins of the state as public secrets.

1

Breaking the Code of Silence

Fieldnotes, June 10, 2010: In the morning we got into the mint-colored minivan with *La Voz de Cataratas* logos and headed toward the Iguazú airport. Kelly and Silvia wanted to write a story about Argentine Air Force pilots who were training in town. When we arrived, the director of the airport informed us that the media were not allowed to take photographs or film outside, strictly prohibiting the journalists from approaching the military planes. So the three of us joined the others—Mario and Jorge from the provincial television station Canal 12, Vivi and Darío from the local cable Canal 5, and two reporters from the regional office of Radio Nacional—who were stranded in the conference room. There was a table with chairs for us to sit down, coffee was served, and the journalists were invited to interview air force representatives. Staying close to Kelly and Silvia, I followed them into a smaller room, where, in the briefing session, the young pilots were given flight instructions before a simulated attack in the province of Salta. With references to a number of maps laid out on the table, they explained to us the details of their tactical mission. When journalists from the other media left, the pilot in charge of the Hercules—a large military transport aircraft—agreed to take us onboard. Despite the prohibitions that the airport officials imposed on the media, limiting our movements in the security zone, Kelly, Silvia, and I were able to get inside the plane. We took turns sitting at the controls in the cockpit, joked with the pilots, and documented our experience using both photography and video. Later, we climbed to the watchtower to wave good-bye to the military planes that one by one took off on their training mission.

Fieldnotes, November 26, 2010: Today over lunch in Ciudad del Este I listened to a conversation between a Paraguayan journalist who worked for one of the town's dailies and his Argentine colleague, a reporter from Puerto Iguazú. They talked about the difficulties of covering drug trafficking in the local media. They both agreed on the existence of clandestine ports along the Paraná River and acknowledged that law enforcement was aiding traffickers. "Journalists who come from outside get away with reporting on organized crime because the authorities know that their visit is temporary," one of them remarked. They arrive and then they leave. In contrast, local journalists, like them, have to stay. The Iguazúense recalled how she was once tipped off about the time and place of a contraband delivery. She made the mistake of informing an acquaintance of hers in the gendarmerie who, as it later turned out, had been involved in the deal. She did not publish the story and, despite her fears, nothing happened to her. The Paraguayan in turn shared his experience of writing a piece on child prostitution in Ciudad del Este. He had pictures showing how the payment was made, how a thirteen-year-old indigenous girl got onto a motor scooter, and how she later returned with the same man. While documenting this for the media, the reporter called 911, but the police never came, reluctant to get involved, he guessed. According to the Paraguayan, the media avoided topics such as drug trafficking and child prostitution because of the *código de silencio*—the code of silence.

This code of silence was the underlying principle in local journalism, as I came to know it during fieldwork on Argentina's northern border. There were no formal guidelines that defined the interactions between news reporters and law enforcement officers—gendarmes, prefects, airport security, or the military. The scope of information that federal forces and regional police units shared with journalists depended on careful negotiations between the individuals and institutions involved. There were places where the media were not allowed and there were issues that reporters could not address, but these forbidden zones and topics had flexible perimeters and definitions. Sometimes an officer would allow a particular journalist to trespass the boundary separating the realm of state secrets, both formal and informal, from the public domain. These breeches were possible when those in law enforcement trusted that the media were on the same side of security-making and would not disclose information that was potentially harmful to their institution and, by extension, to the government. This complicity turned interactions between security forces and journalists into a game of hide-and-seek, where the code of silence as the organizing principle distinguished what could be talked about publicly from what was to be avoided. The excerpt from my fieldnotes cited above demonstrates that the code of silence was particularly marked when it came to media coverage of drug trafficking, contraband, and other organized crime. But it was just as important in everyday situations, where law enforcement officers and reporters constantly measured their relationships on the murky terrain between public secrets and public knowledge. In this chapter I discuss how my professional involvement with the news media in Iguazú complemented my ethnographic fieldwork, allowing me to approach the code of silence, which circumscribed knowledge production about security and crime on the border, from two parallel yet critically different perspectives.

FROM JOURNALISM TO ANTHROPOLOGY

I was a journalist before I became an anthropologist. Not by training, but by occupation. During college years I sometimes wrote articles and commentaries for the press, and before I ever set foot in Latin America I worked for an online newspaper in my hometown of Vilnius, Lithuania. My job was to write stories on timely issues, often based on interviews with sources in the government, the private sector, and civil society. I attended press conferences. I traveled abroad, covering presidential visits to foreign countries, from Ukraine and Bulgaria to Azerbaijan and Turkey. My work took me from the neat and fully equipped press offices of the European Parliament in Strasbourg, where I spoke to Lithuanian representatives, to backstreet internet cafés in Minsk, where I clandestinely typed my field diaries about the election and opposition protests in Belarus. Although the time I worked as a journalist was brief, during those months I was immersed in its distinct *habitus:*[1] the quick pace of the newsbeat, the constant pressure of deadlines, the framing of stories to make the headlines, the importance of recognizing trustworthy sources, and the balance between being accountable to the story, to my editor, and to the public. Even though my experience was limited, it taught me how being a journalist was more than a professional identity. For many, the pursuit of breaking news was a way of life. For some, especially those working under oppressive government regimes or in unstable zones of conflict, it could easily be a death sentence.

Journalism is markedly different from other genres of knowledge production, scientific or fictional. It is a mode of storytelling that requires its practitioners to follow a particular tempo of work and to adhere to a standardized narrative script. It is tightly linked to political interests and the market logic, yet it claims objectivity and aspires to truth. While working for the media, I witnessed how journalists maneuvered the discrepancies between the empirical and the normative reality, deciding on what was truth and what they wanted to be truth. News had performative power; therefore, some stories were preferred over others. In a country like Lithuania, which had recently restored its independence, the media was used to protect fragile state institutions rather than destabilize them. Many journalists, whether they worked for public or private news outlets, shared in this silent pact, deploying the media in national statecraft. They turned away from some questionable behaviors of government officials if they thought that exposing them would do more harm than good for the country. Driven by political and economic interests, directors and editors of media companies were often at the forefront of these efforts to screen potential news, imposing their agenda in the newsroom, but reporters also engaged in self-censorship. As far as I could tell, blind spots in news coverage that resulted from this selective reporting did not conceal any serious breaches of government duties. Yet their very presence taught me that journalism was something else than transparent diffusion of information. I came to see media production as a powerful means of manufacturing legitimacy and, as such, a vital component of state security.

In 2006 I left my job in the media to pursue a graduate degree in anthropology. The move from Lithuania to the U.S. didn't completely cut me off from journalism. Now and then I still recorded commentaries for the radio and wrote articles for the press, even though these contributions became fewer over time. As an anthropologist with a background in journalism, I saw an obvious affinity between the two cultural fields of meaning-making. Ethnographic research and investigative reporting require some form of "deep hanging out" in the community in order to produce knowledge. That knowledge, based on information gathered through interactions with people, then circulates through publications and visual materials, from photographs to films. There is great variation within ethnographic and journalistic writing genres, but most anthropological texts are very different from stories published in the press. Only sometimes—as in the case of long-form, narrative storytelling—do they blend. Writer and journalist Ted Conover, whose book about a prison in New York state, *Newjack: Guarding Sing Sing* (2000), won the 2000 National Book Critics Circle Award in General Nonfiction and was a finalist for the Pulitzer Prize, argues that contemporary journalism encourages the production of longer, subjective stories that resemble nonfiction novels.[2] Conover has been blending anthropological and journalistic genres in his work ever since he wrote his first book, *Rolling Nowhere: Riding the Rails with America's Hoboes* (1984)—a first-person account of riding freight railroads across the western U.S. that was based on his ethnographic honors thesis. He names Truman Capote, Ernest Hemingway, Anne Fadiman, and Sebastian Junger as other examples of this literary journalism, or creative nonfiction, popularized by the *New Yorker, Esquire,* and other magazines. Conover himself regularly contributes to the *New Yorker,* as well as to the *New York Times Magazine* and to the *Atlantic Monthly.* Still, these similarities between anthropological ethnography and investigative journalism are often potential instead of actual. Anthropologists spend years in their fieldsites, acquiring local awareness and habits, including learning the local language. In remote corners of the world as well as closer to home, they search for holistic explanations of cultural phenomena and usually write long, heavily theoretical works that circulate among their colleagues and students. Journalists, on the other hand, have a different work tempo. Foreign correspondents in particular are often parachuted to places where something newsworthy is happening and use the help of stringers and translators to talk to select local representatives. News reporters focus on urgent matters that are relevant to the publics of the media they work for, framing their stories in ways that attract the largest audience, and delivering information in short, easily accessible bits. Although investigative reporters can work on their assignments for extended periods of time—just as long as anthropologists conduct their fieldwork—with around-the-clock demand for news, such in-depth investigations as Conover's, Fadiman's, and Junger's are the exception rather than the rule for contemporary journalistic practice.

Anthropologists interested in news media distinguish ethnography and journalism by their different temporalities, audiences, and institutional logics, which include ethical considerations, financing, and disciplinary regulations (see Bird 2005, 2010; Boyer 2010; Boyer and Hannerz 2006; Hannerz 2004; Hasty 2010; Pedelty 1995; Vesperi 2010). Journalistic time is "thin"—both in terms of the tight schedules that define the everyday routine of news reporting and in terms of the limited duration of their relevance before stories become "old news." Ethnographic time, on the other hand, is "thick"—anthropologists engage in extended fieldwork, the pace of their research is slow, they produce dense empirical and theoretical text, and the results of their investigations are more likely to have enduring effects through teaching and subsequent studies. These divergent temporalities are a result of anthropology and journalism being subject to distinct "disciplinary apparatuses" (Pedelty 1995). According to Pedelty, "discipline is an active, productive, and creative form of power" (1995:6), which in subtle ways effectively controls what knowledge is produced. Anthropology is also characterized by more humanistic approach to sources (Bird 2005:302). The code of ethics of the American Anthropological Association calls upon ethnographers to protect the privacy of their research participants, who are often disguised—given new names and located in unspecified or fictional places. This anonymity is feasible because for ethnographic purposes, people's individual identities are less relevant than the general patterns of social behavior emerging from fieldwork. For the journalist, however, the story comes first, and in pursuit of the story, ethics of privacy and safeguarding of sources can become negotiable (Bird 2005:307). When compared to the limited readership and delayed audience responses that anthropologists are used to, the scale and immediacy of public reaction is also an important distinguishing feature of mass communication (Vesperi 2010:7). Considering these differences, Dominic Boyer (2010:9) suggests that between news journalism and ethnography there is a productive "division of labor": time-sensitive, intense flows of information characteristic of contemporary news make the kind of work that anthropologists do—slow and oriented to details—ever more relevant.

Despite these distinctions between anthropology and media, their similarities are also undeniable, even to the point of being uncomfortable. Ethnography of journalism is "a practice of representing practices of representation" (Boyer and Hannerz 2006:6). As an investigation of a parallel craft, it is a reflexive engagement in "studying sideways" (Hannerz 2004). Reflexivity becomes acute when anthropologists who write about news-making have a background in journalism. Elizabeth Bird, Ulf Hannerz, Per Ståhlberg, and Jennifer Hasty are only a few prominent media ethnographers who have trespassed this professional divide. Yet neither the blending of genre nor that of authors erases the boundary, as Hasty acknowledges: "For an anthropologist schooled in controversies over the politics of ethnographic representation, there is something profoundly uncomfortable about the practices of news media, something vaguely reflective of our own discursive practices, more purely politicized but also more politically compromised than anthropology" (Hasty 2010:133). Anthropologists are often critical of journalists for their involvement with state and corporate interests, but we, too, Hasty argues, are equally immersed in the muddy relations of power. After all, both anthropology and journalism are professional regimes of knowledge production that use interpersonal engagement in the field to create strategic representations of the world. In the words of Pierre Bourdieu, social science and journalism are two fields of cultural production that "lay claim to the imposition of the legitimate vision of the social world" (2005:36).

When in 2008 I began preliminary fieldwork on Argentina's north-eastern border with Brazil and Paraguay, none of these considerations about the blurred boundary between anthropology and journalism mattered to me yet. In the planning stage of this research project, my decision to focus on journalists was mostly pragmatic. The local media offered a layer of protection, establishing distance between me, as a researcher, and the organized crime and violence that I wanted to study, but couldn't do so directly. Working with journalists was first and foremost a methodological solution to the problem of doing an ethnography of border crime. I could follow news reporters to police stations, crime scenes, and court hearings; I could attend press conferences and listen in to interviews with security officers and crime victims, all the while being relatively safe in their company. Soon, however, I became aware that the very production of knowledge about illegalized practices, organized crime, and violence merited attention. The journalists that I was accompanying in their daily routine skillfully navigated between information they received *on the record* and what they learned *off the record,* narrating some events as news stories and hiding others. Sometimes, for example, they reported on drug trafficking or cigarette contraband, quoting numbers of prohibited merchandize captured by the prefecture on the river or by the gendarmerie on the bridge. Other times—as when one reporter and I witnessed a load of smuggled oranges being transported through a clandestine passage—they neither said nor did anything. For them, when it came to crime on the border, news-making depended on recognizing the invisible but critical boundary between public secret and public knowledge. During the early days of research, as I watched journalists work and began noticing how the code of silence defined what events were newsworthy, my interests shifted from the study of border crime per se to the complex entanglement of knowledge production and the making of security.

FROM ANTHROPOLOGY TO JOURNALISM

There is one question that was important from the start of my fieldwork in the Triple Frontier, but its significance grew over time, culminating when I sat down to write this book. Did the same code of silence that regulated the work of local journalists reporting on crime and security on the border apply to me as an ethnographer? In what ways did it affect me? In what ways it did not? There was no simple answer. On the one hand, my experience confirmed the commonly held view that disciplinary guidelines for anthropologists and journalists unevenly shape their access to local knowledge and their ability to circulate it in the public domain. As anthropologists, we can usually get away with writing about illegal practices because we hide or change the names of people and locations, making them unrecognizable to the public, particularly to law enforcement and to competing, potentially violent groups or individuals. In our search for broader societal trends and more comprehensive explanations, we are less likely to expose the identities of those who share their stories with us. Yet the representations we produce can—and do—have negative effects on the communities we promise not to harm. From the point of view of Iguazúenses, disappointed with the criminalization and securitization of the border, the line between journalistic and ethnographic representation has been blurry. Without knowing how their stories would be interpreted and what purposes they would be used for, many people still prefer the safety of silence, whether they talk to a reporter or to an anthropologist. The trust necessary for writing a critical ethnography of security that addresses the code of silence requires months and even years of deep hanging out. Once relationships of trust are built, however, we are confronted with questions about the politics and ethics of ethnographic representation. To explain the effects these concerns have had on my work, I will describe how I first learned the common sense of knowledge production in a securitized border space through my professional engagement with the media and how later these experiences shaped the scope of this ethnographic book.

Initially, my participation in journalistic production was very limited. Beginning with the second year in the field, I occasionally wrote for *La Voz de Cataratas,* the major digital newspaper in Iguazú. My first article was a report about the Fundación Mundo Sano, a nongovernmental organization that conducted scientific research on dengue and malaria in the border area. I observed how workers set up mosquito traps in neighborhoods around town and how they analyzed specimens in the lab. I also wrote about the Iguazú division of the national gendarmerie, one of only two locations in Argentina where service dogs were bred and trained to detect drugs. These descriptive reports were prompted by encounters during ethnographic fieldwork. They gave me an opportunity to contribute to the media that I was studying and that I knew always needed more stories. Later I began writing critical commentaries about events happening in Iguazú. For example, during a prolonged power outage, which was a common occurrence in the summer of 2011, I visited health centers and interviewed doctors who were throwing away vaccines and other medications that expired without refrigeration, criticizing the precarious infrastructure and its hazards to health. When for a few days after a blackout Iguazú had no running water, I published a news piece about a brush fire in the terrain belonging to the federal police, noting that they acted irresponsibly by ignoring burn prohibitions. The editor of *La Voz de Cataratas* added my name to some of these articles, but others she left unsigned. Anonymity is widely used as a method of protecting journalists from potentially adverse reactions to their stories. In Iguazú these safety measures were merely symbolic: in the town, where journalists were known by their first names, where their cars were easily recognized when parked on the street and where their personal cell phone numbers were often made available to the public, it would not have been difficult to identify the author of a piece.

These interventions in news-making allowed me to form a different kind of relationship with Iguazúenses, thereby helping my ethnographic project. Comparing the depth of knowledge that people shared with me as a journalist and as an anthropologist I could better understand the principles underlying the code of silence. Often residents were more comfortable talking about outlawed practices, such as illegal adoptions or bribes to customs officers, in intimate ethnographic settings than they were when asked on behalf of the press. But generally Iguazúenses hesitated before addressing these questions with anyone who could share their stories in public, making the distinction between an anthropologist and a reporter obsolete. At the start of my fieldwork it did not matter whether I introduced myself as a social scientist or a journalist—people did not trust me either way, which limited our conversations to topics that were considered "safe," like tourism. When later I began hearing stories about corrupt border officers, about the impunity of law enforcement, and about the smuggling of food and electronics, it was again all the same whether I was an ethnographer or a reporter—by then people had come to trust me. They expected that I already had enough common sense not to disclose sensitive information in ways that could harm the community I had become part of. The boundary between those who shared in the public secrets of life on the border and those who were denied access to local knowledge was not based on their professional identities. The code of silence protected Iguazúenses from unreliable outsiders.

The difference between anthropology and journalism as two modes of knowledge production was more palpable during my interactions with the government and with the security forces. Like the residents of Iguazú, some public officials talked more openly during ethnographic interviews than when they gave comments to the media. The chief of the federal police, for instance, explained to me in an interview how rising crime ("In this town all that happens are *cosas de barrio* [neighborhood stuff]") is related to politics ("There is no Giuliani here"); criticized law enforcement in Paraguay ("The difference between Paraguay and Argentina is that in Paraguay *la vida no vale nada* [life is not worth anything]. Here people die too, but it is different."); showed his admiration for Brazil ("We can't even compare with the federal police of Brazil. Have you seen their building? Please! They just press a button and call a helicopter. They have money."); and expressed his frustration with government bureaucracy in Argentina, lamenting how difficult it was for him to have his cell phone replaced—none of which he would repeat publicly. This police chief had good informal relations with the media, never refusing to meet with his closest contacts in the press. His public statements, however, were few and brief, stripped off context, and void of interpretation. When approached by news reporters, officers in the security forces regularly used two code phrases—"for/on the record" and "off the record"—to clarify what part of the information that they were sharing could be made public and what details were to be kept secret. While for ethnographers, this distinction didn't apply— nobody asked me to separate their stories into pieces that I could and could not include in my book—journalists in Iguazú heard the two code phrases that marked the contours of permissible news narratives every day. They respected this distinction. It allowed reporters to build relationships of trust with their sources, which facilitated media coverage of routine law enforcement activities. But journalists who feared violating the boundaries of public knowledge authorized by the security forces left some issues out of public debates. Their complicity reinforced the code of silence.

Ethnographic fieldwork was without a doubt very important for understanding the perspective of law enforcement, which was generally not shared with the media, but there were situations when local journalists had privileged access to information from the police. With few notable exceptions—such as the chief quoted above—many officials in law enforcement and security forces had no interest in talking to a foreign anthropologist and ignored my requests for interviews. Under these circumstances assignments to write news pieces for the local media provided me with an alternative access to important data. For example, in 2010 when I was looking for official statistics about crime in Iguazú, the regional police were wary to share them with me, uncertain how they would be used in my anthropological research. Presenting crime statistics to reporters, in contrast, was a common practice. The police knew how to use the media to demonstrate the efficacy of their work. Therefore, I approached the editor of *La Voz de Cataratas* about writing an article on crime prevalence in Iguazú and used this assignment as an excuse when asking for annual statistics from law enforcement. It still took repeated visits to the police press office, but eventually they gave me the requested numbers. Once my article, "The Year of Crime," was published in the daily, I could freely use this data in the ethnographic account.

From the legal perspective, both journalists and social researchers have equal access to public information. However, at the time I lived in Iguazú, a law mandating government institutions to provide records to the media did not exist in Argentina. When deciding how much they wanted to share and with whom, public officials had complete discretion. Sometimes they justified their refusal to provide information by referring to bureaucratic guidelines that required them to get authorization from their superiors on the provincial or federal level before talking to the press. Although these rules were often nothing more than excuses, they were effective in stalling the exchange of information. Officials in law enforcement and the justice system shared their knowledge arbitrarily, discriminating not only between local reporters and a foreign anthropologist, but also among the reporters themselves, treating some to more data than others. News-making was deeply embedded in uneven relationships between the media and their sources in the government and security forces. By switching my role from ethnographer to journalist, I was able to better recognize these distortions.

PROXIMIDAD

Writing for *La Voz de Cataratas* was only one form of professional engagement that I had with the media in Iguazú. In mid-2010, when I spent most days at the headquarters of the local television channel, C.V.I. Canal 5, from where I accompanied reporters on their news-gathering trips around town, I met Javier Rotela. Born in Eldorado, located a hundred kilometers south of Iguazú, Javier had a degree in video production and video editing from the Instituto Superior Antonio Ruiz de Montoya in Posadas. After graduating, he moved to Iguazú and began working for the television company. At C.V.I., where we met, Javier's job was to browse through raw video footage brought in by reporters and integrate it, together with news announcements prerecorded in the studio, into the evening *noticiero* (news program). I regularly stopped by his office in the afternoons when the news team returned to the station to hand over their tapes and before they left for the second round of news-gathering in the evening. Javier was a fervent critic of the media in Iguazú, disapproving of its poor quality and political undercurrents. We agreed that local journalists lacked professional training, resources, and independence, which made it unlikely that they would examine complicated social issues, much less anything related to organized crime. But criticism was not enough—we wanted to know whether an alternative was possible. That was when we settled on the idea of an investigative television program.

We called it *Proximidad,* which refers to the law of proximity—the principle of organization in Gestalt psychology holding that, other things being equal, objects that are near to one another in space or time are perceived to belong together as a unit. The name captured what we thought the program should be about: it focused on topics that were part of a broader field of local concerns, offering to look at them from diverse angles in the community. Produced as a series of seven one-hour documentaries, *Proximidad* was aired weekly from September to November in 2010. For Javier and me, this program was a collaborative undertaking, which meant that we chose themes together and we both participated in most stages of its production. Some tasks we divided to make use of our individual strengths: Javier had better technical knowledge, so he filmed six out of the seven episodes and edited all our video footage, while I had more time to investigate the topics and more experience conducting interviews. Our plan was to explore issues that were important to the community, yet for different reasons they were absent from the public sphere. We did not want the program to be a local version of alarmist mass media coverage of the tri-border area, dominating foreign and national press. But we were equally reluctant to focus too narrowly on matters that were irrelevant beyond Iguazú, as doing so would have attested to the limitations of local journalism. Our goals were summarized in these opening lines of *Proximidad*:

> Journalism is more than information. News stories leave questions that need answers; suggest ideas that lead to discussions; introduce theories that warrant investigation. We live and work here, in Puerto Iguazú, and we approach topics that are important to our community. Every week we offer you a new report. We verify, we analyze, we present—to let you form your own opinion. An encounter between opposite arguments. A crossroad of different angles. One focus. One X. Proximidad. Periodismo de investigación.[3]

As a collaborative project between a media producer and an anthropologist, *Proximidad* was an experiment of professional engagement. But our program was also experimental on another level: it was an intervention that sought to break the code of silence, which limited public debates in Iguazú.

Javier and I made *Proximidad* from scratch. In search for cables, lights, microphones, and other equipment we spent weeks traversing variety stores in and around Iguazú. Prices for electronics in this region were high and product supplies were very limited. When we could not find the items we needed from local vendors, we went to look for them across the border in Ciudad del Este, where large shopping centers were crammed with low-cost commodities—minimally taxed foreign imports, national brands, and numerous fakes. We were able to purchase the rest of our equipment there: mostly miscellaneous things like video cassettes, DVDs, and a camera tripod, not exceeding the quota for shopping abroad and saving us from trouble at the Argentine customs. Our most important and most expensive tool, the video camera, I had brought from the U.S. To have our program broadcast on Canal 5 we also had to pay owners of the television channel a standard monthly fee for airtime, amounting to 750 pesos (approximately US$175).

With costs accumulating, we needed to find sponsorship to finance the program. Many business establishments in Iguazú—hotels, restaurants, food stores, law firms, medical clinics, and other private entities— were paying for advertising in the local media. By the time we started *Proximidad*, I knew that in some cases this was a polite way to handle extortion: business owners used ad money to silence the media, effectively preventing public discussion of inconvenient subjects such as

FIGURE 4. The preview of *Proximidad* in the broadcast studio at C.V.I. Canal 5. Puerto Iguazú, September 2010.

widespread *trabajo en negro* (the practice of paying employees off the books). In this context it did not surprise us that it was difficult to convince anyone to support *Proximidad*. Entrepreneurs were reluctant to finance a new investigative program, uncertain how it would affect their economic interests. The general manager of a supermarket chain who wholeheartedly endorsed the need to improve the quality of local journalism bluntly told me he could not risk investing in *Proximidad* because if our investigations were to cause anger among Iguazúenses, they might respond by boycotting his stores. Fortunately, we managed to find two sponsors that gave us just enough money to cover the fee for airtime.[4] The rest—including all equipment, fuel, and time—was at our expense.

In the initial episodes we addressed issues that were at the time broadly debated in Argentina. The first program examined whether mandatory military service, known as *la colimba,* which Argentina abolished in 1995, would solve the purportedly interrelated problems of decreasing youth morality and growing crime rates, as some national politicians suggested. With memories of the last military dictatorship still haunting Argentines, it was a challenging question all over the country. But in Iguazú, where federal security forces had heavy presence and where many residents had family members working for them, any issue related to the military was particularly sensitive. Looking for different perspectives on the matter, we interviewed public and private high school seniors and their teachers. We also attended the military recruit training camp and spoke to a number of high-ranking officials in the army and the naval prefecture. The morning after the episode aired on television, everyone in Iguazú was talking about it: from people in the streets who stopped us to offer their opinions to other journalists who summarized our arguments in their programs. Encouraged by such positive feedback, in the second episode we sought reactions from the local community to the legalization of same-sex marriage in Argentina, the first country in Latin America to do so. We interviewed representatives of state and religious institutions and we talked to same-sex couples that, afraid of losing their government jobs, asked us to modify their voices and blur their faces to make them unrecognizable in the video footage. We also dedicated an episode to the crisis of urban waste management, which included documenting the construction of a modern recycling plant to be run by a local cooperative. We filmed politicians and municipal employees in their offices, as well as people who worked at the landfill, against the toxic fumes of burning trash. As *Proximidad* gained popularity, Iguazúenses began approaching us with information, asking to investigate issues that ranged from the problems faced by the veterans of the Malvinas-Falklands War to the selling of drugs at the entrance to the indigenous Mbororé community. Some of the leads we pursued, while others proved impossible—due to limited resources, time constraints, and the overarching code of silence, from which, as we soon learned, we could not escape.

Unquestionably the most difficult episode we produced was about informal fosterage, illegal adoptions, and child trafficking, which I discuss in detail in chapter 6. For weeks we waited and were often turned away by government officials who, in the absence of legislation guaranteeing the media access to public information, enjoyed freedom from the press. By stepping on the boundary between legal and illegalized practices that lacked social consensus and, therefore, were neither legitimate nor illegitimate, our journalistic investigation tempered with and tested the code of silence. This attempt to address a contentious topic by moving it from the domain of local common knowledge to that of the public sphere was fraught with complications. Not only were the scars of previous media coverage, which accused the region of being a conduit for child trafficking, still visible and painful; there was also profound ambiguity regarding the ethical and legal status of some widespread practices.

In this context of uncertainty it was not surprising that most Iguazúenses preferred to stay out of trouble, which to them first and foremost meant avoiding talking to the police and to the media. During the production of this episode—the only investigation of illegalized practices that we completed before *Proximidad* was shut down—we had to make some difficult choices about what information we could use in the program, weighing the potential consequences of both inclusions and omissions. We decided to create an assemblage of interviews with people who had encountered illegal adoptions as biological and adoptive parents, human rights activists, doctors, lawyers, civil registry employees, and politicians. But the story was inconclusive—our narrative raised more questions than it gave answers—and reaffirmed the boundary between public secrets and public knowledge that we had tried to overstep.

Producing *Proximidad* was different from writing for *La Voz de Cataratas* in that these two forms of media production—video and text—provided unequal levels of exposure. By seemingly direct reference to social reality, in the terminology proposed by Charles L. Briggs (2007), video, like photography, works as an "indexical icon," (re)producing that which it represents. Visual stories can be read as "forms whose features provide a reliable way of knowing acts that are hidden from us—and whose reality we accept by virtue of their indexical connection to an act of narration," Briggs writes (2007:324). Because of the proximity of the visual narrative, it has important implications for the politics and ethics of representing crime and violence. Images that document such themes as race and gender, for example, risk reifying social categories and legitimizing policies that reproduce suffering and inequality. Yet, as Philippe Bourgois and Jeff Schonberg note in their photo-ethnography *Righteous Dopefiend,* which includes a series of photographs depicting homeless heroin addicts, censoring images of taboo behaviors for the sake of positive politics of representation would distort the painful effects of marginalization, poverty, violence, and oppression (2009:15). Ethnographers and journalists alike can use the power of images, stemming from their emotional, aesthetic, and documentary qualities, to more effectively portray unacceptable social phenomena in social science analysis and news reports. Compared to written text, however, visual narratives have profound implications for the subjects portrayed, making ethical reflection a necessary component of such engagement.

Participating in the production of visual stories is complicated for those who are behind the camera just as it is for those who are positioned in front of it. In their interactions with the media, government officials and

Iguazúenses were more aware of the presence of the camera than a digital voice recorder. The camera was considered more *immediate*. Press reporters scribbled down notes or recorded interviews that they transcribed back at their desk in the office; news articles were often published the following day if not later in the future; and print media offered anonymity by frequently using generic categories such as "a resident," "a government employee," and so forth, as substitutes for individual identities of their sources. In contrast, although video was edited and could be manipulated to disguise people's faces and voices, television news was often broadcast live, and together with documentary films, they were widely believed to show unfiltered and unaltered images of the world.

Since video was accepted as the least mediated and the most accurate form of evidence, it is not surprising that for Iguazúenses, being interviewed on television constituted a more serious violation of the code of silence than if they talked to a newspaper or radio reporter. Video matched their claims with their identities. Print media was limited to citing people's statements in writing and radio added the authenticity of their voice, but only television attributed their words and their voice to an image that was unmistakably theirs. This synergy was dangerous in situations where the protection of public secrets was the common sense of everyday life. Discomfort with visual media, as opposed to print journalism, also extended to government institutions. On several occasions, when I filmed operations of the security forces—once when the gendarmerie was doing a raid at a downtown variety store suspected of selling contraband electronics, and another time when a large tree was burning in the terrain belonging to the federal police, to name just two examples—officers threatened to confiscate my camera. Although by law journalists were not required to have special authorization to film in public places, in practice their rights were circumstantial. Depending on their personal connections and the disposition of individual officers, reporters had unequal opportunities to document the activities of law enforcement and the security apparatus. As a foreigner, at least initially less entangled in the ties of social obligations that crisscrossed the community, I was usually allowed to do even less than local journalists. However, different forms of media production had discordant perimeters of the permissible. This was made clear to me when, prohibited from filming one police incident, I wrote an article about it. Although my text criticized the negligence of law enforcement, *La Voz de Cataratas* did not receive negative feedback from the police after its publication. The written text appeared to be less damaging to the fuerzas than potential video images.

There is no one reason why *Proximidad* ended earlier than we had planned. Certainly, program production was not an easy task. As we began investigating controversial themes, from child trafficking to land occupation, it was harder to find people who were willing to talk "on the record." Going forward required more of our time and more financial resources that we did not have. Javier worked full time as the news editor for Canal 5, a job he needed to support his family, but he spent every morning filming *Proximidad,* for which he earned nothing and actually incurred further expenses. We had not yet advanced far on the episode about the local politics of illegal settlements—I had just interviewed the director of the municipal land department—when a public figure discretely warned me about the potential consequences were we to continue with the program. The threat was not of violence, but of legal action. At first, Javier and I disagreed on what to do next. I wanted to continue with this episode and go to the outskirts of town to talk to illegal settlers, but he argued that it was too dangerous. Even when I suggested filming the interviews alone and preparing the minute-by-minute outline of the program, he refused to edit the footage. "You know why?" he asked me. "Because if anything happens . . . you will get on the plane and take off. I have to stay on living here." These words left an imprint in my mind— for their bitter honesty. They resonated with the dialogue between two journalists quoted at the beginning of this chapter, marking the outsiders from the locals. With *Proximidad* we tried to probe the code of silence, but in the end our efforts proved that media production in this small border town was less a heroic act of exposing public secrets as breaking news than it was a practice that largely depended on concerns about security. "I don't want to make certain people upset because I don't know whether I may need them for another project," Javier said. At issue for him were both personal safety and economic well-being. When on the day of my birthday Javier stopped by my apartment to return the camera and hand over a bag of cassettes with our video footage, it was the sad ending to my active involvement in local media. Though I did not immediately see it this way, the failure in journalism became an invaluable part of this ethnography.

COLLABORATION AS ENGAGEMENT

Much has been written about engaged anthropology. Scholars in the discipline have accepted that our responsibility lies not only with the academic community, which provides us intellectual, administrative, and financial support, but first and foremost with the people who agree to share their lives with us. Ethnographic fieldwork is "mutually formative," writes João Biehl in the first pages of *Vita: Life in a Zone of Social Abandonment* (2005:11); it produces a dialogic form of knowledge. Ethnographers working with people who live under conditions of structural violence (see, e.g., Farmer 1992, 2003; Bourgois 2003; Bourgois and Schonberg 2009, Fassin 2007, 2013a, among numerous others) have used their research to advocate for policy reforms and to foment a broader, issue-focused dialogue between community members, clinicians, government agencies, civic groups, social scientists, and other parties.[5] Some activist anthropologists have allied themselves with the communities they study, working on specific local projects that provide practical solutions for those stuck at the intersection of their aspirations for justice, security, and human rights, which are not always compatible (see, e.g., Goldstein 2012).

In a way, the work of a public anthropologist resembles that of a journalist: both want to communicate critical insights about social life, particularly addressing those who wield political and economic power. But the methods of scholarly and journalistic knowledge production are not easily reconciled. After publishing *Enforcing Order* (2013a), an ethnography on urban policing in the *banlieues* of Paris, Didier Fassin saw how difficult it was to maneuver the boundary between the realms of academia and the media. Journalists have to package their stories in formats that we ethnographers—usually much less limited by constraints of time and space—find too confining. Rather than backing out, however, Fassin made a call for "critical public ethnography": a conversation between ethnographers and their publics, which "generates circulation of knowledge, reflection, and action likely to contribute to a transformation of the way the world is represented and experienced" (Fassin 2013b:628). As anthropologists, we find ourselves wedged in between the people we write about and those whom we write for. Often, rather than entangling ourselves in the webs of obligations to the broader society, we are inclined to stand with those about whom we write, to advocate on behalf of communities that accept us into their midst, that teach us their ways of life, and that share their most dire problems, even though it is not always easy (particularly for those who study groups that behave in ways we don't agree with, such as engaging in violence). The work of a public anthropologist is based on the premise that all these groups of people—those we interact with during research and those who are potential readers of our ethnographies—are inevitably connected, and we should not discard our role as intermediaries between them. As Fassin put it, carrying on fieldwork we accumulate many debts to different parties; "making it into an intellectual production is repaying them—at least in part" (2013b:640).

It is important that after completing our research we present our work to diverse publics—including, and especially, the people we write about. But in situations that permit such arrangements we should also approach the process of fieldwork as a form of engagement, based on partnership and entailing obligations. Such collaborative fieldwork can be equally rewarding for everyone involved. In anthropology of news media, "epistemic fellowships" can be built around what Amahl Bishara (2013) describes as ethnographers and journalists "writing alongside" one another. While living in northeast Argentina, for periods of time I worked together with local reporters and published several stories on matters that were relevant to the residents of Iguazú. Besides interviewing them, on several occasions I also asked my journalist peers to reflect on their lives in the tri-border region by writing something for a distant academic audience in the U.S. and in Europe, where this book would most likely be read. Kelly's letter, from which I quote in the introduction, was her response to such an invitation. Still, writing *alongside* each other risks becoming writing *past* each other. Except for rare, truly collaborative texts where authors mold their separate identities into one narrative voice, "writing alongside" leaves one author distinguishable from another. Anthropologists and journalists might be present next to each another in the same place at the same time, but the audiences they write for usually do not overlap. In video production, in contrast, the roles of team members can be more difficult to tell apart: each episode of *Proximidad,* for example, resulted from our joint efforts to select topics and create content for the program, which was made for the community of Iguazú.

A television program as a form of knowledge production is very different from an ethnographic text. I can compare my experience of writing news articles for *La Voz de Cataratas* with writing this book by looking at the ethics, temporalities, and logistics that define journalism and anthropology as two separate even if closely related disciplines. But a similar comparison with *Proximidad* would be incomplete because it would not treat television as a distinct medium. To render filming, as a process, and video, as a form, visible in this ethnographic text, I had to bring them forward. All but one of the chapters of this book follow the standard layout, in which news production in Iguazú—print journalism, radio, and television—is the content of anthropological analysis.

Such ethnography of news journalism is attentive to differences that exist between modes of media production, but its baseline remains the written text. In chapter 6, however, I make the form of video and the process of filming more prominent. By subjecting ethnographic material to the structure of "takes" used in motion picture production, I juxtapose the flow and the depth of an ethnographic narrative and the ruptured, incomplete mode of storytelling characteristic of video-making. Blending the production of fieldnotes (writing) with the production of "takes" (filming) highlights differences in process as well as in form between ethnographic research and journalistic investigation. Such an unusual organization of the chapter, when the structure of video is brought into ethnographic writing, adds to the overall argument of this book: it shows how and why the two forms of representation are unevenly affected by security concerns.

Media anthropology has a history of cultural activism. Visual ethnographers like Faye Ginsburg and Terry Turner, pioneering this mode of collaboration, designed and participated in indigenous media projects that used video as a form of expressive culture and political engagement, empowering disenfranchised groups (Ginsburg, Abu-Lughod, and Larkin 2002). Strictly defined, activist research requires the existence of a conscious political alignment with a group of people and interaction on dialogic terms (see Hale 2006). In addition to activism and advocacy, there are other, perhaps less radical but not less meaningful, forms of public engagement that anthropologists have been pursuing, including social critique, sharing and support, teaching and public education, and collaboration (Low and Merry 2010). Although during ethnographic fieldwork in Iguazú I actively participated in projects that served the local community and though this book contains political critique, the most significant form of engagement that underlies my work was the production of *Proximidad*. As a collaborative undertaking, *Proximidad* mattered in several ways. On the one hand, the program contributed to the Iguazú media sphere by starting vibrant public debates on significant matters that had been silenced in the community, including the role of the military in contemporary Argentina and the rights of same-sex couples. On the other hand, two episodes—one about the construction of the municipal waste management plant and one about education and health care in the Mbororé community—despite containing critical views, were used for promotion and advocacy, attracting public attention to the recycling cooperative and to the indigenous school. *Proximidad* not only expanded dialogue on neglected

FIGURE 5. Javier during filming of the episode on waste recycling. Puerto Iguazú, September 2010.

topics in the public sphere, but also brought other tangible, albeit modest, benefits to the community.

As I note throughout the book, *Proximidad* also had profound implications for my research. Despite differences between anthropology and journalism, their goals are similar (Bird 2010:5). Aware that each of these forms of knowledge production has limitations, we can experiment with combining them in order to tell difficult stories to more people. It may well be that the problems we encounter in the process are the most critical part. What I learned while writing for *La Voz de Cataratas* and collaborating with Javier on the making of *Proximidad* informs the ethnography and analysis presented here. As a journalist, I was often frustrated by the absence of laws that would ensure public accountability and transparency. Scholars have shown that these projects are ideological and contradictory and that they contribute to, rather than eliminate, the production of public secrets (see, e.g., Hetherington 2011). Yet from the pragmatic perspective of the media in Iguazú, accountability and transparency were highly desired as improvements to the status quo. Until formal mechanisms through which government institutions would be obligated to share information with the public were created, reporters were left at the mercy of particular officials who limited the scope of news. But as an anthropologist I was able to see how, in the context of increased government and mass media surveillance of the tri-border region, local journalists were also complicit in maintaining the code of silence. Their tactical switches between information "on the record" and "off the record" and deliberate uses of visibility and invisibility were intricately connected to security, which in Iguazú required experienced maneuvering between public secrets and public knowledge. Without *Proximidad* I wouldn't have learned just how difficult this news-making process can be.

2

Dispatches from the Wild

And finally: the light of civilization will shine
on these dark regions.

—Rafael Hernández, *Cartas misioneras*

A LAND SURVEYOR'S JOURNEY

"An immense nomadic population inhabits the forests, poor, naked, barbaric, without knowledge of industry, sociality, patria, religion, this absolute source of all human legislation, nor of any other element useful for
settling down and preparing the social, intellectual, and moral progress for
the succeeding generation," wrote Rafael Hernández (1973 [1887]:147–
148). It was 1883, and Argentina had just nationalized the territory that
would later become the province of Misiones. President Julio A. Roca sent
Hernández, a land surveyor, to locate and measure colonies to be founded
in those remote northeastern borderlands. During the months the expedi-
tion spent in Misiones, often clearing their path through the enchanting,
impenetrable forest using machetes, Hernández wrote letters to *La Tribuna
Nacional,* a national newspaper based in Buenos Aires. Known as *Cartas
misioneras,* these letters tell a story of adventures and encounters. Hernández and his companions were foreigners in these lands. The letters convey
their admiration of the exotic flora and fauna, and Hernández carefully
documents the ways in which these subtropical varieties could be culti-
vated and successfully integrated into national development schemes. One
letter is dedicated exclusively to the qualities and production of *Ilex para-
guariensis,* or yerba mate, which is used to make "mate," a caffeinated
beverage popular throughout lowland South America. Hernández also
collected samples of sixty-nine varieties of wood and pointed to the poten-

tial use of local textile plants, timber, aromatic and medicinal herbs, and crops, including cassava, maize, beans, rice, and sorghum. As for the local people, Hernández was skeptical: he saw them as illiterate, "starving and semi-savage" (46). Traveling ever deeper into the interior of Misiones, he wrote, "The miserable life that these poor indigenous lead is inconceivable to a civilized man. Their clothes are tattered. They don't know footwear. Very few of them have ever eaten meat" (97). He was puzzled: "What is this? Who triumphs here? Civilization or barbarism? Between the man and the wild: Who is the brute?" (104).

When his letters were published in the paper, Hernández assured readers that his descriptions of Misiones were objective. He narrated what he saw, "very rarely letting his pen give in to impulses of impressions or feelings" (8). Almost a century later, in 1973, in the prologue to *Cartas misioneras,* Federico A. Daus called Hernández a significant personality in the intellectual conquest of the Argentine territory. He was an *agrimensor-periodista,* a surveyor-journalist. Charting new lands suitable for agricultural production, Hernández also sketched the area in public knowledge. It was at the end of his fifth letter, written from Santa Ana in August 1883, that the surveyor-journalist most concisely outlined his vision of replacing the savage life of the Argentine frontier with the state of civilization:

> So let us work—Let us work in Misiones, let us cultivate its lands—let us exploit its natural treasures, and where today only a wild, ignorant, and poor population exists (with notable exceptions)—which feeds of wild fruit and a limited cultivation of maize and cassava, which traverses the jungle naked, on foot, and lacks any elements of sociability, we will see flourishing cities rise; instead of savage shrieks of the wild, we will hear machines screech; the commerce will produce prodigious results, enriching those who buy and those who sell, those who produce and those who consume, and finally: the light of civilization will shine on these dark regions, allowing us to live in harmony in a community of aspirations, customs, and language with our own countrymen, strengthening the bonds of solidarity for the aggrandizement of the Patria. (p. 59)

CIVILIZATION VERSUS BARBARISM

The opposition between civilization and barbarism that Hernández invokes in his letters is a powerful idea that has shaped our understanding of the state and of security. In one of the cornerstone works of Western political philosophy, *Leviathan, or The Matter, Forme and Power of a Common Wealth Ecclesiasticall and Civil* (2002 [1651])

Thomas Hobbes traces the formation of the social contract to people's aversion to violence and their yearning for security. Describing the state of nature, in which humans hypothetically lived before they decided to surrender to a single authority of the state, he wrote, "During the time men live without a common Power to keep them all in awe, they are in that condition which is called Warre; and such a warre, as is of every man, against every man."[1] Hobbes explained: "Whatsoever therefore is consequent to a time of Warre, where every man is Enemy to every man; the same is consequent to the time, wherein men live without other security, than what their own strength, and their own invention shall furnish them withall. In such condition, there is no place for Industry; [. . .] and consequently no Culture of the Earth; [. . .] no Arts; no Letters; no Society; and which is worst of all, continuall feare, and danger of violent death; And the life of man, solitary, poore, nasty, brutish, and short."[2] The creation of the state is justified as a means to contain and avoid violence. While previously people had to rely on their own physical strength to protect themselves from harm, the Commonwealth took over the provision of collective security in exchange for their obedience to the sovereign.

In this narrative, security prevails over liberty, just as civilization prevails over barbarism. Yet, even for Hobbes, violence is only displaced, rather than eradicated: the state wields "coercive Power, to compel men equally to the performance of their Covenants, by the terrour of some punishment, greater than the benefit they expect by the breach of their Covenant." Since Hobbes wrote the *Leviathan* in the seventeenth century, violence has been consistently incorporated into the theory and practice of the developing modern state. Not only does the state, by definition, hold the monopoly to the legitimate use of force within its territory, as Max Weber (2004 [1919]) suggested, but it has also created legal frameworks that allow the government to use exception as the rule (see Agamben 2005; Schmitt 1985), justifying violence against the same people who agreed to the hypothetical social contract, as a way of protecting themselves from each other. To generate support for their violent actions, authorities continue to invoke the Hobbesian narrative, juxtaposing the order of the state with the threat of anarchy. In the case of Argentina, this master plot, which so effectively bolsters the state's power and strengthens government's control over society, has deep national roots, traced to the writings of the country's post-independence public intellectuals.

Argentine liberal thinkers of mid-nineteenth century used the concepts of "civilization" and "barbarism" to explain and legitimate statecraft

in the hinterlands. This uncompromising duality as the ideological frame-
work for state-building is the legacy of Domingo Faustino Sarmiento.
In 1845, decades before he became the country's seventh president,
Sarmiento published *Facundo: Civilización y barbarie (Civilization and
Barbarism),* a book that became one of the most influential works in
Latin American literature. Through the story of Facundo Quiroga, the
fictional counterpart of Argentine military and political leader Juan
Manuel de Rosas, who ruled the country by terror and violence until his
overthrow in 1852, Sarmiento suggested that the civil unrest in Argentina
was caused by the tensions inherent in the dichotomy between civilization and barbarism. He saw the land as a primary source of the country's
problems, its vast emptiness providing the conditions for barbarism,
which characterized the life of gauchos, caudillos, and the ethnic mix of
Spanish colonists, Afro-descendants, and indigenous peoples. In Sarmiento's vision for the country, there was no place for these backward inhabitants of the pampas. Civilization and culture had to be imported to
Argentina by immigrants from northern Europe. Nicolas Shumway, the
author of *The Invention of Argentina* (1991), writes that Sarmiento and
his generation saw the country as "so sick that only drastic cures [could]
work, be they the violent surgery of eradicating portions of the society—
Indians, gauchos, or 'subversives'—or the insertion of healthy tissue in
the form of foreign immigrants."[3] Argentina's public intellectuals in the
early independence period viewed their writings as part of larger political
processes, and the divisive narrative of civilization over barbarism, which
was initially developed through literary texts, soon became the formal
agenda of the state.

Sarmiento's book laid the intellectual groundwork for strategies that
he embraced as Argentina's president, justifying the campaign known as
the *Conquista del desierto,* or the Conquest of the Desert. Consistent
with Sarmiento's vision of the Argentine landscape as a dormant, unex-
ploited desert that bred values associated with barbarism, in the 1870s
the Argentine government began a campaign of military conquest, followed by massive immigration and modernization. Gauchos and the
indigenous peoples were driven off their land by dislocation and extermination, and the "deserted" space was turned into productive, "civilized"
land, available for capitalist development to build Argentina's export-
oriented economy. Directed by military general Julio A. Roca, the campaign was primarily aimed at establishing Argentine dominance over the
pampas in the south and in the west of the country. But its repercussions
were felt in other corners of the state, including the northeast. It was the

same general Julio A. Roca, between 1880 and 1886 serving as the president of Argentina, who later sent Rafael Hernández to explore the options of developing Misiones. In *Cartas misioneras* the surveyor-journalist echoed Sarmiento's civilizing policies by calling for the screech of the machines to replace the "savage shrieks of the wild."

Governments throughout Latin America have long used the discourse of civilization over barbarism, or order over savagery, to legitimize military intervention and other forms of state violence (see Briggs and Mantini-Briggs 2003; Coronil and Skurski 2006; Gordillo and Leguizamón 2002; Nugent and Alonso 1994; Taussig 1992). In Argentina, the use of violence as a popular tool of statecraft continued throughout the twentieth century. In the early 1900s, the discourse was employed against anarchists and other labor activists accused of posing threats to the security and stability of the nation, and from 1976 to 1983 it was adopted by the military to wage the "Dirty War" against the alleged "subversives" (Feitlowitz 1998). Fernando Coronil and Julie Skurski note that the discourse of civilization over barbarism conceives of history as the ongoing effort to take control of the natural and social geography, spatially advancing from the civilized center toward the savage periphery of the state. This conquest can never be complete: "In an effort to buttress its legitimacy and to strengthen its control of dissent, the democratic regime has kept alive the image of threats that reside concealed within the polity and at its borders, seeking the chance to return" (Coronil and Skurski 2006:86). Though Coronil and Skurski were describing the nationalist discourse particular to Venezuela, their insights have wide reverberations across the continent, including in Argentina. What looks like a failure of the state—both old and new menaces threatening its integrity and challenging its existence—can be the ultimate sign of its power. The prominent discourse of the government, the armed forces and the media focused on the ideal of order, wrote Michael Taussig about the civil conflict in Colombia, even though it was obvious that these very forces "have as much to gain from disorder as from order—and probably a good deal more" (1992:17). Maintaining the possibility of a threat legitimates policies of boundary-making, social cleansing, and militarization, justifying the endless expansion of the state security apparatus (see also Masco 2014).

There is an essential link between state control over its territory and citizenry, on the one hand, and media representations that provide legitimacy to policies of securitization and militarization, on the other. The dichotomy between the declared order of the state and its opposite—lawlessness—persisting at the territorial and social edges has been one of the explanatory frameworks that the mainstream media use in their coverage of state margins around Latin America (see Coronil and Skurski 2006; Penglase 2007). In the Argentine Northeast, from the early writings about the region to the front pages of today's metropolitan newspapers, the view from Buenos Aires has passed through the same lens that focuses on a clash between the civilization of the state and the barbarity of its unruly, disorderly frontier. Such Hobbesian ideology of control preceded and subsequently reinforced the development and application of the national security doctrine during the 1976–1983 military dictatorship and the more recent U.S.-driven global discourse of the "war on terror."

This chapter shows how stories in the Argentine media have played into processes of state-building in Misiones. I suggest that the press is an important part of the political optics of rule that James Scott (1998) calls "seeing like a state." According to Scott, the state ignores the complexity of the social landscape and applies the principles of abstraction, standardization, and legibility in the name of establishing control. The media contributes to this optical governance. News production relies on thematic, logistical, economic, and political frameworks that reduce the physical and social geography of the country into a legible narrative. In the case of the Argentine Northeast, this standardized national script is built around the opposition of civilization and savagery, state versus frontier, and order against violence on the porous borders. News media adapt to and reproduce this uniform outline, excluding inconsistencies and nuances from their stories and enabling legal and political government intervention.

Definitions of savagery and lawlessness have evolved since the nineteenth century to target new kinds of dangerous subjects. Still, the basic premise of "seeing like a state" has not changed in the media. Over a century after Hernández encountered the "semi-savages" inhabiting the remote borderlands, the Triple Frontier continues to be portrayed—in Argentina as in Brazil and Paraguay—as a backward corner of the state where insecurity and violence triumph over law and order. News narratives ignore the fact that "the savage frontier" has been the creation of the center, that like other frontier regions it has been shaped by the politics, economics, and culture of Latin American societies, and it has shaped them in return (Markoff and Baretta 2006:58). In this chapter I explain how the Triple Frontier came to be. This historical perspective will show that in Argentina the nexus between news-making and security-making that I explore in the rest of the book precedes the development of the global security paradigm in the late twentieth and early twenty-first centuries. The particular history of state advancement in the tri-border region, legitimated by the master trope of civilization over barbarism, facilitates contemporary securitizations by providing an already established, effective script into which stories about emergent threats can be inserted.

MAKING MISIONES

Together with Corrientes, Chaco, and Formosa, Misiones forms part of a geographical and historical region known as Nordeste Argentino, the Argentine Northeast. At 29,801 square kilometres (just over 11,500 square miles) in size, it is the second smallest province in the country, tucked in between Brazil and Paraguay (see map 1). Because of its peculiar location in relation to the Argentine national territory, the province has been portrayed both as a penetrating wedge, or *puñito* (fist), pushing its way between neighboring states, and as a dislocated arm of the nation-state's body (Ferradás 1998:40). To the west, on the other side of the Paraná, the province of Misiones borders the Paraguayan departments of Itapúa and Alto Paraná. To the north and to the east, separated by the Iguazú, Uruguay, and Pepirí Guazú Rivers, as well as a twenty-kilometer-long land border, are the Brazilian states of Paraná, Santa Catarina, and Rio Grande do Sul. To the south, Misiones edges on the Argentine province of Corrientes: marked by the Itaembé and Chimiray streams and thirty kilometers of land border, this corridor is the province's only direct connection to the rest of the country. Approximately 80 percent of the perimeter of Misiones is an international borderline. Such unusual geography goes hand in hand with the complex social history of the region. Both were factors that made state-building in the tri-border area a long and tedious process.

Historically inhabited by the Guaraní, who changed their settlement sites and had dispersed political authority, the region at the merger of the Paraná and Iguazú Rivers had flexible and fluid boundaries (Lewis 2006:19). Colonization did little to change these patterns. When in 1494 the Treaty of Tordesillas divided the Western hemisphere by drawing the line between Spanish and Portuguese oversees territories, what is now the border area between Argentina, Brazil, and Paraguay remained sparsely populated and isolated. Instead of fixed limits, perimeters of political authority continued to fluctuate. The region was remote from the economically desirable silver mines in the Andes, from the Spanish political centers in Lima and later Buenos Aires, and from the coastline settlements and plantations of the Portuguese. It was what geographer J. R. V. Prescott (1987) calls a *frontier*: not a well-defined official boundary line, but a zone that—from the perspective of the colonizing states—separated settled areas from uninhabited land. State power was radiant from the center of political control and it diminished at the margins of the colonial territories.[4] The tri-border region was a hinterland, where the sovereign powers of the Spanish and the Portuguese were weak and overlapping. In the colonial era the closest settlement to the intersection of the Paraná and the Iguazú was Asunción. But due to unreliable routes of transportation and communication, the future capital of Paraguay developed broad autonomy from the Spanish Crown and did not help to establish colonial authority in the region.

Left outside of the emerging interest spheres, the tri-border area remained beyond the reach of formal law. It was a no-man's-land. As in other Latin American frontiers (Markoff and Baretta 2006:57), the absence of firm governmental control made it into a harbor for outcasts, attracting those whom the spokespeople of the civilization labeled as deviants or criminals. The most notorious of these vagrants were the Portuguese *bandeirantes* (followers of the banner). In the seventeenth century, from their home base in the São Paulo region, they carried out slave-hunting expeditions known as *bandeiras,* traveling to the south and west of the Tordesillas Line between the Spanish and the Portuguese dominions. Bandeirantes captured and enslaved indigenous people, among them the Guaraní, who were considered more docile than other tribes in the region, like the Tupi and the Guayakí.[5] The Spanish Crown, seeking to extend its colonial authority over this unruly frontier, enlisted the help of the Jesuit Order. The Jesuits gathered the Guaraní into settlements known as *reducciones* (mission towns), converted them to Christianity, and defended them from the Portuguese slave hunters. Throughout the seventeenth and eighteenth centuries, none of these actors—the traveling raiders, the missionaries, and the Guaraní—were proper "subjects" of the state. In the Althusserian (1972) sense of the term, an individual becomes a subject through the process of hailing, which is the key component in the ritual of ideological recognition. But the inhabitants of the tri-border area, rather than being subjected to interpellation from the states, existed parallel to them and outside of their laws. They maintained the autonomous character of the frontier, which the colonial administrations continued to see as wild and dangerous.

Argentina was the first to revolt against the Spanish authority in 1810; Paraguay followed suit in 1811, and Brazil separated from Portugal in

1822. Territorially based nation-states brought with them a new understanding of power. It was no longer gradual or radiant from the center to the margins, as in colonial times, but was seen as equally dispersed over the territory. To use Weber's often-quoted definition, only the state—and only *one* state—could claim the "monopoly of legitimate physical force as a means of government within a particular territory" (2004:38). Declarations of sovereignty were followed by an arduous process in which the new states tried to establish effective control over their lands. After the War of Independence, Argentina was torn by a series of civil wars between Buenos Aires and the provinces that lasted throughout the nineteenth century. During this period Misiones remained a disputed territory. The Triple Frontier was seen as a potential space where any of the three independent postcolonial states might advance. As Frederick Jackson Turner (1962 [1893]) notes for the U.S. westward expansion, at stake was more than establishing control over the land: the existence of the frontier conditioned legislation, which developed the powers of the national government. This frontier hypothesis is important for understanding the historical process of state-building in Misiones and explaining why the Triple Frontier continues to be a significant factor in shaping security politics in Argentina. Frontier-making is an effective tool in statecraft: it underlies the development of the military and other infrastructures and legitimizes centralized government control over its territory.

Establishing state authority in this remote region was not an easy task. In his letters to *La Tribuna Nacional* and in his final report to the government, Hernández defined Misiones as both naturally and culturally different from the rest of the country; Misiones was what Argentina was not. But Hernández was not the only—and not the first—to write about obstacles to state-building in the Northeast. When in 1881 Alejo Peyret, a French-born Argentine writer, agronomist, and administrator, was commissioned to conduct a study on potential development in Misiones, he, too, published letters in *La Tribuna Nacional*. Peyret described his impression of being at the merger of Paraná and Iguazú Rivers:

> We can launch a bullet at any of the three States. But no human vestige indicates the limits of the three nations. These big rivers run through the desert. We have not met, we will not meet any man during our excursion.

> Whose is this territory? It belongs to the tapir, to the toucan, to the dusky-legged guan, to the wild boar, to the tiger and other animals.

> They are the indisputable owners of this virgin jungle. (220)

At the end of the nineteenth century the portrait of Misiones in the Argentine press focused on its exotic, wild nature, untouched by development. Though legally the territory belonged to three separate states, there were no signs other than the rivers to mark these international boundaries. Peyret heard rumors about plans to build a town on the Brazilian side, and in his correspondence argued that the Argentine government should do the same. "The corner of Iguazú would be a very convenient place to establish a town, which would undoubtedly become of great importance," he wrote (220). A town, insisted Peyret, is one of the first steps that must be taken to colonize "this deserted territory." This reference to the desert in *Cartas sobre Misiones* is not accidental— it was one of the key concepts, next to civilization and barbarism, used to explain and legitimate state-building in Argentina's hinterlands.

As the name of his famous land-grab campaign, "the Conquest of the Desert," suggests, Sarmiento considered the Argentine landscape to be "empty." Although the campaign's primary target was the South, where the state engaged in eradicating the nomadic life of the gauchos and indigenous peoples to make way for private land ownership and the development of an export economy, the writings of Hernández and Peyret called for the same prescriptions to be applied to the Argentine Northeast. The state had to take over control of its territorial margins by subjugating the land—through railroads, river transportation, and privatization. Compared to the Andes of Patagonia, which were charged with the symbologies of sovereignty, Argentina's northern borders occupied a secondary place in the national imaginary. But here nature posed similar problems and required the wild to be tamed. Writing about another "desert" in the social landscape of the Argentine Northeast, the Gran Chaco, Gastón Gordillo and Juan Martín Leguizamón (2002:25) show how the nineteenth-century expansion of knowledge about the region, in the form of exploratory expeditions and mapping of space, went hand in hand with military conquest. Pilcomayo River, which marks the international boundary between Argentina and Paraguay, was considered to be the quintessence of the "last frontier" in the Gran Chaco. The river, whose course shifted over time, was a "rebel" with regard to the geopolitical will of the nation-state (Gordillo and Leguizamón 2002:30).

The last significant changes to the geopolitical map of the Argentine Northeast happened during the War of the Triple Alliance (1864/5– 1870). Known for being the bloodiest conflict in Latin American history, the war was waged by the allied forces of Argentina, Brazil, and Uruguay against Paraguay. Paraguay was dramatically defeated in the war, losing more than half of its population and considerable portions of its territory. In the aftermath of the conflict, Brazil added the annexed lands to expand Mato Grosso, while Argentina substantially enlarged Chaco and Misiones. Following the War of the Triple Alliance, a decades-long rivalry over the control of Misiones erupted between the nearby Corrientes Province and the Argentine federal government, which ended when in 1881 the government in Buenos Aires nationalized the contested territory. By the end of the nineteenth century, the region's international borders were formalized: in 1878, U.S. president Rutherford B. Hayes arbitrated the demarcation of Argentina's boundary with Paraguay, and in 1895 U.S. president Grover Cleveland helped set the boundary with Brazil.

In 1953 the National Territory of Misiones became a province and, when in 1958 its constitution was approved, state-building in the region was officially over. Yet Misiones continued to be simultaneously an integral part of the Argentine state and always drifting away from its control. The story of an incomplete project—a state that fails to exert control over its borders, where competing actors and ideologies challenge its laws and authority—can be effectively conjured up by the government to justify its policies and actions in the name of security. Narratives of the fissures and failures of the state, circulated in public discourse, legitimate institutions and practices that strengthen it. Among these, an important vector of early state intervention, aimed at closing the frontier, was establishing reliable connections between the political center and the territorial periphery.

RIVER, RAIL, AND ROAD

Like the mid-nineteenth-century liberals that preceded them, Hernández and his contemporaries, who were sent to explore strategies for developing Misiones, were worried that nature was an obstacle to state-building because it hindered access to the region. Already in his first letter, Hernández insisted that the government must prioritize building communication and transportation routes and infrastructure, placing particular emphasis on enabling navigation along the Paraná. "When this is achieved, the territory of Misiones would stop being a mystery, and the grandiose spectacle that it offers, not less than the generous riches of its soil, would attract numerous industrial, commercial, agricultural, and tourist populations," wrote the surveyor-journalist in his correspondence with Buenos Aires (Hernández 1973 [1887]:29). His advice was taken seriously, and during the nineteenth century Argentina, Paraguay, and Brazil started building communication and transportation lines into the region, literally extending their authority to the politically divided frontier. In Misiones, by the early 1900s infrastructural development was beginning to show results. Effective connection with the capital was a precondition and the foundation for one of the pillars on which the state in Iguazú was built—its tourism economy.

In 1901, onboard the steamship *España,* the first group of tourists from Buenos Aires made the long journey upstream the Paraná in hopes of seeing the Iguazú Falls. Known to the Europeans since the mid-sixteenth century, when Spanish explorer Álvar Núñez Cabeza de Vaca described how their cascades hit the rocks with so much force that they could be heard from far away (Núñez 1902 [1555]:22), the waterfalls had remained a mystery to the outside world, a legend they heard about, but few could dream of visiting. Potential travelers were deterred by the difficulties of crossing the jungle by land, and Apipé Falls on the Paraná presented obstacles for boats. Finally, in 1901, using the newly opened river route, the group of pioneer tourists successfully reached the northern tip of Misiones. But they were soon disappointed. The steamboat that brought them could not advance against the current of the Iguazú River and had to be docked a few yards upstream from its merger with the Paraná. Nor could the passengers walk the remaining twenty or so kilometers on foot. In the words of local historian Carlos Villalba, "After [suffering] extreme shortages and traveling in the most rudimentary of canoes," only three of the group managed to catch sight of the waterfalls; the rest "made do with getting to know the beauty of the exuberant subtropical jungle that both sheltered and invaded them" (Villalba 2010:13). Among the travelers was a woman by the name of Victoria Aguirre who belonged to the elite circles of porteño society. She was impressed by the stories about the waterfalls shared by three travelers who managed to get through to see the cascades, and decided to donate 3,000 pesos to the governor of Misiones to finance the clearing of a path to the falls. To mark her legacy, September 10, 1901, became the symbolic founding date of the town of Puerto Iguazú, which was initially—as a tribute to the generous traveler—called Puerto Aguirre. Completed in 1902, the road to the falls was also named in her honor. Victoria Aguirre Avenue to this day is the major urban artery, connecting the town's main plaza to the national highway, which leads to the park.

In addition to the river route, Misiones became more accessible by land. The railway, which was built in 1912, ran 1,100 kilometers from Buenos Aires to the capital of the province, Posadas. Compared to the four to eight days required for a boat trip upstream the Paraná, travelers by train could cover the distance in only thirty-six hours (Amable et al. 2008:127–128). The railway also sped up postal communications and contributed to regional economic development. In 1913, a ferry began carrying train cars across the Paraná from Posadas to the Paraguayan river port of Encarnación, where they continued their voyage to Asunción. This connection between the railroad networks of the two countries increased Argentine exports to Paraguay. Posadas became a commercial center, where resources from the north of the territory—yerba mate, wood, and citrus fruits—were collected and prepared for shipment to their urban destinations. But the connection by train between the capital and the remote province was unreliable. A century after the railway opened, the journey still took around twenty-six hours one way. The train, known as the *Gran Capitán (Great Captain),* ran the route between Buenos Aires and the south of Misiones twice a week. It did not go further into the interior of the region, so travelers had to proceed north to Iguazú by either river or road. In the early 2000s, the train had an uncertain future, plagued as it was by violations of safety regulations, worn-out rails, mechanical breakdowns, and frequent delays due to bad weather conditions.

Commercial cargo ships, many of them transporting soybeans from eastern Paraguay, still use the Paraná for navigation; however, throughout the twentieth century the road gradually replaced both the river and the railway to become the major route to the tri-border region. National Route 12 stretches from Zárate near Buenos Aires through the provinces of Entre Rios and Corrientes, to Iguazú, where the Tancredo Neves International Bridge unites it with the Brazilian road network (see map 1). In Misiones, for over three hundred kilometers the two-lane highway runs parallel to the Paraná. When it was built, Route 12 ended in Eldorado; the dirt road that extended a hundred kilometers north to Iguazú was not paved until the mid-1970s. Another important highway, National Route 14, emerges from the intersection with Route 12 in Entre Rios and runs north parallel to the Uruguay River, through Corrientes and the eastern part of Misiones, to Bernardo de Irigoyen, located on the border with Brazil. National Route 101 winds along the border between Argentina and Brazil from Bernardo de Irigoyen to Iguazú National Park in the north. By the end of the 1930s, automobiles, passenger buses, and trucks, loaded with yerba mate and wood, traversed the roads of the province. In 1949, when the ferry service across the stream of Urugua-í was enabled, the first buses started circulating between Posadas and Iguazú. By the 1950s Misiones had a road network that extended to approximately two thousand kilometers. Although less precarious than the river and the railroad, land transportation in Misiones, especially north of Posadas, was challenging. For decades asphalt roads were few and many dirt roads were inaccessible for long periods of time each year due to rain. Today, as the most common route to the border area, Route 12 only competes for popularity with air traffic. International airport Cataratas del Iguazú was inaugurated in 1972, when it replaced the first airport in the area, built in the 1940s, and now multiple direct daily flights connect Iguazú to Buenos Aires.

THE SPILLOVER EFFECT

Once the transportation and communication infrastructure in Misiones expanded, it was easier for the government to develop this subtropical province. At the start of the twentieth century, the regional economy heavily relied on the exploitation of natural resources, including timber and palm hearts (Ferradás 2004:420). As Hernández and his contemporaries predicted and prescribed during their explorations, yerba mate has become the main crop grown in Misiones, where it is harvested in approximately eighteen thousand plantations (Klipphan and Enz 2006). Controlling over 8 percent of the territory in the province, Alto Paraná— the largest landowner in the region—annually produces 350,000 tons of pine cellulose. The province also supplies 30 percent of Argentina's tobacco. Locally grown citrus fruits include oranges, lemons, tangerines, and grapefruits, which are sold in Misiones and transported to other parts of the country.

But Iguazú has never been an important part of the regional forestry and agriculture industry. Here, natural resources have served sightseeing, and by the 1950s and 1960s tourism began replacing extractive industry as the major economic activity in the area (Ferradás 2004:421). Considering that the town was originally named in the honor of a tourist, this may be no surprise. In 1906, only five years after the visit of Victoria Aguirre, the first hotel was built. In 1913 authorities began investing in housing for a subprefecture, the police, a radio and telephone station, a primary school, and some basic infrastructure. In 1928, the national government acquired seventy-five thousand hectares of

FIGURE 6. Puerto Iguazú National Park, June 2009.

land, designating it for the creation of a national park and for the construction of a military colony (Villalba 2010:16). Officially founded in 1934, Puerto Iguazú National Park helped preserve the shrinking *selva paranaense*—one of the ecological regions in the once large Atlantic Forest. In Portuguese known as Mata Atlântica, the forest extended along the Atlantic coast of Brazil, from Rio Grande do Norte in the north, to Rio Grande do Sul in the South, and inland as far as Argentine Misiones and Paraguay, and was home to a number of endangered species.

Besides its primary function of ecological conservation, the national park also had an indirect but notable impact on urban growth in Iguazú. Daniel Crosta, who in 2009 served as the park's general manager, explained:

> In 1930s and 1940s the national park administration was responsible for urban development in Puerto Iguazú: They constructed the water system, installed electricity, built the hospital, built schools, built the police station. The park started all these projects because it was the only institution of the state that existed in the area at that time. [. . .] In 1970 the park administration decided to cede all that used to be the village of Iguazú over to the province, and it became the town that it is now.[6]

For most of the twentieth century, Iguazú developed as a procurement base for national park employees. In the beginning, visitors to the park were few—the long and expensive trip to see the waterfalls required an investment of time and money that not many travelers could afford. The town grew, but slowly. Because administrative boundaries in the region changed, existing census data do not allow for accurate estimates, but, where comparable, statistics demonstrate a steady increase in the area's population. In 1920, Puerto Aguirre had 1,176 inhabitants, roughly half of whom were Argentine nationals and the other half foreigners.[7] By 1947 the number of residents in the department had reached 23,512. When the province of Misiones adopted its constitution in 1958, the territory was divided into seventeen new departments, affecting the results of the next census. In 1960, the Department of Iguazú officially had 12,499 inhabitants, reaching 17,122 ten years later. The last census was conducted in 2010, when 82,227 people were reportedly living in and around Iguazú, a dramatic increase from its 31,515 residents in 2001.[8]

Rapid development of the tourism sector and the service industry, accelerating at the turn of the twenty-first century, encouraged both urban and rural migrants to relocate to Iguazú. Throughout the years the town's economy, which always relied on the national park, has become almost entirely dependent on tourism to the falls. "Tourism gives all of us in Iguazú enough to eat," one local journalist said. This vital connection between the town and the park was emphasized in every conversation I had with Iguazúenses—older residents and newcomers alike. They explained it as a spillover effect: "Tourism works like a wheel. Hotel employees receive salaries by taking care of guests, then they go to the supermarket to buy food for their families, so the store owners get money, which they spend someplace else." Directly or indirectly, the whole town is dependent on the flow of cash generated by the tourism industry.

Like the passengers on the *España* in 1901, contemporary tourists make the trek to Iguazú to see the waterfalls. In 2011, the number of visitors to the park exceeded 1 million people, and, according to the estimates made by the town's paper, *La Voz de Cataratas,* the park brought in almost 70 million Argentine pesos (approximately US$14.5 million) in revenue.[9] Visitors usually spend one or two days exploring the waterfalls and engaging in activities offered in the area, from inflatable boat rides to ecological train trips, and from hiking and adventure tours to full-moon walks. Located along the highway before the entrance to town, other attractions draw their attention, including the casino, the museum of woodcarvings, and the Aripuca—a giant replica of the trap that the Guaraní used for capturing wild animals. Some embark on a short boat tour to Fortín Mbororé, where the indigenous community puts on music and dance performances and where tourists can purchase Guaraní crafts as souvenirs. Fascinated by the tropical nature and exotic people of northeastern Argentina, most travelers overlook the haphazardly expanding Iguazú, which is out of their way—the road they take links the airport directly to the national park without passing through the urban center. Only a fraction of park visitors are curious to see the town that their money makes possible.

CRIMES AGAINST THE NATION-STATE

The narrative of state-building in the tri-border region has another side that is less visible, but at least as important, if not more so: the history of militarization. When in 1928 the federal government purchased terrain in northwestern Misiones, it was for two strategic purposes—to create the national park and to establish a military zone. To this day the proliferation of luxury hotels, souvenir shops, and restaurants cannot conceal the presence of an extensive border security apparatus in Iguazú, the second pillar of state-building in the area. Local law enforcement falls in the hands of the regional unit of the Misiones police, which has three substations, a special operations squad, a traffic patrol, and a women's police division. The police deal with common offenses that Iguazú residents encounter—everything from car accidents to thefts to homicides. But parallel to this system of local policing exists an extensive network of federal forces, unaccountable to municipal authorities and impenetrable to public scrutiny. This security apparatus in Iguazú is comprised of the naval prefecture, the national gendarmerie, the federal police, the airport security police, and the Ninth Mountain Infantry Regiment of the Twelfth Jungle Brigade of the Argentine Army. Three of these institutions—the gendarmerie, the prefecture, and the federal police—have overlapping jurisdictions over federal crimes, such as drug and human trafficking, contraband, counterfeiting, and money laundering.

Established in 1912 as Ayudantía de Puerto Aguirre, the naval prefecture was one of the pioneer institutions in Iguazú. Today it occupies a large area on Tres Fronteras Avenue and is in charge of patroling Argentina's border with Brazil, running along the Iguazú River, and the border with Paraguay, along the Paraná. Accountable to the Argentine National Ministry of Security, it is responsible for navigational safety and for controlling the maritime boundary. According to Héctor Vera, who in 2009 was in charge of the institution, in an approximately

FIGURE 7. Civic-military parade to mark the two-hundredth anniversary of the founding of the Argentine Naval Prefecture. Puerto Iguazú, June 2010.

twenty-kilometer-long strip there were twenty-six trails, known as "piques," used primarily to smuggle vegetables, meat, electronics, and cigarettes across the river. Though, as I show in chapter 5, the prefecture was mostly concerned with capturing drug traffickers, it confiscated any goods brought into Argentina without authorization. Cigarettes were by far their most popular catch. The chief official described the prefecture's work to me in the following terms: "The patrols are always out. It is a daily task, which is only visible when there are results. They [Paraguayan traffickers and smugglers] are studying what we are doing—as we are studying them [. . .]. In Paraguay they have a lot of technologies. They intercept our radio transmissions to determine whether we are going out [on patrol] or not. This job at times has no results."[10]

In 1941, almost three decades after the arrival of the prefecture, the national gendarmerie was the second federal force to open a division in Iguazú. It cordoned off a large area along Victoria Aguirre Avenue, only a few blocks away from the town center. Every year in July, on the day of its anniversary, the gendarmerie sends out a press release to the local media reminding the town's residents that it was founded "to contribute to the maintenance of national identity in border areas, to preserve the national territory and the integrity of the international boundary."[11]

The gendarmerie has jurisdiction over Argentina's national infrastructure, primarily borders and highways. In Iguazú, the gendarmerie was at first stationed on the Tancredo Neves International Bridge, connecting Argentina with Brazil, and later established a secondary checkpoint on the national highway, linking the border area with the rest of the country. In a 2009 interview I conducted with the commander of the Thirteenth Squadron, General Edgardo Riva said that the most important federal crimes that the gendarmerie detects in and around Iguazú are the trafficking of drugs and people. While common crimes "only affect people," the commander explained, federal crimes "are crimes that affect the nation-state." According to the gendarme, both drug trafficking and human trafficking in this northeastern Argentine province were facilitated by its geographical proximity to Paraguay.

The federal police was the last of the federal agencies to arrive to Iguazú, opening its delegation in 1990. At the time of my fieldwork the agency was located on a quiet street in residential barrio Villa 14, operating from a small and unpretentious building compared to the extensive offices that belonged to the prefecture and the gendarmerie. This police unit worked with federal crimes: from drugs and contraband to counterfeit money and documents. "Argentina's federal forces historically have mixed jurisdictions," said Oscar Fenocchio, head of the federal police delegation in Iguazú, when I asked him to explain what seemed to me like overlapping mandates.[12] In Buenos Aires the federal police are in charge of all federal crimes, but in the provinces crimes that are committed or intercepted on the river and other waterways fall under the jurisdiction of the prefecture, whereas the gendarmerie and the federal police share the jurisdiction over the land. "We mix a little," he admitted. The federal police in Iguazú also participate in the activities of the Tripartite Command—an international collaboration that brings together Argentine, Brazilian, and Paraguayan intelligence officers and operatives to fight against organized crime. Like other officials of the security forces that I talked to, Fenocchio unabashedly assigned the blame for the region's criminal record on Paraguay.

Paraguay is South America's major producer of marijuana. Because it shares a 367-kilometer border with Misiones, the province has long been one of the key access points through which marijuana reaches Argentine and international markets. Large loads travel via the Paraná, which provides a natural route for shipping drugs and conveniently connects Paraguay with Brazil and Argentina. In the north, on the Paraguayan coast along the Brazilian border, marijuana is wrapped in watertight bags and floated down the river toward Rosario and Buenos Aires.[13] Alternatively, marijuana is hidden in vehicles and smuggled across the border through official checkpoints. Cocaine, too, is primarily a foreign commodity in Argentina, despite discoveries of several local processing labs that used smuggled coca leaves. Like marijuana, cocaine typically travels across the border and to its final destination one of two ways. Large cargoes are transported in trucks, hidden in secret compartments or disguised within other goods, or they enter by aerial route, loaded onto planes that land on clandestine airstrips or drop their shipments, creating what one Argentine federal judge referred to as *"lluvia blanca"* (white rain).[14] Smaller quantities are carried by people known as "mules" who tuck them into their luggage or under their clothes, or swallow and carry them inside their stomachs. Though no clandestine airstrips or *lluvia blanca* have been reported in Misiones, Route 12, which for 1,580 kilometers stretches between Iguazú and Buenos Aires, is known as one of the major land routes for transporting both marijuana and cocaine.[15]

According to 2012 *International Narcotics Control Strategy Report* (INCSR), which uses information provided by the Argentine National Ministry of Security, from January through October 2011 government forces seized over 87 MT of marijuana, most of it in the Triple Frontier and along Argentina's western border with Chile. Argentine security forces also reported seizing 5.8 MT of cocaine, which suggested a continuing decline from previous years, when the authorities intercepted over double that amount. This downward shift in cocaine seizures was attributed to disagreements between the Argentine government and the U.S. Drug Enforcement Agency, constraining the latter's operations in the country.[16] At the time this book was written, both states continued to talk about the increase in cocaine transit through Argentina, explaining it as a consequence of intensive counternarcotics efforts in Colombia and Mexico, which forced traffickers to look for alternative routes out of South America. The INCSR noted that by 2012, Operation Northern Shield, which extends radar coverage to deter illegal flights used for drug trafficking along Argentina's northern border, had been only partially implemented. This lack of security infrastructure, in addition to the redeployment of federal forces from border zones to urban policing, is cited as a significant impediment to the operational effectiveness of Argentina's security apparatus in combating drug trafficking.

However, government statistics do not provide an accurate measure of crime and must be evaluated within the broader context of global and national security politics. The amount of marijuana and cocaine seized does not reflect the extent of contraband. There is no reliable information regarding how much of these drugs successfully reach their final destinations. According to some estimates, less than 10 percent of trafficked drugs are caught on the border. Yet in the global security regime, these statistics are used as a vehicle of communication and political accountability. The *International Narcotics Control Strategy Report,* which I quoted for estimates of marijuana and cocaine seizures in Argentina, is published by the U.S. Department of State. In accordance with the Foreign Assistance Act, the annual report describes "the efforts of key countries to attack all aspects of the international drug trade."[17] Based on these numbers, the U.S. government determines how well countries are adhering to U.S. drug prohibition and enforcement policies, certifying countries as "cooperative" or "noncooperative," and thus eligible or ineligible to receive U.S. economic and military assistance. As Peter Andreas (2000) notes, the INCSR rewards the most immediate and visible operational "successes," primarily arrests and seizures, so drug-exporting countries prioritize law enforcement efforts that produce these results instead of initiatives that have longer term but less visible effects, such as judicial reform.

Rather than being an accurate portrayal of the amount of drugs passing through Argentina's borders, the numbers included in the INCSR point to the tactics used to justify security initiatives. Andreas, who studied the U.S.-Mexico border, saw the interactions between state practices and illegal crossings in terms of a "game," a rehearsed ritualized performance. He wrote, "Feedback effects of state practices on both sides of the border helped to create the very problems for which increased law enforcement has been promoted as the solution" (Andreas 2000:12). Both the Argentine and U.S. governments identify the Triple Frontier as susceptible to drug trafficking, using statistics to legitimate the militarization of the area. As a result, Misiones has become the scene of a highly politicized, self-justifying, and self-perpetuating cycle of law violation and law enforcement, which locks the traffickers and the border control apparatus in a perpetual fight and leads to an escalation of the problem.

Drug trafficking is the new major narrative that the metropolitan media, especially the foreign press, use to represent Misiones. The tri-border area continues to be a wild and dangerous frontier, where "barbaric" traffickers have replaced the indigenous "savages." The media employs the optics of "seeing like a state," reproducing a geography of security that coincides with the agenda of federal authorities. This view is beneficial to both. On the one hand, the government uses the discourse of threats, which the media allege exist at the state's borders, to justify security policies. On the other hand, such spectacular stories attract attention from nationwide news outlets, increasing the popularity and budgets of media companies. However, the chronicle of drug trafficking has not diminished the significance of the earlier story—about the exotic nature of Misiones, which both attracts and threatens tourists. Mainstream media continues to focus on Misiones through two lenses: the first emphasizes "nature," the second—violence. In what follows, I further unpack these two thematic plots in the press coverage of the Argentine northeastern border.

REGIONAL CORRESPONDENT OF NATIONAL NEWS

"From Buenos Aires they [the editors] usually ask me for news related to tourism. Articles about child malnourishment, dengue fever, security, or crime are often results of my own initiative," explained the Misiones regional correspondent for the Argentine newspaper *Clarín*.[18] It would not be an overstatement to say that Ernesto Azarkevich forms the national public opinion about Misiones. Except for when *Clarín* publishes news agency information or when, on rare occasions, a special correspondent is sent to the area, Ernesto writes everything that appears in the largest Argentine daily about the province. He is a native of the place who works for the most widely read metropolitan paper, embodying the potential contradictions that exist between local and national news-making. Before I came to Argentina I learned most of what I knew about Misiones from reading Ernesto's articles. Not surprisingly, I had been trying to meet with him ever since my fieldwork began. How did he decide what to write and what not to write about? Was he self-conscious about contributing to the portrayal of Misiones as a wild and violent frontier? How much did the agency of one journalist affect the frame through which national media saw the region? These questions were critical to me, yet for over two years after I arrived in Argentina I had no opportunity to raise them. Ernesto was not coming to Iguazú while I was there, and other ways of contacting him failed.

Then one evening in the summer of 2011, when the end of my fieldwork was fast approaching, Kelly asked me whether I had any pending plans. I told her about my intent to meet Ernesto. I knew that Kelly was skeptical about his writing, criticizing it for being too distant from the realities of the region. But she often sent him photographs and other local information from Iguazú, sparing him the five-hour journey to the northwestern edge of the province. Ernesto owed her a favor, she said. So when Kelly, together with other journalists from Iguazú, was invited to a press conference in Posadas, I accompanied her on an overnight bus ride to the provincial capital. There, at an outside café in the shopping mall on the main pedestrian boulevard, Kelly finally introduced me to *Clarín*'s regional correspondent.

Ernesto was born in San José, a rural town south of Posadas, adjacent to the Misiones border with Corrientes. When he was growing up, he said, his parents had a yerba mate plantation. Once a week, on Saturdays, they went to town to buy groceries and newspapers, which, from the age of six, Ernesto eagerly read. After finishing secondary school, he moved to the provincial capital to continue his studies. At that time, Universidad Nacional de Misiones (UNAM, the National University of Misiones) did not offer a degree in journalism, so Ernesto enrolled in a newscasting program. In 1991, invited by one of his professors, he began working for the major provincial daily, *El Territorio,* at first covering sports, then moving through interior and general news desks until he found his vocation in crime reporting. Five years later, at the age of twenty-four, Ernesto applied for a regional correspondent's position at *Clarín,* and, despite competition from more experienced colleagues, he got the job. *Clarín* used to have a regional office in downtown Posadas, but since its closure in the aftermath of the 2001 economic crisis, Ernesto works from home, where he tailors stories from Misiones to the liking of *Clarín*'s nationwide public.

My data show that during roughly two years, from April 2008 to June 2010, almost one-third of the articles *Clarín* published on Misiones focused on different forms of criminal activities, including drug contraband, murder, human trafficking, child abuse, document forging, and government and police corruption.[19] The second most covered topic was nature, both as an object of aesthetic consumption (waterfalls, flora, and fauna) and as a subject of danger in the form of diseases (yellow fever, dengue, leishmaniasis) or natural disasters and wilderness accidents. Numerically less significant but still notable was the issue of broken connections between the remote border region and the rest of the state, such as delays of the train *Gran Capitán,* road blockades, and vehicle collisions on the highway. Table 1 shows in more detail the breakdown of these tendencies to portray the area as a tropical paradise, ridden with crime, violence, and disease. In the twenty-first century Misiones, as seen by *Clarín,* is as exotic and dangerous as it was for the readers of Hernández's and Peyret's letters in *La Tribuna Nacional.*

Published by media corporation Grupo Clarín, *Clarín* is the largest Argentine newspaper and one of the best-selling dailies in Latin America.

THEMATIC CATEGORIZATION OF ARTICLES ON MISIONES FROM *CLARÍN* BETWEEN
APRIL 8, 2008, AND JUNE 14, 2010

Topics	No. articles	Percentage
Crime and violence	77	28.3
Human trafficking	9	3.3
Drug trafficking	19	7.0
Homicide	16	5.9
Child abuse and illegal adoptions	8	2.9
Other (assaults, document forging, state violence, terrorism, corruption)	25	9.2
Disease and natural disasters	37	13.6
Politics (including official visits)	58	21.3
Tourism	39	14.3
Transportation issues (train delays, road blocks)	14	5.1
Education	10	3.7
Commerce	6	2.2
Infrastructural failures (power outage)	1	0.4
Sports (rally)	11	4.0
Culture	8	2.9
Other	11	4.0
Total articles mentioning Misiones:	272	100%

It is usually described as fiercely oppositional to the Kirchner government. The tensions between the federal administration and the Grupo Clarín media conglomerate began in 2008, when the company supported the agricultural sector during its confrontation with the government. President Cristina Fernández de Kirchner, who in 2007 succeeded her husband, Néstor Kirchner, as the head of state, accused Grupo Clarín of monopolizing the media market. In 2009 the National Congress approved Argentina's new broadcasting and communication services law, which sought to replace dictatorship-era legislation dating back to the early 1980s, and to break up monopolies in the media market. But Grupo Clarín, which owns newspapers, television and radio stations, and cable and internet services, was so strongly affected by this law that the conglomerate framed the legislation as a personal vendetta by the Kirchner administration. The company called it an assault on the freedom of the press in Argentina. The battle that ensued between the government and critical media outlets became a concern for international organizations, including the Inter-American Press Association and the Committee to Protect Journalists, worried that the fight deprived people of objective information on vital political and economic issues. While judicial appeals prevented the law from coming into full effect for a few years, the government stepped up attacks against the media conglomerate. It went as far as publicly questioning the identity of the children adopted by the company's owner, Ernestina Herrera de Noble, requesting proof that they were not the children of the *Desaparecidos* (the Disappeared), those who had been forcefully taken from their parents, tortured, and killed under the 1976–1983 military regime. President Fernández de Kirchner also made accusations that *Clarín,* together with another major Argentine daily, *La Nación,* had illegally acquired the company Papel Prensa, the only producer of cellulose that was used as raw material for print newspapers, during the dictatorship, suggesting that the monopoly of the press has roots in state violence. In October 2013 the Supreme Court ruled that the new broadcasting law calling for decentralization was constitutional. Its effects in making the Argentine media sphere more pluralistic will only come gradually.

At the time of this writing, in addition to *Clarín* and the center-right *La Nación,* other nationally circulated papers in Argentina included the left-leaning *Página/12,* the conservative *Ámbito Financiero,* the populist *Crónica,* and the sports daily *Olé.* Several regional newspapers, such as *La Voz de Interior* from Córdoba, *La Capital* from Rosario, *La Gaceta* of Tucumán, and a few others, also have a recognized place in the print media industry and readership beyond the boundaries of their provinces, but this is not the case for the press in Misiones—*El Territorio* and *Primera Edición,* both of them located in Posadas. The country has a highly developed radio and television-broadcasting infrastructure with over a thousand radio and forty-two television stations, five of which are nationwide networks. Many of the most popular broadcasters are owned by multimedia conglomerates. For example, Grupo Clarín owns *Clarín, La Voz de Interior,* Radio Mitre, Canal 13, and cable news channel Todo Noticias; Spanish broadband and telecommunications provider Telefónica, the largest fixed-line operator in Argentina, also controls the television network Telefe and Radio Continental; and Uno Medios owns Radio Rivadavia, América TV, and Rosario's *La Capital,* among other television channels, radio stations, and newspapers. Public media are administered by the state and include Radio Nacional and television station Canal 7, also known as TV Pública. The Argentine government also has a national news agency, TELAM. Although national and international organizations that monitor the freedom of the press and protect journalists' rights have expressed concerns about continuing conflict between the government and critical media, and the absence of clear rules in how government advertising is distributed, which influences news coverage by punishing critics and awarding supportive outlets, the Argentine media sphere is regarded as one of the most independent, vibrant, and diverse in Latin America.

There is no question that politics is an important variable in determining what issues are included in the nationwide media. As Mariquita Torres, director of the Radio Nacional branch in Iguazú, said, "National media are not national in the sense of representing the whole country. They are national by their outreach. Currently, the powerful multimedia only includes Misiones when they are interested in punching the government."[20] Ernesto admitted that their job in *Clarín* was to find what the government wanted to hide. Therefore, since 2008 the editorial policy of the newspaper—to fight against the policies of the Kirchner administration—coincided with what is commonly seen as the structural function of the media: being a "Fourth Estate," a watchdog responsible for monitoring the performance of the government and holding it accountable to the people.[21] But the tendencies noted in the news coverage of Misiones were not particular to the editorial politics at *Clarín*, and so they cannot be reduced to the media conglomerate's disagreements with President Kirchner—the same optics were shared by all nationwide media in Argentina.

Mainstream press journalists are blunt in acknowledging that they report some issues over others. For example, Lila Luchessi, who, when we met in 2008, was working for the porteño daily *Página/12* and teaching at the University of Buenos Aires, explained to me: "The coverage that national agencies give to local or provincial news depends on whether it is connected to some kind of interests of these media."[22] In the case of Misiones, connections that exist between Buenos Aires media and political and business sectors result in representing the region in terms of its nature or criminality: "The national media views *la tierra colorada* as either totally exotic, that is, it can be an object of tourism, or it appears in a criminalized form."[23] Narratives of wilderness sell for the tourism industry; narratives of violence sell for the state. To rephrase Luchessi's observation in terms of Herman and Chomsky's (1988) propaganda model, exotic nature and crime are the two news topics from Misiones that successfully pass through the "filter" system, foregrounding the political economy of the Argentine mass media.[24]

The same criteria apply to news photography. A photojournalist living in Misiones and freelancing for both *Clarín* and Reuters told me that his editors mostly asked for images illustrating human trafficking, child trafficking, and drug trafficking. When we spoke during the 2009 photography contest in Iguazú, he said he had recently covered two stories in the northeastern province: one about cocaine and another about seven tons of marijuana, confiscated not far from Iguazú. He noted that cultural diversity and cultural integration were also newsworthy in the eyes of his editors, as when the Guaraní voluntarily joined the Argentine military, or when the first bilingual schools opened. But matters that were only relevant for the locals would not sell in Buenos Aires or in Europe. Based on his experience, Reuters preferred coverage of issues that were interesting to their European publics, which included celebrity visits to the Iguazú Falls, traffic accidents involving tourists from European countries, and environmental concerns.

The media agenda did not solely depend on tailoring themes to make them attractive to the national and international news audiences. It is also important to consider financial and logistical aspects. Brian Byrnes, who in 2009 was freelancing for CNN, CBS, the *Washington Post,* and *Newsweek,* related the issue of underrepresentation of Misiones to the financial costs of reporting, which are tightly linked to the spatial configuration of the media network.[25] Like Byrnes, most foreign correspondents in Argentina are stationed in Buenos Aires and only cover regional events when these have a spillover effect and when the costs of news production are relatively low. Stories that develop far from the capital are less likely to be included in the national and international news narratives for two reasons: because they have limited social, political, or economic effects in other parts of the country and because significant geographical distance causes logistical and financial inconveniences for reporters.

Ernesto struggles with the same problem, albeit on a smaller scale. Even though he works as a regional correspondent at *Clarín,* he rarely leaves the provincial capital to cover news events in the rural areas. *Clarín* is primarily a porteño daily. Ernesto explains, "This means that the biggest weight, the biggest importance always goes to what is happening in Buenos Aires, to the detriment of the interior. Misiones is a peripheral province, a very tiny province, where *Clarín* does not have massive sales."[26] For their part, most small, private media organizations in rural Misiones, including in Iguazú, have what Ernesto calls "local vision." He criticizes their stories for being *"desaprovechados"* (wasted) because too often articles focus on local news without considering their wider implications for the Argentine state. Unless journalists in Misiones make explicit connections between what is happening in the border area and its repercussions in the rest of the country, their narratives fail to draw the attention of the nationwide news audience. There are exceptions, of course—some local news have a designated spot in the mainstream media's agenda. "The waterfalls are always there," says Ernesto.

MOSQUITO CONSPIRACIES

Nature has an important share in the representation of the region both nationally and globally. Particularly in weekend or holiday supplements, Argentine metropolitan media, including *Clarín,* publish travel guides and advice about Misiones with images of enchanting subtropical nature. Narratives draw attention to sounds, smells, and tastes—all the senses that nature awakens. "The spectacular falls are a magnet for the senses. It is because everything is intense in the jungle of Misiones. From the merciless sun to vegetation of incredible forms and sizes. From clamorous waters to the most colorful land," begins one piece in *Clarín*'s travel supplement.[27] "Everything is overabundant in Misiones. The colorful land, the jungle and the water. And the taste of fruits and fish," notes another article, titled "Misiones Cuisine is Rich in Taste, but Also in Legends"; this one from the food supplement.[28] Other publications, as their titles indicate, repeat these themes: "An Approach to the Misiones Jungle, Its Mysteries and Its Sounds," "Drops Falling over the Hot Land," "In the Kingdom of the Big Waters," "Surprises in the Jungle," "In the Heart of the Jungle."[29] Nature is called a paradise, a promised land, luring visitors to explore its native treasures.

Travel stories about the mystical beauty of the jungle stay in the supplements. But when nature turns capricious and threatening, where it is transformed from a peaceful object of admiration into a menace, it is worthy of the main edition. In May 2009, due to prolonged draughts in southern Brazil and northeastern Argentina, the amount of water in the Iguazú Falls significantly dropped, and the metropolitan press was quick to sensationalize it. "The Waterfalls Are Almost Dry" ran the headline of *La Nación,* one of the major nationwide dailies.[30] The article included a photograph depicting a few trickles instead of the usual torrential cascade. Iguazúenses still remember this news as a threat to the regional tourism economy. Later that same year, in September, a tornado in San Pedro, a town known for its araucarias, in the eastern part of the province, became an even bigger story. The tornado caused eleven deaths, most of them children, and left sixty people injured. Then in March 2011, a boat taking tourists on a ride to the waterfalls capsized in Iguazú National Park, resulting in two fatalities, both American citizens; it was all over the news. Fortunately, natural disasters and emergencies like these—dramatic events that become important on the national and on the international scale—are rather rare.

Wilderness has another implicit danger: disease. Following Mary Douglas's analysis in *Purity and Danger* (1966), medical anthropologists have shown how the culturally nurtured distinction between cleanliness and dirt, which racializes space and creates what Briggs and Mantini-Briggs (2003:10) call the dichotomy between "sanitary citizens" and "unsanitary subjects," is superimposed on the boundary between the state and the non-state, or civilization and barbarism. The humid subtropical climate in Misiones facilitates the spread of vector-borne diseases, primarily dengue, yellow fever, and leishmaniasis. The mainstream media, always on the lookout for issues that concern the general public, is proficient at perpetuating the narrative of dangerous illnesses. In their stories journalists, who are used to relying on established communicative cartographies, essentialize the connection between disease and the sociospatial terrain of the state, portraying the border area between Argentina, Brazil, and Paraguay as an epidemiological frontier. The following example illustrates this point.

On March 4, 2008, *Clarín* reported that a farmworker in rural Misiones had been diagnosed with yellow fever. The newspaper noted that earlier that year Argentine health authorities had found seventeen dead monkeys—animal hosts for the virus—in the nearby area.[31] Although yellow fever has never been eradicated in Brazil, in Argentina the disease has claimed no official human victims since 1841. The media depicted the renascent disease as originating both from across the human/nature divide (from monkeys to humans) and from across Argentina/neighboring countries divide (from Brazil and Paraguay to Argentina). Alerts that yellow fever has reappeared immediately became global news. Immunological maps that show potential danger zones for the disease were redrawn. The Argentine state started a centralized nationwide immunization campaign; everyone living in Misiones or traveling to it was ordered to get a vaccine.

Argentine mass media collaborated in the state's efforts by promoting vaccination and raising awareness about the virus.[32] But the other effect of these stories was to perpetuate fear. Many journalists in Iguazú saw the alarmist coverage by their porteño counterparts in terms of conspiracy against the province. They reasoned that Iguazú Falls competes for tourism revenue with Bariloche and other destinations in the

Argentine South, which, not by coincidence, was the home base of Néstor Kirchner: before becoming Argentina's president, Kirchner was the governor of Santa Cruz, his native province in Patagonia. As Kelly often repeats, during the *temporada alta* (high tourism season), especially right before Holy Week, when many vacationing Argentines choose to spend their holidays in Iguazú, something bad always happens in the area, be it a drought that depletes water from the falls or a disease outbreak. When national media sensationalize the coverage of these events, tourists are purportedly redirected from the country's north to the south. Kelly and other Iguazú journalists suspect that by circulating negative news about Iguazú, Argentina's metropolitan media, even if indirectly, contribute to the private interests of the ruling elites.

While it is futile to attempt to verify allegations of government-media conspiracy, the mere popularity of this myth deserves attention. Briggs and Mantini-Briggs (2003) noted that during the cholera epidemic in Venezuela, a number of conspiracy theories circulated among the Warao in the highly affected Delta Amacuro region. In one of the most popular versions, the government was accused of planning the epidemic in order to get rid of the indigenous community and take over the area's natural resources. Rather than discarding them, Briggs suggested that conspiracy theories are excellent objects of reflection because they raise important questions about official practices of purification and hybridization and constructions of scale (2004:183). From this viewpoint, the prevalent belief that the government and the national media were escalating the danger of yellow fever and other tropical diseases in Misiones in order to concentrate tourism profits in Patagonia should be understood in terms of anxieties and insecurity among Iguazúenses stemming from a history of socioeconomic and political marginalization of the region. Their mistrust of the federal government was so strong that some locals even questioned the purpose of the vaccination campaign. They suspected that the government used yellow fever as a pretext to inject them with unknown medications that would ultimately make them worse.

The case of yellow fever was not unique. There were other reported disease outbreaks, regularly providing Kelly and her colleagues with opportunities to reiterate their conviction about conspiracy. In 2009, a scare about leishmaniasis, a parasitic disease that is transmitted by sandflies, which move between infected animals and people, brought speculations about the need to exterminate local dogs in Misiones.[33] As the news circulated, causing unease, Corrientes—the only connection

FIGURE 8. At the inauguration of the dengue prevention campaign, Misiones Governor Maurice Closs poses with personnel from the Argentine Army. Puerto Iguazú, February 2011.

by land between Misiones and the rest of the country—banned the entry of dogs from the north. The following year, danger reemerged in the form of dengue fever. News about what was called the "unavoidable impending epidemic" started in December 2009.[34] Later that summer, in February 2010, the number of dengue patients attended daily in the local Martha Schwarz hospital in Iguazú rose to sixty, exhausting its resources.[35] The Misiones Ministry of Health described the situation as "complicated, but under control," putting the blame for the epidemic on Argentina's insecure borders. In an excerpt from Ernesto's *Clarín* article, we can see how the media further develops the idea of dengue being a "foreign," "imported" disease, spreading through the country's porous border with Paraguay deeper into Argentina: "Dengue virus came from Paraguay at the end of last December. It was imported by a former gendarme who visited the neighboring country and contracted the disease. Since then, cases multiplied and today they are primarily concentrated in eight barrios of Puerto Iguazú, the majority of them at the edge of town."[36]

Stories of tropical disease imply the failure of the state in taming nature. Centuries ago in the European colonies throughout Latin America many illnesses, including yellow fever, were viewed as an enemy to civilization, to be conquered in the name of progress (Wiley and Allen 2009:273). In what is perhaps the most widely known case, the U.S. government and the Rockefeller Foundation fought against *Aedes aegypti* mosquitoes, which are the carriers of both dengue and yellow fever, in Panama. Putting the Aedes population under control was a prerequisite for closing the natural frontier in Central America and building the Panama Canal. Ironically, in the tri-border region the proliferation of mosquito-borne diseases was not a matter of nature's wilderness, but was directly linked to the construction of the Itaipú Hydroelectric Dam on the Paraná. Only a few miles upstream from Iguazú, the still-water reservoir created by the dam became a perfect breeding environment for mosquitoes. Anthropologist Carmen Ferradás showed how the combination of changes brought about by the construction of the dam, deforestation related to soy production, and population migration contributed to the spread of dengue virus in the region (see Ferradás 2004). It was development, associated with the state of civilization, that caused the epidemic, rather than its alleged chief enemy—untamed nature.

But such alternative explanations, which make connections between disease outbreaks and larger political and economic development projects, did not make it to the front pages of the mainstream media. During the yellow fever and dengue epidemics in Misiones, the Argentine government called for the formation of a broad coalition between federal and provincial state institutions, municipal authorities, the military and regional police forces, schools, and the media, among other actors, to implement campaigns aimed at prevention, eradication, and monitoring of these diseases. Iguazú was designated as a critical zone for the spread of dengue because of its proximity to high-prevalence areas in Brazil and Paraguay and its susceptibility due to the frequent movement of people across the borders. When in the beginning of 2011 no new dengue outbreak was reported, local journalists in Iguazú celebrated this civilian-military strategy as a success story. Concerns about the securitization of the disease, which gave the military even broader authority to intervene in local affairs, were only occasionally shared in private conversations. Nobody addressed publicly the implications of enlisting the armed forces to fight the dengue mosquito in the town's outlying barrios, where the state's alleged "unsanitary subjects" lived. Instead, I heard some of the town's inhabitants blame their fellow Iguazúenses, saying that residents of poorer neighborhoods, dirty and uneducated, contributed to the spread of the disease because they failed to keep their homes clean and left open water containers outdoors.

Local media participated in the social coalition–driven campaign against dengue by publishing guidelines for appropriate "sanitary citizen" behavior. Thus, despite their honest intentions to inform the public about ways to prevent the epidemic, without realizing it they, too, were making poverty into a crime against public health. The government's decision to deploy the security forces to spray neighborhoods with toxic agents to eliminate mosquito larvae was the easiest solution to a complex social problem, which allowed discussions of government responsibility, untoward effects of development projects, and causes of poverty to be left aside.

SPECTACLES OF POVERTY AND VIOLENCE

Dengue outbreak was not the only occasion on which the media contributed to the criminalization of extreme poverty in the region and legitimated state involvement to deal with its effects. When in October 2010 two children in the rural Misiones town of Montecarlo died from malnourishment and the national media turned their heightened attention to the province, journalists both challenged and, often unintentionally, justified the need for more extensive government intervention. The Argentine Ministry of Health announced that 1,300 gravely malnourished children were now under the medical and social supervision of the newly created governmental program Hambre Cero (Zero Hunger). Nonetheless, Misiones governor Maurice Closs, quoted by *Clarín,* admitted that the situation was bad: "Obviously some of these kids will die because infant mortality is a problem, it is reality."[37] Together with popular broadcast media such as the cable news channel TN and Canal 13, both of which belong to multimedia conglomerate Grupo Clarín, the daily attacked the government, pointing to the ineffectiveness of the Hambre Cero program. To some extent, they showed the problem to be the result of structural violence, emphasizing the extreme poverty of the region as the underlying cause of child malnourishment. However, their reporting from the area soon turned to looking for cultural explanations of children's deaths. As the scandal escalated, the outraged Misiones government fought back against what it claimed were "false accusations" from the national media.

But the metropolitan press was committed to the story line. The cause of malnourishment was found in *reviro,* a traditional meal made from wheat flour and water and then fried in fat. In Misiones there are annual festivals and competitions dedicated to preparing the dish, which is the

FIGURE 9. Inauguration of a primary school in Barrio 1ero de Mayo, a peripheral neighborhood of Puerto Iguazú, in September 2010. Behind local government officials, gathered for the occasion, stand the precarious houses of the neighborhood's residents.

staple food of the poor and part of the cultural heritage of the region. On November 14, 2010, a popular midnight program on Canal 13, hosted by Chiche Gelblung, included a report called "Scandal in Misiones because of the News on Hunger." The theme of the evening was food, as the caption read: "Is reviro pride or misery?" The report focused on the death of a child whose daily meal was reviro. A beautiful blond reporter was shown visiting the houses and pointing out the conditions of poverty under which the families in Montecarlo lived. She lifted children's shirts to show their inflated bellies. She asked the children if they had ever eaten *milanesa*, a breaded meat filet popular in many Latin American countries. Like the savages that Hernández met in Misiones at the end of the nineteenth century, who, unlike "proper" Argentines, had never "eaten meat," some children in the program responded they did not know what a "milanesa" was. Mothers interviewed by the journalist admitted they could rarely afford to buy meat. The camera moved to Ángel. At thirteen kilos (28.9 lbs.), the nine-year-old boy was severely underweight.

In voiceover, Gelblung commented on the conditions of survival of these families: "Children live under the threat of death. Illiterate parents don't know how to administer medicine [. . .]. Seven children used to

live in this house. Now only six remain." The voice continued, emphasizing the extreme poverty: "In the house of these children there is no
gas, there is no electricity, there is no drinking water. They don't even
have bathrooms." Criticism of the failures of the state and inadequate
governmental policies merged with blaming the victim. Illiterate, poor
Misioneros, used to eating reviro, which has little nutritional value, die.
They die because of both state neglect and their own ignorance. Gelblung was the contemporary counterpart of Hernández, pointing to the
barbarity of the jungle population and instructing the state about what
needed to be done to create sanitary citizens out of those whose lives, in
Hobbes's words, were "poor, nasty, brutish, and short."

To report on the deaths of children, *Clarín* sent a special correspondent and a photographer to Misiones who prepared a series of news articles. Ernesto helped them with production. But he was critical. "When
did the issue of malnourishment in Misiones come up? When somebody
died. Malnourishment has been here for decades."[38] The regional correspondent of the major Argentine daily said that local problems gained
national prominence suddenly, in cases where the story had a potential
for a greater impact. He had written about malnourishment before, but
until an extraordinary event, such as the death of a child, could conjure
up a spectacular narrative, the porteño paper had no space for structural
violence and other systemic problems in Misiones.

On the other hand, Ernesto did not agree with his Iguazú-based colleagues that *Clarín* allegedly worked alongside the Kirchner administration, conspiring to lure tourists away from the Argentine Northeast and
redirect them to the south. The newspaper was fiercely opposed to the
federal and provincial governments, which in 2011 belonged to political
allies. He explained: "Last year there was a series of important news
stories about dengue, which had wide repercussions, because the government tried to minimize the scale of the epidemic in the area. So,
together with a photographer, we went to Puerto Iguazú to do field
work, talk to the people, visit the local hospital. We realized that the
situation was much worse than the Misiones Ministry of Health admitted."[39] Though journalists in Iguazú saw alarmist coverage of the dengue epidemic and the deaths of local children as intentional attacks
against those living in the border area that further worsened the effects
of enduring state neglect, and they tried to downplay the significance of
both problems, for *Clarín* the focus on dengue and on malnourished
children was a means to criticize the government in the form of blaming
it for the structural abandonment of the remote province. This example

shows that local and metropolitan media may expose the inadequacy of government policies in contrary ways. They also have a different understanding of newsworthiness: while the former, as I show throughout this book, have an interest in protecting the good reputation of the border area, which is directly related to their social and financial well-being, the latter's motivations are circumscribed by editorial policies that are tightly connected to economic and political interests of the mass media.

Tendency to favor bad news over good is a central pillar of media logics, which explains journalistic fascination with disease outbreaks, natural disasters, and other deadly incidents. But Ernesto is also biased toward negative stories because crime and security are his professional specializations. The editors in Buenos Aires often ask him to send news articles featuring Iguazú Falls, but he typically uses his own initiative when it comes to reporting on crime and violence in the region. He began by writing for the crime section while still a young reporter at *El Territorio* in the 1990s. When we met in 2011, in addition to being the regional correspondent at *Clarín*, Ernesto worked for a posadeño news daily, *Noticias del 6*, where he exclusively covered crime. "It is true that Misiones is the port of entry for Paraguayan marijuana," he said, when our conversation finally turned to discussing crime, adding that it was difficult to know the extent of the problem, when even the security forces admitted to catching less than 10 percent of the drug flow.[40] Cocaine, too, was trafficked through the area, including across the bridges of Santa Cruz and Tancredo Neves. But organized crime in the tri-border region was not limited to drugs, and Ernesto talked at length about human trafficking, about Paraguayan women and girls who are brought into the country through clandestine crossings and then taken to Córdoba, Buenos Aires, and the south of the country, where they are sexually exploited. "A few days ago there was a publication about 250 girls that were rescued and attended at the center for trafficking victims here, in Misiones," he recalled, concerned about this issue.

More than organized crime, however, it is the "savage" lifestyle that earns the province a place in the mainstream Argentine press. In these news stories Misioneros are portrayed as both uneducated and aggressive. The following titles from articles that appeared in *Clarín* and *La Nación* between 2008 and 2010 show the tendency to depict the area as a space of shameful crime and appalling domestic violence: "Couple Accused of Selling Four Children Denounced," "Child Shoots His 9-Year-Old Cousin," "Former Mayor Attacks Two Salesmen with Knife because They Did not Give a Discount," "Misionera Who Was Sold for 100

Pesos Rescued," "Teacher and Her Mother Assassinated in House in Oberá," "Woman Detained for Buying a Child," "Brutal Murder of Aboriginal Child in Misiones."[41] Through such sensational, often graphic publications, Argentine metropolitan media emphasized the absence of moral norms regulating everyday life on the border. During my fieldwork, such coverage of interpersonal violence and common crime in Misiones was more prominent in the domestic media sphere than were stories of drug trafficking or human trafficking, which were preferred by the foreign press.

OLD PLOTS, NEW STORIES

The media's "seeing like a state" implies thematic, logistical, economic, and political schemes that reduce the physical and social geography of the country into a legible narrative based on the rhetorical opposition between civilization and barbarism, order and porous borders, state and frontier. The frontier, though it connotes the process of state-building and the advancement of governmental control over "no man's land," is never completely closed. Even after the state demarcates its territorial boundaries, it can return to using the narrative of potential threats at its borders. Such discursive reopening of the "savage frontier" serves to justify government intervention in the form of tightened military control. Now and again Argentine mainstream media, based in Buenos Aires, have been used as vehicles to circulate this story line, legitimating the expansion of state security and regulatory apparatuses. Although characters in news coverage change, the basic script undergoes only minor modifications: where once Hernández saw naked and illiterate savages, unfamiliar with the social norms of civil society, the Argentine metropolitan media now identifies marginal subjects who are incapable of following public health prescriptions and who cheat the state by trading in the informal economy. The easily legible media script effectively serves interests the media share with Argentina's governmental and business sectors. In the twenty-first century, national and foreign media still represent the Triple Frontier as a peripheral, dangerous place and, hence, a threat to security.

As a major Argentine newspaper regularly publishing news about Misiones, *Clarín* participates in reproducing the story of the wild and dangerous border. Its coverage focuses on the topics of nature and crime, perpetuating the image of the province as an exotic tourism destination and a place of violence, not much different from how Hernández, Peyret, and others saw it over a century ago. However, Ernesto's writings about Misiones do not resemble alarmist stories published by the U.S.-based media, to which I will turn next. As the gatekeeper between Misioneros, concerned with local issues, and the nationwide news public of *Clarín,* Ernesto knows how to maneuver between the two modes of seeing, translating between the vantage points of different scales. His is a nuanced approach. Born and raised in Misiones, he is familiar with the structural inequality that affects people in this remote province; yet he is also aware of the broader national debates into which local events must be inserted in order to be recognized and acted upon. By writing about the waterfalls and common crimes, he continues to reproduce the national communicative cartography that assigns Misiones the status of being an exotic and insecure border province. Although these two themes—nature and crime—are addressed as distinct plotlines, they are intricately connected. In the next chapter I explore how the regional economy, based on tourism to the waterfalls, determines how journalists who live and work in the tri-border area translate and renegotiate the global discourse of the frontera caliente.

3

Global Village of Outlaws

The city absorbs air, sun, and water, and through the
network of arteries underground, immediately transforms
them into blenders and televisions, into arms and drugs,
into counterfeit money and intoxicating perfumes.

—Hernán López Echagüe, *La Frontera*

BORDER ANECDOTES

There are two authorized routes to get from Puerto Iguazú, Argentina,
to Ciudad del Este, Paraguay.

The first one is by ferry. To reach the port of Iguazú, one must descend
a curvy road down the steep riverbank, overgrown with lush jungle vegetation, pass in front of the historic "Cabildo"-style headquarters of the
Iguazú National Park, one of the first constructions in the area, dating
back to May 25, 1937, and move on past the modest new offices of
immigration and the naval prefecture. On most days, there is a long line
of look-alike minivans with tinted windows, winding like a serpent
down the hill to the port. It is common knowledge that the back-and-
forth movement of these vans shapes the circuit of everyday contraband,
where minimally taxed electronics and cigarettes from Paraguay are
brought into Argentina, and state-subsidized products, including food
and fuel, are taken in the opposite direction. The schedule is not strictly
enforced. When ready to leave, the ferry drifts with the flow of the
Iguazú River until its reddish-brown waters merge with the strong dark
current of the Paraná, and, with its motors fully engaged, the ferry
crosses the river. On the other side, one climbs up the steep shore of
Presidente Franco, situated precisely at the intersection of the three
countries and often called the "City of the Three Borders," and continues a few miles north, toward Ciudad del Este, by road. In 2010, the
ferry ticket cost 7 pesos, or 6,560 guaraní (less than US$2) each way.

The alternative route involves crossing two bridges. First, there is the Tancredo Neves International Bridge, between Argentine Puerto Iguazú and Brazilian Foz do Iguaçu, which was built in 1985 and named in honor of a Brazilian president-elect who died of a severe illness before being able to take office. Next is Puente del Amistad, the "Friendship Bridge," on BR 277, since 1965 connecting Foz do Iguaçu to the very heart of the bustling commercial center of Ciudad del Este. This bridge is the lifeline for land-locked Paraguay's imports and exports. Public buses for Ciudad del Este leave from the Iguazú bus terminal, making stops along the way to pick up early-morning commuters. Many of them carry *equipos de mate*—thermoses with hot water and gourds with yerba mate to make tea. In their hands are large shopping bags, to be filled with clothes and household items in the street markets and malls abroad.

Opting for this second route, Claudio Altamirano, who was an active member of the Iguazú Journalists Association, Kelly, and I boarded a white public bus with the colorful stripes of the Argentine and Paraguayan flags on its sides. As soon as the bus reached the Argentine border checkpoint, without any instructions the passengers got off and hurried through migration control holding their ID papers, which were worn down from frequent use. They were familiar with the routine identity verification on the Argentina-Brazil border, implemented since 2001, after the National Directorate of Migration took over control of the bridge from the gendarmerie as part of the measures at strengthening security. The line moved fast and those who stood at the front were back on the bus in no time, taking up the seats. The rest of the commuters, slower to return, had to stand in a fully packed bus for the remainder of the trip. Brazilian migration control does not check Argentine buses that go directly to Paraguay without making an official stop in Brazil, so we sped along the wide tree-lined avenues of Foz do Iguaçu, past an imposing structure housing the Brazilian federal police, until we approached Puente del Amistad. Suddenly traffic became very slow: many cars, trucks, buses, and motor scooters were squeezing onto the bridge from merging roads and lanes, heading for Paraguay.

As the only bridge across the Paraná in the stretch of hundreds of kilometers between Encarnacíon and Guairá, it is notorious for congestion. Besides heavy commercial transport, the bridge is the route of *contrabando hormiga,* the "ant contraband." Thousands of people carrying plastic bags full of cheap Paraguayan goods form what Argentine writer and journalist Hernán López Echagüe called "a dense human horizon" (1997:22). In 2011, on average 15,222 people crossed the bridge from

Foz do Iguaçu to Ciudad del Este every day.[1] This was nothing compared to the 1990s, the celebrated golden age of Paraguayan commerce,
when around thirty thousand people and twenty thousand vehicles were
estimated to circulate across the bridge daily. In the midst of traffic on
the bridge, Kelly and Claudio called to a street vendor acrobatically
maneuvering the crowd of pedestrians and cars, and bought *chipas,* the
popular, soft cheese-flavored buns made of manioc flour that are an
everyday staple in the region. The bus was moving very slowly, allowing
the passengers time to get in and out of small conversations. It would
have been much faster to walk the remainder of the third-of-a-mile long
bridge on foot, but the driver did not stop to let anyone out.

Two hours later, our bus triumphantly entered Ciudad del Este. Paraguayan migrations and customs authorities did not stop it to check the
documents or possessions of those it had just brought into the country.
When they arrive in Ciudad del Este across the bridge from Foz—unlike
when they take the ferry from Iguazú—residents of the tri-border area do
not pass migration control unless their destination is beyond the vague
limits of the border zone, further in the country's interior. At the checkpoint, the bus slowed down and several uniformed officers peeked inside
the bus through the windows, rapidly scanning its passengers for anyone
or anything suspicious, and permitted our driver to proceed. Having
made this trip multiple times—in a public bus, in a cab, in a government
van, and on foot—I saw how navigating the borders involved having
practical knowledge, or the know-how, of crossing the checkpoints:
knowing in what situations to stop at migration control or at customs,
and when it was not necessary. Official rules existed, some of them written in bold letters on signs at the entrance and exit of each country, but
usually only those who were not familiar with the process—outsiders—
bothered to read them and follow the formal protocol of international
border crossing. Brazilian and Paraguayan authorities generally allowed
residents of the area to move from Foz do Iguaçu to Ciudad del Este and
back with minimal interruption. Between these commuters and enforcement agents, bureaucratic rules were flexed. In the interest of practical-
ity, some laws were readjusted based on the situation on the ground.
Here, efficiency and speed in monitoring the flow of people, vehicles, and
commodities across the bridge were preferred to the kind of scrupulous
inspection that would halt the traffic—and negatively affect regional
commerce—on both Paraguayan and Brazilian sides of the border.

Because of such uneven patterns of control at international checkpoints, foreign journalists have described the experience of crossing the

two borders that separate the three countries as a quintessential tale of the chaos and lawlessness of the Triple Frontier. U.S.-based reporters in particular have used vivid metaphors to express the peculiarity and porosity of the borders. In 1998, *Los Angeles Times* staff writer Sebastian Rotella published a column with the memorable title "Jungle Hub for World's Outlaws." Rotella worked for the *Times* for over twenty years specializing in coverage of the U.S.-Mexico border and terrorism, and he served as *L.A. Times* bureau chief in Buenos Aires. Seventeen years old, his article on the Triple Frontier is still widely cited in American government reports and academic publications about the region. The story Rotella tells fulfills the promises of its captivating title. He describes how organized crime linked Ciudad del Este to international mafia and terrorist networks, unleashing violence in this border area. In the article, local residents are portrayed as nothing like the "ordinary" (in Latin *ordinarius* signifies "orderly")—disciplined and law-abiding—citizens of the state. At the end of the twentieth century their "barbarism" no longer implied nakedness and illiteracy, which were featured in the letters Hernández wrote for *La Tribuna Nacional* more than a hundred years earlier (see chapter 2). Still, Rotella's borderlanders were anarchic and violent, and he presented their lives as surreal:

> The triple border was a global village of outlaws: Lebanese terrorists, Colombian drug smugglers, yakuza hoodlums from Japan, Nigerian con artists. The Tai Chen ruled by fear in the trash-strewn downtown, a Latin American casbah seething with smugglers, merchants and shoppers haggling in Spanish, Portuguese, Arabic, Asian languages and indigenous Guarani. [. . .] Everyone is loading, unloading, counting money, chattering into cell phones and walkie-talkies. Security men with shotguns guard doorways and armored cars. Women in Islamic head scarves and Buddhist monks in robes and sandals add splashes of surrealism to the crowds.[2]

Rotella argues that the Triple Frontier has become "an alarming enclave of lawlessness" where "the polyglot mix of thugs epitomizes a foremost menace of the post–Cold War world: the globalization of organized crime." He compared the area to the U.S.-Mexico border, which he knew better and which was more familiar to *L.A. Times* American readers: "The anarchic energy of Ciudad del Este recalls Tijuana. But imagine a Tijuana without nightclubs, beaches, factories or big hotels, a small and especially grim Tijuana stripped of almost everything except bare-knuckled border commerce." Here "just about everything that is not biodegradable is fake. [. . .] At rows of cigarette stands, vendors wrap boxes in waterproof plastic and strap them onto smugglers' backs. Backpackers hurry toward Brazil on the crowded two-lane bridge over the Parana River, as brazen and numerous as illegal crossers at the U.S. border." In the column Rotella cites a cigarette vendor whose comment summarizes the chaos and criminality of the place: "We need to clean up this country. [. . .] This is the United Nations of crime."

A decade later, John Kreiser of CBS News still referred to the region as "one of the most lawless places in the world" and "a smugglers' paradise."[3] He said that the CBS News crew crossed the bridge twelve times without immigration authorities ever checking their passports or customs control inspecting their luggage. Kreiser also mentioned that the area was "a safe haven for terrorists." While in the 1990s the main concern expressed about the region, repeated as adage in the media, was the prevalence of organized crime and petty contraband, after September 11, 2001, the informal business of manufacturing false identity documents and lax border checks became an index of terrorist activity and the primary motive for increased militarization and surveillance of the Triple Frontier. Writing for the *New Yorker* in 2002, Jeffrey Goldberg began his article about Hezbollah activities in the region by recounting his experience with Brazilian federal police officers in "jeans, sunglasses and bulletproof vests," armed with AK-47s, patrolling the "wide, muddy, and sluggish" waters of the Paraná, moving fast to avoid snipers.[4] "They're just waiting for us to leave the river," Goldberg quoted the chief as saying when they spotted a group of shirtless men staring at their boat from the shore. "Then they'll start across." The police seldom patrol at night. It would be too dangerous, he was told. But Goldberg was less interested in contraband. He was after Hezbollah and their fund-raising operations in the region. Unnamed officials told him that the Lebanese Shiite group, backed by the Iranian government, ran "weekend training camps on farms cut out of the rain forest."

Circulation of such thrilling stories worried local journalists like Kelly and Claudio. They objected to sensationalist reporting by their international colleagues, whose articles were widely read abroad and resulted in a negative impact on the regional tourism industry. At last, in November 2010, associations representing Argentine, Brazilian, and Paraguayan media workers organized the First International Journalists Meeting of the Triple Frontier.[5] The goal of the event was to critically discuss the coverage of inherent problems such as contraband, drug trafficking, and terrorism, in what the organizers called the "demonized" region. Over three days the meeting rotated between venues in neighboring cities. It was considered to be an opportunity to strengthen ties between journalists of the three countries, to forge alliances for peer protection, and to create networks for sharing information. Local authorities, concerned with the image of the region and its economic repercussions, welcomed the event. For them, news-making based on reporters' knowledge and firsthand experiences of the place was more legitimate than sensational narratives produced by foreign correspondents, who molded their stories from already available discourses. Talking on behalf of the provincial government, the Misiones press undersecretary said that "the critical analysis of journalists who are perfectly aware of the reality in the area" was more valuable than "border anecdotes."[6]

Late for the opening speeches due to our delay on the bridge, Kelly, Claudio, and I arrived just in time for the first panel, entitled "Common Topics on the Journalistic News Agenda of the Triple Frontier: Myths and Truths," held in Hotel Casino Aracay. The first to speak was Ricardo Arrúa, a journalist from Misiones' oldest daily, *El Territorio,* and the president of the Media Workers and Communicators Forum of Misiones. He began by saying that there was no international terrorism in the area, despite it being on the agenda of many media organizations. Arrúa acknowledged that there was trade in counterfeit products; there was money laundering; there were immigrants from the Middle East who sent remittances to families suffering from economic hardships back in their home countries. But, he said, investigations have not confirmed that these remittances were used to finance terrorism, nor have alleged sleeper cells or training camps been located. "It continues to be a generalized myth," said Arrúa, who then asked: "How come they did not have to prove there was terrorism in the region, but we are now forced to find evidence to demonstrate it does not exist?" As the meeting unfolded, participants discussed the conditions of crime and the circumstances of violence in the tri-border area. They challenged the geography of blame, relocating responsibility for the structural problems in the region on government policies in the three states. Journalists even argued for a redefinition of the term "terrorism," suggesting the concept of "social terrorism" to emphasize the structural state-directed violence on the border.

This chapter traces how the Triple Frontier has become the subject of security talk as an alleged "global village of outlaws"—a haven of organized crime and a remote hideout for terrorist financiers and sleeper cells. These discourses have given fame to the region, marking the remote border area on the map of political strategists, security analysts, and press reporters. The talk of terrorism circulated across institutional boundaries, and, as it moved between global, regional, national, and local scales, the meanings, practices, and effects of security have been questioned and renegotiated. The Triple Frontier is both an experiential and a discursive category. Emphasizing the link between discourse and experience, anthropologist Begoña Aretxaga defined experience as an "ongoing construction always placed within the arena of existing discursive fields and social practices" (1997:17). Working on the frontlines, where the global discourse about organized crime and its connections to terrorism clashes against the daily concerns and struggles of politically and economically marginalized communities, local journalists in the tri-border region are in an ambiguous situation, balancing between security and news-making. In this chapter I show that in addition to circulating talk of terrorism, journalists play an important role in translating security discourse across the scales and regimes of knowledge: they rewrite global narratives to fit local situations; they selectively reject, adapt, and modify stories; and they attempt to create a feedback loop in which local actors have an effect on how global security is understood and practiced. Although their efforts to change the sensational narrative have had little success, by closely examining the process of translation and negotiation of the global security discourse from inside the allegedly insecure border milieu we can better appreciate the role of the media in mitigating securitization of emergent threats and reassessing the meaning of security as the lived experience within journalists' own communities.

THE OFFICIAL STORY

In the global news geography, the border area between Argentina, Brazil, and Paraguay was first highlighted as a haven for organized crime and terrorism in the 1990s, after the bombings of the Israeli embassy and the Jewish community center AMIA in Buenos Aires. The media circulated two broad explanations for the AMIA attack (see Greenberg 2010). According to *la historia oficial* (the official story), the bombing was carried out by an Iranian-backed Hezbollah cell operating out of the tri-border area; *la pista siria* (the Syrian lead) suspected the involvement of President Carlos Menem and focused on the role of officials and criminal organizations in Buenos Aires, allegedly acting in conjunction with the Syrian government. Argentine journalists were skeptical about the government's version of events and pursued the Syrian lead. In contrast, the U.S. media prioritized the official story put forth by the Menem government, tracing the links from the scene of the bombing in the capital to alleged terrorist groups active in the tri-border area.[7] After 9/11 the Triple Frontier fell under an even closer scrutiny by American security analysts and intelligence agencies. Since then the U.S. government has on numerous occasions reiterated that the region is a refuge for international terrorism. On September 25, two weeks after the attacks on the World Trade Center and the Pentagon, writing for the *New York Times*, Larry Rother reported from Ciudad del Este that FBI agents and police officers were scouring the area for evidence that it had become a haven for Islamic terrorists.[8] Shortly thereafter, CNN broadcast images of a photograph of Iguazú Falls inside a house belonging to Al Qaeda in Afghanistan, unleashing rumors about the links between Al Qaeda and the Triple Frontier (Seri 2004:92; Karam 2011:263). News media also suggested that Al Qaeda might have begun to establish a network in the South American border region back in 1995, when Osama bin Laden and Khalid Sheikh Mohammed reportedly visited the area, and that its activities were linked to the trafficking of arms, drugs, and uranium, as well as money laundering, in association with Chinese and Chechen mafias (Hudson 2003). Rumors of terrorist activity were publicly confirmed in November 2001 at the Iberoamerican Summit, held in Peru, when Brazilian minister of international affairs Celso Lafer acknowledged that there were sources financing international terrorism in the Triple Frontier (Seri 2003). Argentine judge Juan José Galeano, the chief prosecutor on the AMIA case, soon concluded that residents in the tri-border region had provided logistical and financial support for the terror act against the Mutual Israeli-Argentine Association, as evidenced by a series of telephone calls between Foz do Iguaçu and Buenos Aires. Hezbollah was named as the perpetrator, and the Triple Frontier, providing a nexus for criminal and terrorist activity, was blamed for being the staging area for the attacks.

In a report published in 2003 and revised in 2010, the Federal Research Division of the Library of Congress established that the Triple Frontier was "highly conducive for allowing organized crime," a place where various Islamic terrorist groups probably engaged in drug trafficking, money laundering, and fund-raising (Hudson 2003). A survey of open-source news media on terrorist group activities, this report referred to the border between Argentina, Brazil, and Paraguay as "the lawless jungle corner" (6). "Ciudad del Este is an oasis for informants and spies; peddlers of contraband [. . .] and counterfeit products; traffickers in drugs, weapons, and humans [. . .]; common criminals; mafia organizations; and undocumented Islamic terrorists," claimed the document (10).

The media watch group FAIR, which monitors bias and censorship of the press, observed that "nearly every article reporting on Islamic terrorism in the Tri-Border Area is honeycombed with qualifying language indicating that, despite a lack of clear evidence, U.S. officials say that there are *probably* links to terrorist organizations in the Tri-Border Area" (emphasis mine).[9] The 2003 *Library of Congress Report* is comprised of references to unconfirmed media accounts, but, once published, it became the source for future references by media and government agencies, further implicating Triple Frontier as a threat-harboring place in need of sophisticated intervention from the apparatuses of security.

Another report, based on a 2005 study funded by the U.S. Department of Justice, examined the links between organized crime and terrorist networks, suggesting that "crime and terrorism in the Tri-Border Area [TBA] interact seamlessly, making it difficult to draw a clean line between the types of persons and groups involved in each of these activities" (Shelley and Picarelli 2005:60). The authors of the study claim that Ciudad del Este has active criminal gang networks such as Yakuza and the Chinese Triads, and is the center of operations for several terrorist groups, including Al Qaeda, Hezbollah, Islamic Jihad, Gamaa Islamiya, and the Colombian FARC. The study suggests that it is logical and cost-effective for terrorists to use the skills, contacts, communications, and smuggling routes of existing criminal networks. For example, the authors explain, Hong Kong–based criminal groups, specializing in large-scale contraband of counterfeit products, deliver merchandize to Hezbollah operatives, who profit from the sale and send the proceeds to fund their activities in the Middle East and beyond. The "sophisticated and reliable document forgery industry" (63) in Ciudad del Este is taken as an indicator of cooperation between terrorists and criminals. With the poor social and economic conditions in the region, the ineffectiveness of Paraguayan state institutions, and the high level of corruption, as many as US$261 million annually have reportedly been raised in the Triple Frontier and sent oversees to fund Hezbollah, Hamas, and Islamic Jihad (Shelley and Picarelli 2005:64). A disclaimer on the front page of the study clarifies: "Points of view in this document are those of the authors and do not necessarily represent the official position or policies of the U.S. Department of Justice." A closer look at U.S. government documents below will show, however, that its official discourse is premised on very similar ideas.

The intricate links between U.S. governmental, research, and media narratives regarding the Triple Frontier are illustrated by the following example. In a feature article in *Military Review,* Lieutenant Colonel

Philip K. Abbott, a U.S. Army chief at the time stationed in Honduras, wrote: "The TBA's exact role in attracting terrorist groups is not entirely clear, but Ciudad del Este's Arab and Muslim community has raised funds through money laundering, illicit drug and weapons trafficking, smuggling, and piracy, with some of the funds *reportedly* going to Hezbollah and Hamas to support terrorist acts against Israel. The FARC also *reportedly* maintains a fundraising presence in the TBA" (emphasis mine).[10] The high-ranking officer, a graduate of U.S. Army Command and General Staff College, considered the possibility of terrorist threat in this South American region: "The TBA's dangerous combination of vast ungoverned areas, poverty, illicit activity, disenfranchised groups, ill-equipped law-enforcement agencies and militaries, and fragile democracies is an *open invitation* to terrorists and their supporters. Undeterred criminal activity, economic inequality, and the rise of disenfranchised groups with the *potential* to collaborate with terrorists present a daunting challenge" (55; emphasis mine). As in other accounts, the language is inconclusive: claims about terrorism are preceded by "reportedly," "potential," "open invitation." In other words, the lack of evidence in the present should not matter if there are possibilities of terrorist activities in the future, and the U.S. should take a proactive, preventative approach: "The potential for terrorism in the TBA and elsewhere in Latin America is clearly no myth. The TBA and several other tri-border areas in Latin America will emerge as ideal breeding grounds for terrorists and those groups that support them" (55). The potential alone is enough to warrant closer scrutiny and preparedness. As Joe Masco put it, writing about the U.S. counterterror state, the objective of preemption means that the state is "devoted to locating and/or conjuring up images of dangers from an unrealized future and then combating each of those alternate futures *as if* they were material and imminent threats" (2014:15).

These reports about a potential future served as a retroactive justification for intensified securitization of the border. In 2002, the U.S. began participating in the Tripartite Command that the Argentine, Brazilian, and Paraguayan governments established in 1996 to address the issues of organized crime and terrorist groups operating in the region. The American government has insisted that the group focus exclusively on terrorism and terrorist financing, diverting attention from other areas of criminality such as smuggling of arms and people, contraband, money laundering, and drug trafficking. Under this framework of international cooperation, the U.S. provided training to underequipped Paraguayan military and police forces, and the four countries carried out joint counterterrorism training operations. Yet, as became clear from the U.S. embassy cables published by Wikileaks, the South American partners did not take U.S. emphasis on terrorism in the Triple Frontier for granted. Brazil has been particularly stubborn. For instance, in 2007 the U.S. embassy in Brasilia quoted the director of the Brazilian Ministry of External Relations Office of Transnational Crimes as saying that Brazil did not consider the 3+1 mechanism the best way to address terrorism concerns. "Brazil participates in these mechanisms 'only out of solidarity' with countries that have been victims of terrorists attacks," read the cable, specifying that the official categorically ruled out expansion of the 3+1 mechanism.[11]

In the cable from the U.S. embassy in Brasilia dated February 6, 2009, American officials admitted that Brazil "parries our efforts by complaining about the supposed sullying of the TBA's reputation, which they say undermines their efforts to promote it as a tourist destination."[12] They lamented that although the government of Brazil "knows that the 3 Plus 1 is not a forum for sharing intelligence and, as a result, that there is a limit to how much the USG [U.S. Government] can provide regarding terrorism-related activities in the region, it uses our reticence to share information in this forum to assert that there is no evidence of terrorist activity in the TBA. [. . .] It therefore dismisses the existence of terrorist activity in the TBA and shuts down most discussions that are explicitly focused on addressing terrorism-related activities." A cable sent in October 2009 reiterated Brazil's position that "the question of financing for [. . .] Islamic groups out of the TBA is a non-issue," and that the "Tri-border Area (TBA) is not a problem anymore."[13]

In this global discourse on security the Argentine government, balancing between its U.S. and Brazilian partners, has found its own niche. It does not challenge the dominant narrative of the Triple Frontier as a terrorist haven, but it redirects what Guillermina Seri (2004) calls "the process of zoning" away from itself and toward Ciudad del Este in Paraguay.[14] In a 1997 interview with CNN, Argentine minister of the interior Carlos Corach, a close ally of President Menem, proclaimed Ciudad del Este to be "a sanctuary of impunity and of international crime" where a hundred clandestine airstrips were used for drug trafficking, arms contraband, and terrorist financing. "The area is completely out of control," said Corach. "There are organizations dedicated to forging all kinds of identity documents from all over the world," he continued, adding that "intelligence services detected the movement of people related to international terrorism and fundamentalist groups." After this public accusation, the Paraguayan border town declared Corach persona non grata. Although the following year, contradicting itself, Ciudad del Este proclaimed Corach a *huésped ilustre* (distinguished guest), it was too late.[15] His provocative statements about the Triple Frontier had become solidified in numerous iterations, and, despite his intentions to put the blame solely on Paraguay, they were applied to the entire border region.

The Argentine government has been cooperating with the U.S. since the 1990s. It acknowledges the reality of the terrorist threat in the Triple Frontier, but it continues attempts to relocate it across the border to the Middle Eastern immigrant communities in Ciudad del Este and Foz do Iguaçu. In September 2007, the U.S. embassy in Buenos Aires sent out a cable summarizing a briefing that top Argentine intelligence officials and analysts had provided to the American ambassador with regard to terrorist threats in the region: "The Argentines emphasized that Hizballah maintains a real structure in the Paraguayan and Brazilian portions of the TBA, which includes individuals who have been active Hizballah operatives in Lebanon and thus pose a higher potential threat."[16] They noted a number of advantages that a border area provides to terrorist activity, including easy ways to make money, widely available forged documents and simple immigration requirements, porous international boundaries, and large informal currency flows. The U.S. ambassador visited Iguazú to discuss "targets of interest" with counterterrorism units at the federal police and at the gendarmerie, primarily investigating "family-based business groups, with origins in and ties to Lebanon, who are involved in the sale of contraband electronic goods, appliances, and clothing, but also deal in the trafficking of persons, drugs, and arms." These groups were not operational on the Argentine side of the border. In Ciudad del Este and Foz do Iguaçu, financial crime investigators told the American ambassador that the main impediment to their ability to control illicit flows was corruption.

The media, especially U.S.-based newspapers and television networks, played an important role in the development and circulation of this global security discourse, focusing on terrorist threats in the Triple Frontier. They recycled claims backed by references to their previous iterations, forming a closed loop. Rather than adjusting to new information, for over a decade the discourse absorbed data into the existing narrative, strengthening it and at times retroactively justifying past events. Michel Foucault wrote that the milieu in which a security apparatus works produces a circular link between causes and effects, "since an effect from one point of view will be a cause from another" (2007:21).

In the Triple Frontier, the apparatus of security is applied to illegal circulations of drugs, arms, and money, but it is itself predicated on circulating discourses of terrorism—formulaic and repetitive, made up of scraps of evidence but effectively legitimating intervention to deal with emergent threats on the border.

Next I turn to the story of one journalist and his book, which became a significant piece in the discourse of lawlessness in the Triple Frontier, causing much commotion in Iguazú. By blurring the line between fact and fiction, this publication continues to affect how residents view reporters who come to the tri-border region from afar with intentions to investigate organized crime.

UNSCRUPULOUS THIEF OF CONFUSING VOICES

The enigmatic border has long lured investigative journalists, but none have become as iconic in the frontera caliente discourse as Hernán López Echagüe. At forty already an acknowledged journalist, López Echagüe had just completed a political biography of Argentine president Eduardo Duhalde, which became one of the country's best-selling and most challenged journalistic investigations of the decade, and, motivated by curiosity and ambition, the porteño was drawn to the border triangle in northeastern Argentina. Soon after arriving in Iguazú in 1996, López Echagüe found more than he had anticipated. In his book, *La Frontera: Viaje al misterioso triangulo de Brasil, Argentina y Paraguay (The Border: A Journey to the Mysterious Triangle of Brazil, Argentina and Paraguay),* he writes:

> After a few months I had trafficked arms and drugs; I had gotten drunk with corrupt gendarmes, and we had sung like wolves and laughed like hyenas; I had received favors from Arab fundamentalists; I had coaxed tourists and residents; I had talked in Guaraní, thought in Portuguese and lied in Spanish [. . .]. Without any authorization I had appropriated fragments of lives. An unscrupulous thief of experiences, of confusing voices. (12)

In *La Frontera,* the journalist alleged border enforcement in Iguazú to be so corrupt that officers in the prefecture and gendarmerie were fiercely competing for clients who engaged in contraband from Paraguay, each trying to propose a better deal. Both of the fuerzas deployed to secure the area were facilitating arms and drug trafficking by extorting a "blind check" at the river port and on the bridge. In his account, saturated with insecurity and paranoia, López Echagüe wrote about his meeting with a Paraguayan journalist who covered organized crime and kept a revolver in his desk drawer to defend against hired killers. He also narrated the horror story of how common barrio kids got involved in trafficking and how easily and brutally they were discarded. When his friends Alcides and Tomasito disappeared after an unsuccessful trafficking operation, the author threatened to disclose the names of those involved in organized crime unless they helped to find them, but his attempt was futile—after the months López Echagüe had spent undercover in this investigation, the corrupt officials refused to believe he was a journalist. Although the book left more questions than it answered, its portrait of the Triple Frontier—as a place of confusion, contradictions, and dangers—marked the region for years to come.

As full of unresolved mysteries as the manuscript was, it cannot compete with the events that unfolded after its publication. Everyone in Iguazú knows about the book—some talk about it with passionate anger, calling the journalist a liar, while others in a hushed voice acknowledge his courage in telling the truth. But it has left almost no public trace. People remember that during those few months he spent in Iguazú, in between hanging out in bars and brothels, López Echagüe would come to the local library to work on his book. Yet the library does not have a copy of his text, even though until recently it was the only book written about the town. When I asked the librarian about this curious case, she invited me to sit down and drink some mate with her. "I didn't know he was a journalist. Stout and dirty, this man would come in the afternoons and write," remembered the woman. Unlike many of his adversaries, the librarian said that López Echagüe's description of Iguazú in the mid-1990s was accurate: "He told the truth. People here always lived from contraband. This was a town of traffickers." The librarian recalled how *prefecturianos* would bring corpses down the street every day. "If you knew the names of the gendarmes or prefects involved in trafficking, you could get killed. In the tiny shops of Brasil Avenue there were boxes full of dollars in cash. *Señores del pueblo* [town authorities] were involved." She said that in his book López Echagüe implicated high-profile officials and businesspeople, showing their links to trafficking, so they sued him. It was then that his books disappeared. "I might have an incomplete photocopy, which I will look for," the woman promised. She also remembered having seen a copy of a copy held at the library in Posadas.

Throughout my fieldwork, when Iguazúenses asked me why I had come to the tri-border area, they would often bring up the name of López Echagüe, usually critically. They said that a lawsuit for libel followed the publication of his book. The more I heard about the por-teño journalist, the more I wanted to know what had really happened to him and his manuscript. With the help of another journalist I was able to get in touch with López Echagüe's wife, who passed my inquiry on to the attention of the author. In his response by e-mail López Echagüe explained to me that the family of a customs official who had been exposed in his journalistic investigation had threatened to sue him, but he assured them that he had witnesses to every claim he made in the book. "If they wanted to go to court, I had no problem with it," noted the journalist.[17] Charges against him were never pursued.

In a postscript to his letter López Echagüe added: "I forgot to tell you that after the book was published the town council of Iguazú declared me persona non grata." This document, like the book and the alleged lawsuit that followed it, was an elusive object—impossible to locate, as if it, too, had mysteriously disappeared, leaving confusing traces about the course of events. Estimating that the declaration must have been made soon after the book was published in 1997, I wrote an official request for a copy from the town council's archives. But after a few days of browsing through the file cabinets the staff could not find anything. They speculated that the declaration must have suffered irreparable water damage when the building that houses the archive was heavily flooded. Or, they reasoned, even if it survived the flood, all rescued documents had been left outside in the sun to dry, where the wind might have picked it up. Gone with the wind! Unable to help further, the council secretary referred me to Antonia Soto from the municipal archives and to Carlos Villalba, the town's historian.

The next morning the town hall, located on Tres Fronteras Avenue, was busy as always during the early weekday hours. Carrying folders of paperwork and their equipos de mate, Iguazúenses were running their errands through the tiny offices of local government. Mrs. Soto greeted me at the entrance to a small one-story building in the backyard, where the municipal archives were squeezed in between transit inspection and the land department. Mrs. Soto refused to give in to the fatalistic expla-nations of flood and wind, and agreed to help me find out what had happened to López Echagüe and to the legal documents I had heard about. We spent a few days browsing through the archives dating back to the period between 1996 and 1998, from the year the porteño jour-nalist arrived to Iguazú to the year following the publication of his work. Mrs. Soto even called the family who reportedly sued the journal-ist to inquire about the dates. Nothing turned up. After flipping through the town council's records and old newspapers, we found only one reference to his book, in the provincial daily *El Territorio:* on December 17, 1997, an article entitled "Today Mega Operation of Control Launched in the Triple Frontier" cited Carlos Corach, the Argentine minister of the interior, who referred to López Echagüe's work as a confirmation of arms and drug trafficking in the border area.[18] Newspapers from January and February 1998 were missing from the municipal archives—Mrs. Soto recalled having been on vacation then, and she had personally compiled this collection—but during summer months the town council is not in session, so it was unlikely that any formal document, yet alone a persona non grata declaration, would be passed during that time. In the end we could not find anything. It appeared that all documents surrounding López Echagüe had inexplicably, even if perhaps unintentionally, vanished in the cracks of the official history, and what was left in their place was the strengthened security apparatus in control of the border.

I made one last attempt to find more details about the porteño journalist from the town's historiographer. But when I ran into Carlos Villalba, the *historiador,* who with extreme precision and great satisfaction cites every date of every local event, big or small, could not even vaguely remember the year of López Echagüe's visit to Iguazú. He said that the writer came over to his house a few times, bringing empanadas and wine. Their interview was included in the infamous book and Villalba was upset that the porteño journalist distorted what he said about trafficking in the area. The author of *Apuntes históricos de Puerto Iguazú (Historic Notes of Puerto Iguazú),* the first complete account of the town's history, he seemed clearly displeased by the memory of the encounter. But to Villalba's knowledge there was never a lawsuit and López Echagüe was never proclaimed persona non grata.

López Echagüe now lives in Uruguay, where he moved in 1998 to escape from recurrent threats resulting from his work in Argentina. He teaches online courses in investigative journalism and, as a brochure to prospective students puts it, "the construction of reality." Participants read Gabriel García Márquez, Rodolfo Walsh, Elena Poniatowska, and Truman Capote, among other notable journalist-writers who have turned *crónica periodística* (narrative journalism) into an art form. Since he began teaching, thousands of students from Latin America, the U.S., Europe, Israel, and Japan have attended his virtual workshops. In response to my inquiry regarding the controversies surrounding his book, *La Frontera,* López Echagüe wrote to me in an e-mail: The book is "a fictional story, a story at times desperate to face the truth, which was impossible to capture in a manuscript I had promised to write. The outline of the book was born out of ignorance of a porteño journalist, from a distance, fed by wrong information from the media."[19]

Faced with the challenge of depicting the situation that he found in Iguazú, his solution was to "flip the book like a glove," to "laugh at investigative journalism that is born in such senseless way," and to enjoy the process of writing. Some, the author said, understood from the very first page that they were holding a different book, one that had no resemblance to his previous investigative work. But others thought he was mad. "My colleagues in the region don't like me much," he wrote. "I think they never understood those pages. Neither did my editors." Despite claiming that the book was a fictional story, the journalist maintained that the manuscript was based on true information and on real situations he lived through. Regarding the eerie confusions about the content of the book and the aftermath of its publication, he wrote: "The only thing you can believe in this region is the certainty that everything is unlikely, everything is an enigma, that everything is a myth. The great Chilean poet Vicente Huidobro said it better: 'The four cardinal points are three, the south and the north.'"López Echagüe mentioned that a colleague had sent him a copy of the persona non grata declaration, but it had been left in his old apartment in Buenos Aires, stored away in a box containing other files about Iguazú. The journalist could not find the manuscript of the book, either, because the computer he wrote it on had since broken down.

This is a short version of a story obscured by the blurred boundary between fact and fiction, between history and memory; a story animated by the ghostlike character of documents that disappeared through the cracks of official records and left confusing marks in the public memory. Once published, the narrative about the mysterious border triangle was no longer contained to Iguazú. It fed the discourse of threat, circulating on national and international scales, establishing the Triple Frontier as a dangerous place, a notorious haven for organized crime and, later, international terrorism. The key elements forming this discourse, a few of which I have included here, are so difficult to trace that the best we can do is try to capture them as they momentarily reappear at points of friction, as they resurface brushing up against the hard edges of reality, causing perplexity, before they once again disappear into the safety of all-encompassing and self-referential security talk. Trying to pin down these elements is a hunt for simulacra. But these simulacra are not lies or fictions; they do not conceal and deceive. They may appear to have lost reference to what they represent, but like the documentation of López Echagüe's story, they are displaced. The circulation of texts about the Triple Frontier was never meant to reveal the secrets of international organized crime. The discourse of the threat of terrorism is only disguised as evidence. Instead of being proof, it is an effect of the constantly expanding security apparatus.

If the regime of security is producing reality rather than being accountable to it, can those who are implicated redefine it? As media producers, journalists are instrumental in the circulation of narratives that justify security buildup, which, once set in motion, absolves them of their responsibility as authors. Confident as a protagonist in the story he was about to write, López Echagüe said he came to Iguazú with the intention to either prove how dangerous it was or relieve the region of the accusations against it; however, he was entrapped by a story he could no longer control. Whether deliberately or unintentionally, as the series of strange disappearances of key documents shows, his manuscript was reshaped and obscured by multiple actors, leaving few public records. The question, then, is whether, once narratives are merged into a coherent and convincing version of reality, the security apparatus locks them into a cycle of perpetual repetition. Or can local knowledge producers effectively destabilize the global discourse of security that frames border residents as threats and shift it away from the tri-border region?

For journalists in Iguazú, stories of organized crime and terrorism were either false accusations or *misplaced* accusations. Those who argued for the latter said that Iguazú was unfairly mixed up with its violent and dangerous neighbor in Paraguay. Thus, the ethnographic journey to find answers to my questions about the agency of media producers took me across the border to Ciudad del Este, the alleged culprit of the region's bad reputation, which, unlike Iguazú, had powerful media and a strong tradition of investigative journalism.

THE POWER OF THE PRESS

The bus driver dropped me off in front of the town hall past the Ciudad del Este's commercial district. Following the directions I was given, I crossed a park and walked toward the municipal library, where I saw the Iglesia Catedral and the Edificio España. There, at the intersection of Rivas Ortellado and Curupayty, I found the regional editorial offices of *Última Hora,* a major Paraguayan national newspaper. I pushed the door to enter, but it did not open immediately: a heavily armed security guard was leaning against it from the inside. Without asking who I was, he let me in and a receptionist took me across the bustling office to meet Andrés Colmán Gutiérrez. An internationally recognized investigative journalist and also the regional editor of *Última Hora,* Andrés greeted me warmly. While serving coffee he explained that the automatic rifle the guard at the door was holding had never been used. More than for any other purpose it was meant to be a warning. Because many companies in the neighborhood hire private security companies—there are as many as ten guards per block—Andrés described it as a "relatively very safe area."[20]

Andrés was born in the small peasant village of Yhú, which in Guaraní means "spring," in 1961; at the age of nine he moved with his family to Salto de Guairá, north of Ciudad del Este, where a land border separates Paraguay from Brazil. "I grew up there, on the border, in a culture marked by a lot of violence, but also a lot of cultural wealth," remembers Andrés. In the 1970s, trafficking and contraband were so intense that he describes the place as "the world of illegality." But instead of emphasizing crime, Andrés is particularly critical of the changes that accompanied large-scale development projects under the Stronato, General Alfredo Stroessner's right-wing military dictatorship over Paraguay from 1954 to 1989. Stroessner staked his regime's claims to modernity and legitimacy on a gargantuan hydroelectric project—the Itaipú Binational Dam over the Paraná River, a joint venture between Brazil and Paraguay, only a short distance from Ciudad del Este. In her reading of formerly classified documents about the dam, known as the "Archive of Terror," anthropologist Christine Folch (2013) uncovered how this hydro-energy development scheme served authoritarian state objectives in Paraguay. The world's largest dam played an integral part in the terror apparatus of the Stronato, operating its own security office, which provided a nexus between military and secret police in Operation Condor countries, primarily Argentina, Brazil, Chile, and Uruguay.[21] In addition to the security and intelligence functions that facilitated the dictatorship's repression of opposition, this hydroelectric project had massive environmental and social impacts on the region. The effects were so dramatic that Andrés called it "the biggest ecocide committed in MERCOSUR."

Another development scheme that irreversibly changed the area's natural and economic landscape was the rise of export-oriented soybean production. The national security doctrine of the Brazilian military regime, which stayed in power from the 1960s to the 1980s, included the concept of *fronteras vivas* (live borders), encouraging Brazilians to move to the country's western borders and develop the region. Advertisements for cheap, fertile land in Paraguay appeared in Brazilian dailies, and some 450,000 migrants settled in this area, forming the *brasiguayo* population. In the eastern Paraguayan departments of Canindeyú, Alto Paraná, and Itapúa, Brazilian migrants, with access to capital and equipment, displaced the Paraguayan *campesinos* that used to live in small settlements cultivating mixed fields of cotton, tobacco, and manioc (see Hetherington 2011). The virgin jungle was destroyed to produce soybeans, Paraguay's most important export commodity. Andrés spoke nostalgically about the effects that these massive development projects—the construction of the dam, the expansion of soybean monoculture, and vast population shifts linked to both of them—had on the region's nature and on its local people. Being a witness to these devastating changes motivated him to pursue a career in journalism.

It was during the Stronato that Andrés started working with the media. Living in Salto de Guairá, he founded and edited a school paper that was well received by the community and began circulating in town. His writing caught the attention of the local radio director, who invited Andrés to contribute to the program. The journalist remembered how one day he spoke up against the building of the Itaipù Dam, which threatened to submerge Guairá Falls. In the 1970s any opposition to the construction project was equated with resistance to the Stronato regime. As you would expect, the governor did not like his on-air comment, and when Andrés was leaving the recording studio, police officers were waiting for him at the door. His classmates organized a rally against his detention, which turned into the first student demonstration in Salto de Guairá. Irritated further, the governor told Andrés that the comment on the radio was "inappropriate" and asked him to silence the students. "This is when I learned the power of the press. I discovered that the press can make the powerful uncomfortable," he remembers. The director of the radio was pressured from above and did not allow Andrés to resume the program. "It was then that I decided I wanted to be a journalist: at the age of fourteen, after my first arrest by the police."

After he graduated, Andrés moved to Asunción to study journalism. Following his father's tragic death in a car accident, Andrés also needed to provide for his family. He thus had the courage to ask the editor of *Última Hora* to give him—a recent high school graduate with no experience in working for a large daily—a job he has held ever since. At the newspaper, Andrés initially specialized in agricultural topics and wrote reports from the countryside. Over the years his hard work in investigative and literary journalism has brought him acknowledgment. Andrés was awarded the Premio Vladimir Herzog de Periodismo y Derechos Humanos and the Premio Nacional de Periodismo Santiago Leguizamón.[22] In 2008, increasingly drawn to work outside of Asunción, Andrés moved back to the eastern part of the country. He was convinced that journalism in Paraguay had to be decentralized and agreed to be in charge of organizing the first regional office of *Última Hora* in Ciudad del Este. This territorial expansion of the paper resulted in an increased presence of regional news in the national daily. Although the Asunción-based newspaper tends to limit regional reporting to focus on issues that draw nationwide interest, Andrés says that his bureau also explores topics that are outside of the established editorial agenda. Often these independent investigations are about illegal activities: Andrés wrote a series of articles on clandestine river ports along the Paraná and, with his colleague Sofia Masi, investigated child trafficking. In part to counteract the effects that investigative focus on organized crime has on the image of the area, the office in Ciudad del Este also has a project called *"la otra Triple Frontera"* (the other Triple Frontier), which supports the writing of positive articles about the region. These news features are included in specialized sections such as "El otro Paraguay" (the other Paraguay) or published in the weekend edition.

Andrés said that despite their efforts to diversify the coverage of the tri-border region, the news from Ciudad del Este was predominantly negative. "The concept of 'news' defines 'news' as something that draws our attention, what is current, what is urgent, what causes greater impact. Unfortunately, I believe that in Paraguay you cannot avoid publishing articles on corruption, on trafficking, on mafia, as these are the dominant issues." The Paraguayan press contributes to creating and perpetuating the image of the Triple Frontier as a dangerous area, but Andrés says that crime in the area is real: "There is a lot of news about crime, which is a normal thing on the border. [. . .] Here [in Ciudad del Este] it is a bigger issue because of the money and interests involved." Recently, the city has experienced a series of kidnappings and assaults. More remote locales to the north of Ciudad del Este, such as Pedro Juan Caballero, have been even more affected as traffickers look for new, less controlled, corridors to transport drugs from Paraguay to Brazil. The media, said Andrés, followed these crime patterns, sensationalizing them and perpetuating a violent image of the region. But, according to him, "common citizens walking in the streets of Ciudad del Este are safer than in Asunción or in Rio de Janeiro, where the risks of being attacked or of having your wallet stolen are higher."

THE CITY OF THE EAST

The legacy of Stronato, Ciudad del Este (the city of the east) is the second largest city in Paraguay.[23] Its population expanded dramatically when in the 1970s thousands of people arrived to do construction work on the Itaipú Dam.[24] Settling on both sides of the border in Ciudad del Este and Foz do Iguaçu, these labor migrants generated a wave of urban development in the area. With easy access to Brazilian and Argentine markets, Ciudad del Este had the potential to become an important regional center of commerce. The Paraguayan government capitalized on the city's strategic location and actively created incentives to attract businesses to Ciudad del Este. Initially some luxury commodities were taxed at near zero rates, and, although over the years taxes have increased, to this day the low taxation rate sets Paraguay apart from its neighbors. Here, in 2010 the value-added tax (VAT) of 10 percent was the lowest in the region.[25] Excise taxes, paid by producers and vendors, and especially popular for goods such as tobacco, alcohol, electronics, and other luxury items, were also very low. For example, some electronics were taxed at a rate of 1 percent; luxury goods, including watches, perfumes, leather, precious stones and metals, and weapons, were taxed at 5 percent; various other items, from air conditioners to televisions to toys, were taxed at 10 percent.

Because of such low rates, businesses in Ciudad del Este have been able to offer favorable prices to consumers. They attract shoppers from across the border, where taxes are significantly higher: the standard VAT rate in Brazil is between 17 and 19 percent, while in Argentina it is 21 percent—over twice as much as in Paraguay.[26] The 21 percent Argentine VAT applies to many electronic products, including phones, digital photo and video cameras, GPS equipment, televisions, microwaves, and other home appliances. Electronics are also subject to Argentina's 26 percent federal excise tax, which is levied on, among other goods, cigarettes and tobacco, alcohol, and luxury items. No wonder many Argentines and Brazilians prefer to buy in Paraguay and travel from around the country to the tri-border area for shopping. Even more important to the city's growth has been the practice known as commercial triangulation, or re-export trade, which involves importing American, Asian, and

European goods to Paraguay, where import taxes are low, and making considerable profits from taking them across the border, usually clandestinely, to Brazil and Argentina. In the "belle époque" of the 1970s and 1980s the economy in Ciudad del Este was generating so much cash that the original plan envisioned in the "March to the East"—to create a garden city with wide avenues and parks—was shoved aside.[27] In the commercial district near Puente del Amistad, "each square meter, where you could build something, was worth gold."[28]

Over the years Ciudad del Este became a strategic enclave for all kinds of businesses. To protect their internal markets from cheaper Paraguayan commodities, the Brazilian and Argentine governments implemented stricter import regulations, pushing a significant part of local commerce underground (see chapter 4). Visitors from as far away as São Paulo still come to purchase cheaper alcohol, cosmetics, and computers, but it is not surprising that with the tax regimes in the neighboring countries remaining so markedly different, according to some estimates, as much as half of Paraguayan imports are illegally re-exported to Brazil and Argentina (Ferrario 2006:2). New customs control mechanisms motivated local businessmen to use contraband routes to bypass official checkpoints. By the 1990s the informal economy in the tri-border area was soaring, providing employment to two-thirds of its residents and earning Ciudad del Este the reputation of being a global contraband hub.[29] Paraguay has become the source of illegalized flows of common goods such as electronics, household appliances, and cigarettes, and a transfer center for trafficking in illicit products, from drugs to fake documents to pirated movies.

Such a booming informal economy has also provided a convenient platform, and a shelter, for other types of criminal activities. In particular, due to its strategic geographic location and expansive black market, the tri-border area has attracted organized crime. "This is the crossing point for arms trafficking, primarily for groups such as Primer Comando Capital and Comando Vermelho in the favelas of Rio and São Paulo," Andrés told me. "This is also the place for trafficking in women, both for Argentina and for Europe, and an area of drug trafficking," he added, explaining that Paraguay is one of the world's major producers of marijuana as well as being a transit route for Bolivian cocaine destined for the global market and increasingly consumed domestically in Argentina and Brazil. The U.S. Department of State notes that these different criminal activities in the tri-border region overlap, for example, when Paraguayan women are recruited as couriers of illegal drugs to Europe, where they are subsequently coerced into prostitution.[30] According to the U.S. government, multi-billion-dollar contraband trade in the tri-border region is fed in part by endemic institutional corruption.[31] The chain of corruption extends from local to regional to national authorities, entangling the country's legislature, its executive, and the criminal justice system. As Andrés put it, "Even looking through the magnifying glass you would not find a judge or an attorney who is not part of the organized crime machinery. This is the reality of the Triple Frontier."

Ciudad del Este is a cosmopolitan place, a cultural melting pot, which Andrés called a dynamic "intercultural laboratory." The presence of diverse ethnic and religious groups has not resulted in conflicts. "If you go one night to the casino of Hotel Acaray, you'll see a Chinese, an Arab, a Paraguayan, a Brazilian, and an Argentine playing roulette. It appears that all are neighbors, friends. There is rich coexistence." The Chinese-Taiwanese community in the border area has about thirty thousand residents; together with Foz, Ciudad del Este also has the second largest Muslim immigrant population in South America, comprised of twenty to thirty thousand people (Hudson 2003:8–9). Islamic migrants from Lebanon, Syria, and Palestine began arriving in South America in the late nineteenth century, and their definitive presence in the tri-border area can be traced back to the 1950s (Karam 2011:253). Many more migrated to flee the conflicts between Lebanon and Israel in the 1970s and 1980s. They were particularly active in commerce, profiting from free-trade zones and other business incentives, as well as trade triangulation schemes. This community "takes Foz do Iguaçu and Ciudad del Este as if they were one city: there are people who live in Foz but have their businesses here, and vice versa," explained Andrés. The U.S. government has expressed concerns that large sums of cash generated in the extensive informal economy in the tri-border area can be easily laundered through regional banking networks to finance Islamic fundamentalist groups in the Middle East. On a smaller scale, family remittances to their relatives, which are a common practice among transnational migrant communities worldwide, come under suspicion for their potential political purposes: "There are many people who have patriotic, cultural, religious sentiments toward their communities, which are in conflict and where political forces use violence in their fight." Andrés says that part of the problem is that the U.S. government's definition of "terrorist" groups blends them with what others consider "liberation" and "revolutionary" movements, and many migrant families who maintain ties with relatives in their countries of origin become automatically classified as supporters of fundamentalism.

"I believe that there is an interest—or there was an interest—on the part of the U.S. administration to create a focus of attention. It is linked to other issues, all of which are speculative. What is true is that every year the State Department repeats a prearranged script that the Islamic community in the Triple Frontier finances terrorism in the Middle East," said Andrés. This myth about the Triple Frontier has developed in relation to geopolitical interests, but he avoided speculation about what those interests might be. Against the opinion of many Argentine journalists, Andrés was skeptical about the Guaraní Aquifer hypothesis, which links security concerns with the issue of water. In the form of a conspiracy theory, this hypothesis postulates that since the Guaraní Aquifer, which spans the territories of Argentina, Uruguay, Brazil, and Paraguay, is one of the largest underground freshwater reservoirs in the world, the U.S. has identified the region as a site for dormant terrorist cells in order to gain control of the scarce resource. According to Andrés, this is a myth created by the press. Paraguayan legislation guarantees that this water, unlike the mineral resources, cannot be sold, and he was not aware of any international company that would be eyeing the aquifer. "The Guaraní Aquifer has not been exploited yet because there is so much surface water. We have the Itaipú Lake, which is one of the biggest artificial lakes in the world, and we have rivers with the largest flow in Latin America: Paraná, Paraguay, Monday. *Agua nos sobra* [we have an excess of water]." That many residents in the area do not have drinking water in their homes due to inadequate infrastructure is another matter.

Andrés took me to see Monday Falls, located in a quiet municipal park south of Ciudad del Este. One of the last remaining blocks of the Atlantic Forest west of the Paraná, this natural reserve is a refuge for flora and fauna displaced by the Itaipú Dam and the soybean monoculture that has colonized eastern Paraguay. From the park we headed to the river port of Presidente Franco, where we faced a long line of minibuses waiting to pass through the Paraguayan customs control and then, in the direction opposite to ours, to head uphill toward Ciudad del Este. The ferry to Iguazú had just departed, so we sat down and waited for the next one. We watched the deliberate current of the Paraná, speculating on what impact a planned second bridge between Paraguay and Brazil would have on what remains of the fragile ecosystem, which has barely survived the large-scale development schemes in the region. Almost an hour later the ferry came back; at least twenty almost identical vans disembarked and, like the group that had come before, lined up at customs for the familiar ritual of inspections. Casually Andrés remarked that the vans were carrying contraband goods—such common knowledge that the media rarely reported it.

I bid Andrés farewell and boarded the ferry, which soon left the Paraguayan shore, heading east across the Paraná and up the Iguazú, back to Argentina. During that half-day talking to Andrés, I was amazed by his breadth of knowledge and experience of life on the border. Raised in an area that was characterized by violence, now a recognized professional whose job is to write stories for the media, he was both critical and accepting of "the world of illegality" on Paraguay's eastern fringe. Andrés did not deny accusations directed at the Triple Frontier by the global security discourse. He admitted that there was organized crime, which he, as a journalist, was also investigating and, hence, drawing more attention to. Yet he also injected common sense into often-sensationalized portrayals of the border as a haven for traffickers and terrorists. As a journalist, he was familiar with the production and the aftereffects of negative media stories. As a local resident, he had a more thorough understanding of the circumstances that precipitated crime and a more nuanced perception of its social consequences.

On this short trip through the very heart of the tri-border region, I was thinking how easily journalists working for foreign media characterized this place as one of the world's great centers of lawlessness. In an article published soon after 9/11, the *New York Times* quoted a Brazilian federal police official who said that "every criminal activity that you can possibly think of flourishes here, from drug and arms trafficking to money laundering, counterfeiting, carjacking, contraband and prostitution."[32] The coverage of the region is almost always sensational, invoking perpetual disorder and danger. What I observed, however, was a discrepancy between media narratives and everyday realities. At times chaotic, certainly not devoid of violence linked to various forms of organized crime, life in the tri-border area was nevertheless profoundly quiet. This inconsistency motivated me to inquire into the feedback mechanism between the global and the local discourses of danger. Circulation of the criminalizing narrative affected media production among border journalists, who experienced firsthand the consequences of news-making that implicated the Triple Frontier as a haven for organized crime and terrorism. Could the voices of those who had different stakes in the outcomes of securitization alter the narrative of the frontera caliente?

THE BORDER OF TERRORISTS

Local resistance to the potential effects of the frontera caliente discourse became public when in 2010 American film director Kathryn Bigelow and scriptwriter Mark Boal announced their plan to make a movie that they initially called *Triple Frontier*. The screenplay of what was described as a *Traffic*-esque action thriller was still in development, but it reportedly focused on five Americans working in the "notorious" border area between Argentina, Brazil, and Paraguay, "a hotbed of organized crime activity."[33] In September 2010, on a trip to select possible shooting locations, Bigelow and Boal visited Foz do Iguaçu and, before long, the discussion of the leading actors began.[34] This news caused an uproar in the region. Some Iguazúenses regarded the production of a high-budget Hollywood movie to be an opportunity to attract money to the area, arguing that numerous action thrillers filmed in Brazilian favelas had not affected Brazil's image or its economy negatively. But most government officials loudly resisted the project. In Argentina and Paraguay, tourism authorities of ranks ranging from national ministries to local institutions declared they would not support the production. "We don't want the movie," said Enrique Meyer, Argentine minister of tourism.[35] Marcelo Ghione, the director of the chamber of tourism in Iguazú, explained: "The film damages what we do every day to promote the destination. I would like them to emphasize the nice things we have, such as the integration and peaceful coexistence. I have been living here for twenty-three years and there have never been attacks that would make us deserve what this film is going to say. We want the film to tell the truth."[36]

The fiercest and most vocal opponent of the film project was the Paraguayan minister of tourism, Liz Cramer. That November morning in 2010 when I accompanied Kelly and Claudio to the meeting of journalists in Ciudad del Este, she was the last speaker on the opening panel. Like the majority of participants at the three-day conference, the minister admitted that the border region was not free from contraband and drug trafficking, but she emphasized that the same problems were common on other South American borders. "I have to sell Paraguay. My job is to make sure that people come and spend. In my job, if people are discouraged from coming, it is bad business." In a room full of journalists Cramer lamented that the media only made negative news about the tri-border region because "beautiful reality does not sell." Laughs and applause rippled through the audience when she called a known author of a book about organized crime that traces the international drug mafia networks all the way to the Triple Frontier "a provocateur." Cramer explained that Paraguay did not have a marketing fund to counteract the negative portrayals of the country. Though there were many positive things to write about, there was no space left for them in the media agenda.

Given that one of the major misunderstandings in the media coverage of the tri-border region has been the alleged radical Islamist activities and funding of terrorist organizations—the international media insisted on the presence of Al Gama'a al-Islamiyya, Al-Jihad, Al Qaeda, Hamas, and Hezbollah—on the second day of the conference journalists from Argentina, Brazil, and Paraguay were invited to Foz do Iguaçu to visit a local mosque. At the entrance of the Mezquita Árabe (Arab mosque), women were handed headscarves and long skirts to cover their heads and legs. Everyone proceeded barefoot, and, once inside the mosque, we sat down on the floor forming a semicircle. The imam addressed the gathered journalists in portuñol. He said that in Arabic "Islam" meant "peace," and that this faith was defined by transparency, which was incompatible with radicalism and extremism. He talked about the five fundamental pillars of Islam, including the *zakat,* an obligation of those who have the financial means to give a fixed portion of their wealth to the poor. Since the media often pointed to zakat and other forms of family remittances by Muslims in South America to explain the link between the tri-border area and terrorism in the Middle East, one of the journalists asked the imam what he thought about this accusation. Likely anticipating the question, the imam politely explained: "It's a question to the politicians of Hezbollah in Lebanon, not to me. I do not have any information confirming such claims." And, to conclude his lecture to the journalists, the purpose of which was to demonstrate that the local Muslim community was open for dialogue, the imam said: "But terrorism has nothing to do with Islam."

From the mosque, the journalists headed to the campus of the Universidade Dinâmica das Cataratas. Many of them considered the panel entitled "Myths and Truths about the Alleged Financing of Islamic Terrorism from the Triple Frontier" to be the most important part of the three-day meeting. The small conference room was so crowded that those who arrived late had to stand in the hallway and listen through the open door. The main speaker on this panel was Brazilian political scientist Arthur Bernardes do Amaral, the author of *A Tríplice Fronteira e a Guerra ao Terror (The Triple Frontier and the War on Terror)*. He pointed out that the border between Argentina, Brazil, and Paraguay is the most problematic of all tri-border regions in Brazil. To show that the area has always been affected by global geopolitical dynamics, Amaral cited a list of events and processes that have shaped the region, including the War of the Triple Alliance, the Cold War, the Lebanese civil war, the bombings of Israeli institutions in Argentina, and the "war on terror." Stigmatizing discourses proliferated when the relationship between the region and Islamist terrorism was established following the investigation of the 1992 and 1994 attacks in Buenos Aires, and were solidified after 9/11. Amaral explained that as a political scientist, he could not say whether there were terrorists in tri-border area. However, he emphasized that the political consequences of the discourse do not depend on whether the discourse itself is correct or not. The guest speaker told journalists they should avoid letting politicians "prep" public opinion through the instrumental use of the media. Instead of creating a cycle of speculation, they should explore the issues based on primary sources; they should ask who the beneficiaries in each situation are: "*Cui bono* [who benefits]?"

Dolly Galeano, correspondent for the Paraguayan daily *La Nación* from Asunción, echoed Amaral's questions: "The Triple Frontier has been defined as suspicious. Why are there accusations? Why is this region stigmatized? What does the U.S. want by characterizing this region in such a way? What are the geopolitical objectives? What are the strategic goals of those who use these concepts? We must pay attention to this. *Que carajo quieren* [What the hell do they want]?" Galeano was losing her temper. "Water?" Reformulating the narrative in which Iraq was accused of possessing nuclear weapons in order for the U.S. to justify the war and take over its oil resources, she suggested that Washington was inventing the presence of terrorists in the tri-border region to secure the freshwater deposits of the Guaraní Aquifer. This conspiracy theory had strong support in the audience. There was general agreement, followed by resentment, that terrorism in the tri-border region was an imposed agenda that no journalist covering South America could avoid. As one participant put it, "There are topics that we journalists have on our backs and cannot shake off. The question is how to face them." He confronted the guest speaker by ricocheting his own question back at him: How did Amaral come up with the idea for the book focusing on the political perspective of terrorism in the tri-border area? He substituted "Cui bono?" with "Who benefits from these investigations"? The sea of hands in the tightly packed room was not receding—everybody wanted to speak on this highly charged topic. But it was already late in the evening and the organizers were trying to close the panel. There was no time for answers to the rhetorical questions, so the animated participants fled the conference venue and continued passionate conversations in smaller groups, disappearing into the night.

But before the panel was dismissed, the director of Radio Nacional in Iguazú raised a final question: "Apart from asking who is interested in creating this region as a risk zone, why don't we, journalists, ask why the World Bank and the U.S. organizations support this meeting? I am concerned about the level of information and control, not of what we can or cannot say among ourselves, but of the strategic goal to make us, journalists, work for their interests while believing we are working for our own." To Mariquita, the meeting, which was financed by the Open Society Institute, the World Bank, and the Knight Center for Journalism in the Americas, perpetuated the same myth it officially intended to dissolve: it called attention to the tri-border region and its associations with organized crime and terrorism. Media headlines following the conference repeated the same refrain of the security talk: "Triple Frontier: A Place Demonized by Governments and Journalists Who Do not Know the Region" and "Terrorism and Crime: Aspects of a Contradictory Reality."[37] Objections to the hegemonic narrative about danger launched from local journalists were included in these publications. However, for Mariquita and others who participated in the event, the content was submerged under the form. The conference, mostly attended by journalists who did not subscribe to the hypothesis of terrorism in the tri-border region in the first place, reaffirmed the discourse it was challenging.

The event also had another message. Panel presentations, discussions, and media coverage marked a distinction between the type of crimes that the tri-border area was accused of in the mainstream media and the different modes of violence that the locals considered to be the real problems in the region. The Paraguayan daily *Vanguardia* extensively quoted Chilean journalist Mónica Gonzáles, who in her opening speech at the meeting outlined this dichotomy from the locals' point of view:

> Triple Frontier has always been a space of terrorists. Previously there were the terrorists of Operation Condor, there was state terrorism, prisoners were taken from one side to another to torture them and kill them in order to get their secrets. Those who traffic women and children are also terrorists because they commit family and social terrorism. So this is the border of terrorists, like all borders are. But they [the media] try to push this aspect so that we would not see the other parts, such as poverty, decimated indigenous population, land disputes, the Russians and the Chechens who come attracted by the business of prostitution.[38]

Founder and director of the Centro de Investigación e Información Periodística (CIPER, Center for Journalistic Investigation and Information) and laureate of the 2010 UNESCO Guillermo Cano Press Freedom Award for her work against the Chilean dictatorship, Gónzalez expanded the use of the term "terrorism" to include forms of terror perpetrated by the state and organized crime groups that exploit the social problems in the region. The legacy of state terrorism during the years of the Argentine Dirty War and Operation Condor is still palpable in Argentina, Brazil, and Paraguay. Some journalists who work in the area had had direct encounters with the military regimes during the early years of their professional careers in the media, which significantly influenced their understanding of news-making against security-making, as I show in the following chapter.

In her speech Gónzalez also emphasized widespread poverty, calling it "unbearable" and "obscene." Where the state and mass media wanted to see foreign enemies, she invoked structural violence: "Here victims of drug trafficking, trafficking of children and women for sex work are invisible. Not only in the Triple Frontier, but in the region as a whole there is a niche of unbearable, obscene poverty." She continued: "Nobody talks about this poverty, as if there were no illiterate people, no poor children who in order to eat and feed their families at the age of eight go to the streets and offer themselves to men. There is always a hand that gives and a hand that takes." In chapter 2 we saw how the focus on "unbearable, obscene poverty," "illiterate people," and "poor children" can also be sensationalized, made into a spectacle, reducing structural violence into cultural determinism. But Gónzalez does not succumb to this explanation. She firmly holds the state—its political and economic sectors, which finance the media—accountable for this situation: "there is always a hand that gives and a hand that takes."

The connection between organized crime and the conditions of everyday life in the tri-border area runs through the stories of local journalists. They work against the background of the global discourse that has vilified the region—impacted by it, responding to it, contesting it, and inevitably reproducing it. As the ever-expanding centrifugal apparatus of security incorporates books, petitions, documents, articles, resolutions, and conference papers that are absorbed into the circulating narrative of threat, the role local journalists play in the regime designed to manage uncertainty is ambivalent. Resisting the effects of the security regime, as seen in the actions of journalists in the tri-border area, in many cases inadvertently results in perpetuating the very story they are attempting to change. The discourse of security absorbs fragments of narratives, extracting morsels that fit its agenda and discarding evidence that appears contradictory and open to interpretation. In the absence of concrete evidence, talking terrorism is speculative. But the weight of arguments is not equal. Depending on the social status and politico-economic significance of the institution that utters a particular version of events, some truths become more real than others. In such an unbalanced landscape of media and power, even denial, repeatedly asserted by the participants in the trinational meeting of journalists, can be interpreted as a confirmation of the story.

TO LIVE ON THE MARGINS

Commenting on the cinematic fascination with the Triple Frontier, *Página/12* columnist Martín Granovsky wrote: "*Vivir al límite* [to live on the edge] is not the same as *vivir en el límite* [to live on the margins].[39] Maybe a few dedicate themselves to the former. Millions of Paraguayans, Brazilians, and Argentines everyday do the latter."[40] This quote summarizes the dilemma that exists when the security discourse is translated from the global to the regional and local milieus. International portrayals of an Islamist terrorist threat in South America focus on establishing the link between Muslim migrant communities in the tri-border region and terrorist organizations operating in the Middle East. This is achieved by the constant repetition of the same line of future-oriented reasoning in official state documents and media reports, rather than by references to tangible evidence and actual events. The vilification of the Triple Frontier was not an immediate result of terrorist attacks in Argentina in the 1990s and in the U.S. in 2001. The discourse of terrorist threat needed time to mature, and a number of actors, both global and local, using fragments of information, participated in making it into a coherent story. This chapter has shown how, once produced, stories take on lives of their own: no matter what the author's original intention is, they circulate across regimes of knowledge—from media to academia, from investigative journalism to fiction—legitimating increased government surveillance and justifying militarized intervention. Indirectly, Argentine, Brazilian, and Paraguayan journalists who organized the meeting to discuss representation of the Triple Frontier in the global media also played a part in recirculating the narrative that they were challenging.

Created and proliferated in this way, the discourse of security is detached from the actual experiences that comprise daily life on the margins of the state. The ethnographic chapters that follow demonstrate that local journalists find it unacceptable to reduce and simplify the often legally ambiguous border practices that are cited as proof of lawlessness in the region into standard news scripts. Not only do they consider it to be a distorted and exaggerated version of reality but also, and more importantly, they see it is a distraction from the real problems that residents of the area deal with. Hence, aware how their words can spin out of control and end up being uncritically appropriated and used by the global security strategists, further implicating their region as a threat-harboring place, journalists try to balance negative representations with features on the positive aspects of living in the border region.

While the global discourse about danger and violence continues to circulate, local media broadcast the message that the tri-border area is secure. Articles such as "Triple Frontier: There Are No Terrorist Organizations" and "There Is No Lebanese Community in Iguazú" explicitly deny the connection between the border and terrorist activities in the Middle East.[41] In May 2011, when Osama Bin Laden was killed in Pakistan, newspapers in Foz do Iguaçu—their articles also reprinted by Puerto Iguazú dailies—celebrated the fact that the region will be once and for all acquitted of harboring him.[42] Ironically, to the temporary relief of many Argentines, Brazilians, and Paraguayans, director Kathryn Bigelow immediately refocused her attention to making a film about the operation to find and capture Bin Laden, postponing the *Triple Frontier* project. "In cinema, as in all fiction, everyone has a right to do whatever they want. Viewers will also use their right to express their opinion. The problem is not when art imitates reality, but, as Oscar Wilde would say, when reality imitates art," wrote Granovsky in his opinion piece for *Página/12*. Referring to information about the 3+1 cooperation between Argentina, Brazil, Paraguay, and the U.S. provided by leaked diplomatic cables, the journalist observed that North American delegates took the existence of terrorism in the region as a given rather than a hypothesis that needed to be proven. Trying to reestablish a clearer boundary between fact and fiction, which in the Triple Frontier has been continuously blurred, the columnist claimed: "A fiction movie has the right to imagine the kingdom of hell. A serious country has to verify it."

Talking about the trinational meeting of journalists in 2010, the Misiones press undersecretary told a reporter from a provincial daily: "This region has normal levels of insecurity for this part of the world."[43] As I show in the next chapter, security on the local level is very different from that defined in national and global doctrines. More than a self-referential discourse based on constructing large-scale threats, such as organized crime and terrorism, here security is interpreted, experienced, and practiced through the relationships that residents have with everyday uncertainties, and through their encounters with urban crime and state violence. For Iguazú journalists, who live and work on the margins of the state, security is a local project that is motivated by their personal experiences and embedded in the economic and social struggles within their community.

4

Small Town, Big Hell

Do I want to be a hero? Will it change my life? Yes, certainly.
I will end up three meters below the ground.

—Horacio Valdés

VISION CORRECTION

The idea of placing security cameras in central locations in Puerto
Iguazú met with significant resistance. In 2010 private television company C.V.I., which had a monopoly as the cable provider, presented the
plan to the town council as a project of *seguridad urbana* (urban security). C.V.I. was installing a fiber optic cable network for high-speed
internet, and the company suggested that as part of the project it could
also set up surveillance cameras at strategic points around Iguazú, such
as busy street intersections. But the town council repeatedly blocked
implementation of the project. Local government was uneasy about
outsourcing the provision of public safety to a private institution, even
though the company insisted it would relinquish the management of the
cameras to the appropriate state agencies. In the context of fears of
violating citizen privacy, the urban security project was called *ojo vigilador* (monitoring eye) and nicknamed "panopticon." In a letter to the
town council, the *fiscal de instrucción*—the prosecutor in charge of conducting preliminary investigations on behalf of the state—cited crime
statistics showing there was no need for enhanced security, especially in
the town center, where law enforcement was effective in maintaining
order. "It would show tourists that we have cameras, but major crimes
occur in the outlying areas, where the more vulnerable population
lives," he wrote, recommending that the councillors decline the project

because it was "una necesidad superflua, secundaria, accesoria y extemporánea para nuestros márgenes" (an unnecessary, secondary, ancillary and untimely need for our borders).[1]

Surveillance has been used as a significant albeit controversial tactic in security and policing strategies worldwide (see Frois 2013; Maguire 2012). The project proposed by C.V.I. is an example of one way in which the media, too, actively participate in the process of securing public space. In Iguazú, however, political rivalries did not allow the government and the media company to come to an agreement. In addition to concerns about citizen privacy, video surveillance was seen as a highly selective means of crime monitoring. The cameras were to be located in the areas that already have strong police presence, not in the outlying barrios, where more incidents occur. Cameras, some argued, would displace crime, not reduce it. Video surveillance would push criminals to the edges of town, where nobody sees and nobody cares. Even more importantly, crime is not always visible: it takes place behind the closed doors of a family home and in the unlit streets of residential or industrial neighborhoods. As a tool, the camera is a technical prosthesis, controlled by whoever is behind it: it can be manipulated to look in some directions and not others, focus on some objects and people, but not others.

It was also feared that ojo vigilador would be discriminatory. But this concern about the panoptical qualities of surveillance over urban space obscures the extent to which the perspective on local reality was already limited in Iguazú. Like the cameras they use, journalists cover crime by *focusing*. The stories they create are selective, and they are framed in ways that serve a particular purpose. Rather than raising alarms about the danger of the Triple Frontier, as the criminalizing discourse of the foreign and national press does, stories Iguazú journalists write convey a sense of security for the community. These focused narratives are shaped by journalists' personal encounters with crime and violence and threats to their own safety. Although, as seen in the previous chapter, news media in Iguazú reject and ridicule the globally circulating narrative about terrorism directed at the Triple Frontier, reporters' concern with other forms of security is both a significant issue and an important goal behind media coverage of crime in the area.

Security on the local scale is very different from that defined in national and global paradigms. More than a self-referential discourse based on constructing large-scale social threats, such as organized crime and terrorism, here security is seen through personal and highly contextualized relationships that residents have with crime and violence.

Daniel M. Goldstein suggests that a critical anthropological perspective should examine security as configured and deployed by local actors in their engagements with each other and with the state (2010:492, 2012:15). When we embrace an understanding of security that is not state-centric and pay attention to translations, negotiations, and adaptations that a number of actors, positioned along a continuum from the global to the local, engage in, the making of security becomes a performative project. In it, journalists play an important role as mediators across the different scales of security discourse and practice. As I have already shown, the media in Iguazú, together with their counterparts in Ciudad del Este and Foz do Iguaçu, have attempted to renegotiate the global narrative that implicates the Triple Frontier as a dangerous place, defying the securitization of the border. But journalists are concerned with security on the local level, anticipating and avoiding danger in their everyday lives in a way that results in greater protection for themselves and their community. For them, security is made at the intersection between the politics of global threats and local reality. Their position is influenced by a combination of factors, which include the criminalization and militarization of the region, their varied personal encounters with violence, and the economic uncertainty faced by the residents of Iguazú.

In this chapter I shift the perspective from the broader discourse of threat to the ethnography of individual ways of experiencing violent crime and interpreting insecurity. Through the stories of journalists who have encountered violence in their personal and professional capacities, I show how it directly affects news production. Local journalists contrast the perils in large urban centers, primarily Buenos Aires, where assaults and robberies are frequent and indiscriminate, and what they see as peaceful life in the Argentine Northeast. Contrary to the popular geography of blame, journalists who moved to the tri-border area from crime-ridden cities saw security as a resource that drew them to the border, and as a resource they were ready to protect. Not surprisingly, in 2011, when residents became increasingly anxious about insecurity in Iguazú, local media reports on rising crime projected the violence onto the national capital, attributing its presence in the tri-border area to recent migrants from the shantytowns of Buenos Aires. In Iguazú crime was seen as a foreign threat to the *convivencia* (coexistence) that the locals had worked out. In their news reporting, journalists inverted the dominant geography of crime and violence, in which the nationwide press portrayed the border as lawless and dangerous, and ricocheted these allegations of criminality back to the urban core.

Ethnography provides an invaluable tool for exploring how lived experiences of knowledge producers both constitute and challenge geographies of blame in the public sphere. In Argentina, as in other Latin American countries, popular discourse often maps violence and crime onto a horizontal plane of the nation-state, where the center and the periphery are presented as two opposite poles (see, e.g., Briggs and Mantini-Briggs 2003; Coronil and Skurski 2006; Markoff and Baretta 2006; Poole 2004). This spatial dichotomy juxtaposes the political capital with its distant borders; the city with the country's interior. In the previous chapter, I argued that, drawing on the discourse of civilization over barbarism, the principal security paradigm locates crime and violence at the margins, territorial and social. In this chapter I show how local opinion reverses this dominant vision. Many Iguazúenses, because of memories of terror during the Argentina's brutal Dirty War, ongoing structural violence that affects the region, and their firsthand experiences of crime, interpret violence as a core feature of the state and map it onto the federal capital. In this reversal, even the criminality characteristic of everyday life on the border, such as the extensive informal market based on smuggling, is secondary to state and structural violence and is a form of resistance to it, as I discuss in chapter 5. This geography of crime and violence, seen from opposite perspectives along the center-periphery axis, underlies discordant interpretations of security. For the government, security is the raison d'être of the sovereign state as it dispatches the military and law enforcement from the center of power toward its disorderly frontiers, but for those who live in the interior provinces and distant borderlands, the deployment of the security apparatus by the state, which has a legacy of violent repression, is seen as a threat that increases their insecurity. Geography of blame for crime and violence is predicated on the opposition of the urban core and the rural periphery, of the center of the state and its territorial margins, even if they are constitutive of each other.

For local journalists, the discourse and experience of crime become intertwined and feed into each other. On the one hand, journalists use news production as a means to challenge narratives that vilify the region and thwart the effects of the geography of blame by questioning and inverting the projections of violence from the national capital onto the border. On the other hand, they also live in neighborhoods where crimes are carried out, sharing the same streets, shops, and schools with suspected delinquents, so their representational tactics are inevitably conditioned by spatial and social proximity and interconnectedness,

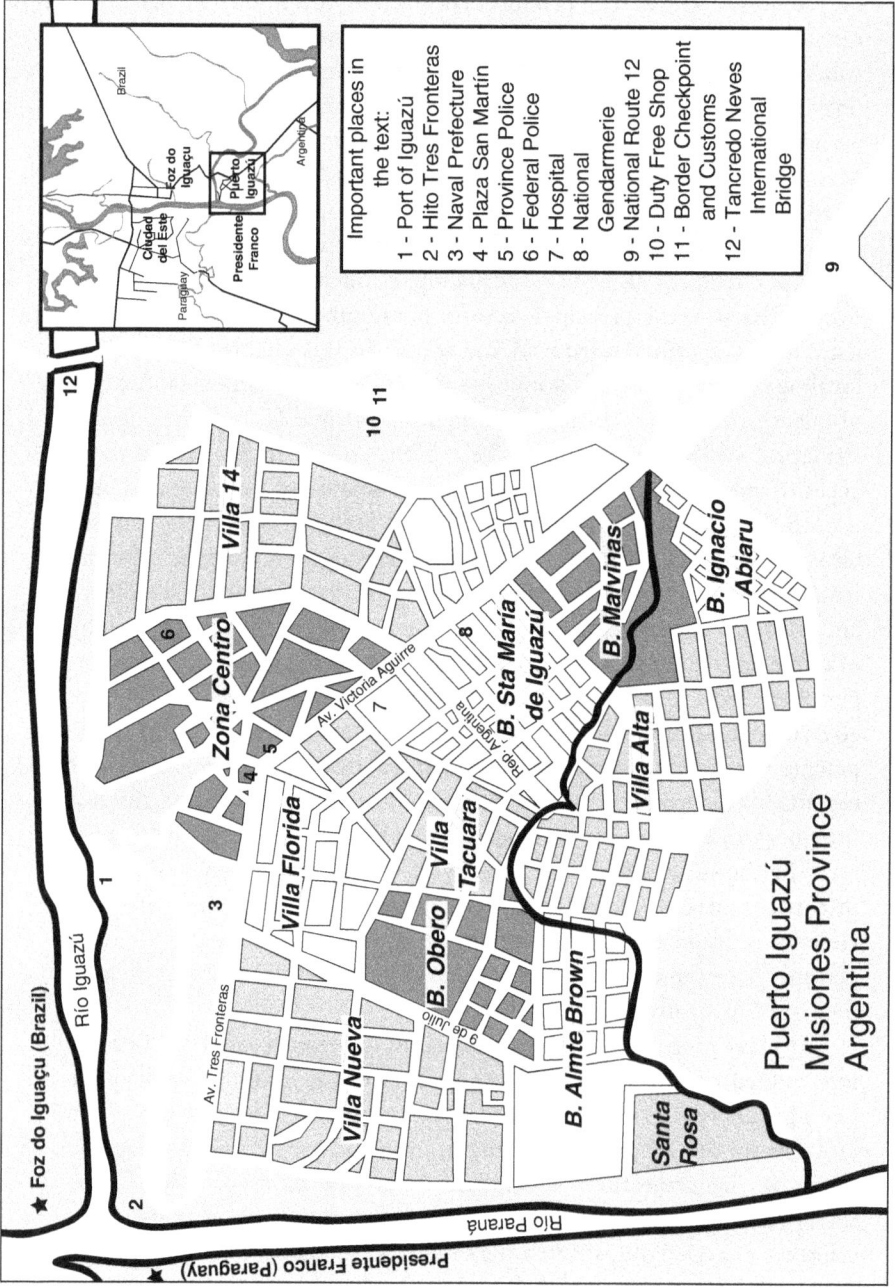

MAP 2. Puerto Iguazú. Cartography by Bryce Davenport.

Important places in the text:

1 - Port of Iguazú
2 - Hito Tres Fronteras
3 - Naval Prefecture
4 - Plaza San Martín
5 - Province Police
6 - Federal Police
7 - Hospital
8 - National Gendarmerie
9 - National Route 12
10 - Duty Free Shop
11 - Border Checkpoint and Customs
12 - Tancredo Neves International Bridge

Puerto Iguazú
Misiones Province
Argentina

condensed within the formula "we are all neighbors." News-making in
Iguazú provides discursive resistance to the frontera caliente narrative,
but this resistance is deeply rooted in and circumscribed by the lived
experiences and everyday practices of local knowledge producers. The
public memory and enduring legacy of state violence, their direct and
indirect encounters with crime, and the rules of complicity and coexistence that entangle members of a small border community all contribute
to what and how local journalists report.

COMPLICIDAD AND CONVIVENCIA

Pueblo chico, infierno grande (small town, big hell), is a popular saying
that I first heard from Horacio Valdés. Horacio has got the look of a
frontline reporter: a carefully trimmed Van Dyck beard, a pocketed
beige vest, and dark sunglasses. Born in Buenos Aires, in early childhood he moved to his mother's native Misiones. Horacio went to the
regional public university in Posadas, where he studied journalism and
specialized in covering crime and police investigations. After an intern-
ship at *Primera Edición,* one of the two major papers in the province,
he was hired to work in the newspaper's crime section. It was in these
early days of his career that Horacio learned about the dangers of doing
journalistic investigations into organized crime. He recalls an experience that taught him, then a young and ambitious reporter, about the
unspoken rules of his profession:

> I was investigating a case related to child trafficking. One day an elderly
> person came to see me in the editorial offices of the daily in Posadas. He asks:
> "Are you Horacio Valdés?" "Yes," I reply. "How can I help you?" He says:
> "Look, I have information that will help you in the investigation." I don't
> know how this man knew what I was investigating. "What investigation?" I
> ask. "The investigation you are doing," he replies and smiles. "Really? What
> information do you have?" I inquire. He says: "I have pictures, documents.
> Everything you need. Will you publish it?" Just imagine! An informant
> comes and tells me all this! It is the best thing that can happen to a journalist.
> It's a front-page story for the daily. "OK, bring me the proof, bring all the
> information that you have, and we'll see. I can't promise I will write any-
> thing before I know what documents you want to show me," I explain.
> "I will come tomorrow," he says, and leaves.
>
> The following day the man brought a box full of photographs of children, of
> clandestine airstrips where planes land, photographs of the places where
> operations are carried out. Everything. Papers related to judges, to gover-
> nors, to politicians. I was speechless: Who is he? Why did he bring me all this

information for free? Usually informants want money. "Who are you?" I ask. "It doesn't matter who I am," he responds, "If you are interested, I will leave all this. Do whatever you want with it." He left me all the materials. Very well known politicians in Misiones were implicated. I went to see my editor and explained the situation. "Horacio, be careful with this," I was told. "What you want to publish is very dangerous."

When I went home that day, my phone rang: "Déjate de joder o sos boleta" [Stop messing around or you are dead]. I don't know who it was. Nor do I know how they got my number. A man called me and threatened to kill me. He said: "You are dead, your mother is dead, and your brother is dead." The next day I told my editor what had happened. "We won't publish this," he says. "Why?" I ask. "First, because your life is in danger. Second, do you know who the person that brought you the documents is? This man has worked for intelligence services for fifty years. That is why he knows what he knows. If you get involved in this, tomorrow you will be dead."[2]

Horacio's example presents the classic dilemma faced by investigative reporters: the need to reconcile publishing a breaking news story with concerns for their safety. According to the Committee to Protect Journalists (CPJ), between 1993 and 2013 four journalists were killed in Argentina; this rate, when compared to that in other countries in Latin America, such as Colombia, Brazil, Mexico, and Honduras, is low.[3] But recently international press freedom organizations have expressed concerns about an upsurge in assaults on Argentine journalists, especially in the provinces. In 2012, Reporters without Borders noted that safety has deteriorated due to the failure of public authorities to take action against frequent threats and assaults carried out by local elected officials.[4] The problem was not new. Impunity for government officials involved in corruption and linked to crime has for decades presented serious obstacles to journalists working for media organizations in small rural communities in the country's interior.

After Horacio graduated, he returned to Buenos Aires. However, the federal capital was not welcoming to the ambitious reporter. "In the interior regions everybody paints Buenos Aires as the city of opportunities. The reality is different, especially for those who come from the provinces," he said. During the three years he lived in the capital, most of the jobs Horacio had were not related to news-making. Then, for a while he worked at a radio and television channel outside of the city, until he finally auditioned at *Telefe,* one of the major private television networks in the country. Unfortunately, this happened in 2001, during the climax of a major economic crisis in Argentina. In December President Fernando de la Rúa declared a state of emergency, precipitating violent clashes between police and protestors, and when he resigned later that month, Argentina fell into chaos. Horacio remembers how the crisis affected media companies: "When the nation-state was in trouble, the door was shut and there was no more money for the media. It is a sad page in the nation's history." Without support from the government, media companies began firing personnel, and *Telefe* withdrew its offer.

Professional hardships were not the only problem Horacio encountered in Buenos Aires. Once, on his way to the bank to withdraw his salary, he was assaulted by armed robbers. "In the federal capital there is a lot of insecurity. They kill you for two pesos. They even took all my clothes," he tells me. It was after this experience of armed robbery that he made up his mind to return to Misiones. Like many other journalists in the tri-border area, Horacio contrasts the danger of living in a major metropolitan area with the tranquility of the primarily rural Argentine Northeast. Back on the border, he briefly worked for the official Misiones government radio station in Posadas, until in 2003 Claudio Alvarez, the CEO and major shareholder of C.V.I. Canal 5, invited him to Iguazú. For seven years Horacio was the reporter and evening news host for the local channel. He quit in February 2010 over a disagreement between employees demanding better working conditions and the owners of the company, who, he says, were more concerned with business and politics than with quality journalism. When I met him, his television career on hold, Horacio was on the edges of the public sphere, working on a tourism radio project. But this interim phase did not last long, and in May 2011 he returned to television, at first as the face of the municipal news program on the new FTA (free-to-air) channel Canal 11, and two years later as the host of a new show broadcast on Canal 5, *Sentido común* (Common sense).

"Iguazú is a very peculiar and a very complex community," observes Horacio. "Being a journalist here is more complicated than in any other place I have worked. It is a very small community. Everybody knows everybody. If tomorrow you say something about someone, you will meet this person in the street the following day. Therefore, there is a lot of *connivencia*. There is a lot of *complicidad* in the media." The Spanish word "connivencia," which like "complicidad" stands for "complicity," is close to another popular Iguazúense concept—"convivencia," translated into English as "coexistence" or "collaboration" and invoking the spirit of getting along. Whereas "complicity" has negative undertones because it constricts the agency of journalists and implicates them in the games of hide-and-seek with the town's authorities, *convivencia,* which has the same effect of withholding some information from circulating in

FIGURE 10. Horacio Valdés conducting a radio program. Puerto Iguazú, September 2010.

public, is seen in a positive light—it is a form of protection for journalists within the community. One reporter put it this way: "This place is tiny. When you try to investigate, to tell the truth, it can have negative consequences for more than half of the town, and that is a problem." Complicity may be forced upon border residents as an informal system of control; but, through convivencia, they internalize it as accountability to their community. "There is a direct relationship among the people because everybody knows each other's story," explains Horacio. In a move that might seem contradictory, he chose to return to the tri-border area from Buenos Aires even though he understood that complicity and convivencia would create blind spots in news-making—a small-town predicament from which he tried to escape earlier in his career. The underside to the sense of personal safety in Iguazú relative to Buenos Aires is that investigative journalism here poses significant risks, as he explains:

> You look around and realize that you are alone. Even worse, you put the life of your loved ones in danger. Then it "clicks": What am I getting involved in? Does it serve me somehow? Will I change anything? Do I want to be a hero? Will it change my life? Yes, certainly. I will end up three meters below the ground. So it gets complicated. When dealing with issues such as drug trafficking, human trafficking, and child trafficking, unfortunately you don't know who is involved. Sometimes they are the people you would least have imagined.

POLITICS OF NUMBERS

According to the Argentine Ministry of Justice, Security and Human Rights, out of twenty-three Argentine provinces, Misiones has consistently had one of the lowest incidence of crime. In 2006, the crime rate in Misiones was at 217.3 per 10,000 residents; in 2007 it fell to 197.33; and in 2008—the last year for which government statistics were available at the time of writing this book—it had risen slightly to 209.2.[5] These numbers show that the province has a significantly lower crime rate than the average for Argentina, which during the same time period stood at 314.2 (in 2006), 309.54 (in 2007), and 329.8 (in 2008). In the city of Buenos Aires, at least three times more crimes per the same number of people were reported for each of the years between 2006 and 2008, while the crime numbers in the provinces of Mendoza, Neuquén, Santa Cruz, and Salta were more than twice higher than in Misiones. Homicides, often used as proxy data for measuring violent crime, reveal similar trends. According to the United Nations Office on Drugs and Crime (UNODC), Argentina's homicide rate, which in 2010 was at 5.5 per 100,000 residents, was considerably lower than that in neighboring Brazil (22.4) and Paraguay (11.4).[6] In 2008, there were 66 homicides recorded in Misiones (compared to 77 in 2006, and 57 in 2007), a very small number out of the total of 2,305 murders committed in Argentina that year. Nationwide almost half of all homicides (1,045) occurred in the province of Buenos Aires; but Santa Fe (where the city of Rosario is located), Córdoba, and Mendoza also had substantial numbers: 274, 134, and 131, respectively. During the same year Misiones reported 476 violations of drug laws—remarkably fewer than the province and the city of Buenos Aires combined (23,121), and the province of Santa Fe, including Rosario (1,421), and comparable to other provinces in the Argentine Northeast: Salta (796) and Chaco (522).

In Iguazú crime statistics are managed by the regional delegation of the Misiones police, whose newly renovated headquarters are located in the heart of town, next to Plaza San Martín. The institution is in charge of five municipalities: in addition to Iguazú, it administers four smaller towns—Puerto Esperanza, Puerto Libertad, Wanda, and Andresito. According to the data provided to me by the police, during the year between January 1 and December 31, 2010, they registered 203 robberies (fewer than half of which were solved), 13 armed robberies, and 437 thefts. Among other common crimes were five homicides, four of which had been solved, 13 deaths and 51 injuries in traffic accidents, 139 other incidents involving injuries, and 18 sexual assaults. Although these numbers were not alarming—in Iguazú the murder rate per 1,000 people was 0.06, only slightly higher than the U.S. average of 0.05 and smaller than, for example, Boston at 0.10 murders per 1,000 residents—anxiety about crime and insecurity was slowly growing to the point that in 2011 crime had become a new major subject of public discussion.

As with data on drug seizures, discussed in chapter 2, crime statistics cannot be taken for granted. They are a quantitative expression of social facts, which are related to but separate from material acts of violence and crime (see Andreas and Greenhill 2010; Caldeira 2001; Comaroff and Comaroff 2006; Tate 2007). Statistics are "technologies of truth" that produce rather than merely represent social reality, and although they are important tools for measuring injustice and wrongdoing, numbers provide only a partial perspective, which can perpetrate symbolic and structural violence instead of mitigating its effects (Merry and Coutin 2014). In the domain of political contestation, the numbers can be manipulated to match specific governmental agendas, such as when the state uses increasing crime rates to strengthen the presence of law enforcement and boost their funding. Crime statistics show as much as they hide: while murders and property crime such as robberies and burglaries are more likely to be accounted for, certain other types of crimes, like domestic violence, often go unreported and, therefore, unrecorded. As a social fact—and a social problem—crime is construed in accordance with the interests of those who wield political and economic power. It is not shocking, then, that crime statistics often reveal profound inequalities between neighborhoods divided by class, race, and ethnicity. In his ethnography of policing, Didier Fassin (2013a) noted that the issues at stake in counting victims are both anthropological and political: on the one hand, which crimes merit reporting depends on fluctuating cultural and social contexts; on the other, reports have a tactical function in terms of anticipated benefits. Because of these "politics of numbers," crime statistics provide an incomplete picture of the actual situation.

Moreover, the perception of danger and the way people talk about crime often do not correspond with its official rates. As Fassin shows in his ethnography of law enforcement in the banlieues of Paris, institutional crime figures may even contradict residents' concerns about and fear of crime, which often stem from the poor image of certain neighborhoods perpetuated in the public sphere by the media and politicians. In her study on São Paulo, Teresa Caldeira suggests the existence of intricate relationships among violence, signification, and order that explain how talk about crime is not only expressive but also productive: the classification and discrimination entailed in the symbolic work of making sense of experiences of violence "helps produce segregation (social and spatial), abuses by the institutions of order, contestations of citizens' rights, and, especially, violence itself" (2001:39). Because of its effectiveness in providing a symbolic ordering of the world, crime becomes a lens through which people talk about things such as economic crisis and unemployment. These everyday discourses about violence, including news stories, commentaries, conversations, and even jokes, are contagious and repetitive, both counteracting and reproducing violence. They lead to a proliferation of class-specific strategies—from window grilles and bars to gated residential spaces to surveillance technologies to private bodyguards—that citizens use to mitigate their escalating concerns about insecurity.

In Argentina, in 2010 and 2011 an increasingly alarming discourse of insecurity saturated the news media, portraying Buenos Aires as a war zone, with almost daily reports on murders, violent assaults, robberies, and assassinations of police officers. According to an article in *La Nación,* which used data from a Gallup poll conducted in 2009, 61 percent of Argentines were afraid to walk alone at night in their neighborhood, compared to the world average of 36 percent, assigning Argentina fourteenth place in global ratings measuring the feeling of insecurity.[7] But this data obscures the stark difference that has historically existed between urban parts of the country and smaller, rural municipalities, where, in comparison to Buenos Aires, people felt safe. Watching crime news on nationwide television channels and weighing their own experiences or those of relatives who were visiting or living in metropolitan areas, Iguazúenses saw the country's capital as the epicenter of crime. This reversal of the dominant geography of blame was consistent with their understanding of Buenos Aires as the source of state violence during the military regime of 1976–1983 and of the neoliberal economic restructuring in the 1990s. Their argument was deeply grounded in their sense of security on the border, based on lived experience. But, since in the public sphere crime was represented quantitatively, in order to validate their corrected vision of the geography of crime they commonly referred to statistics. Consider this assertion from Horacio:

> If you do the math, if you analyze the statistics, you will see that in Buenos Aires there are attacks every twenty minutes. In the federal capital, in conurbano bonaerense, there are almost as many assaults as in the civil war in

Colombia. But the national media want to show that in the border area, in the Triple Frontier, there are guerilla fighters and mafia groups. They do exist. Obviously they exist. But it is not as they say, that drug traffickers pass in front of you carrying cocaine. In the capital there is more crime than here, there are more robberies than here, there are more deaths than here, in the Triple Frontier, in the "hot" area.

Thus, the state assigned them the role of suspicious border dwellers, balancing on the edge of law and crime, and Iguazúenses ricocheted the accusations of violence back to the capital. Their own experiences combined with stories they heard from other people or saw on metropolitan television networks only confirmed to them that, compared to the quietness of Iguazú, the situation in Buenos Aires was much worse.

For Horacio, the fear of crime and of the potential for violence in conurbano bonaerense was exacerbated because his brother was a gendarme. As a member of a special command unit, Horacio's brother was deployed to different places around the country to deal with conflicts on national highways and other assignments directly mandated by the president. In 2010 their unit was to be sent to the outskirts of Buenos Aires, where gendarmes were to help police maintain security in one of the most dangerous neighborhoods in the country—barrio Ejército de los Andes, nicknamed Fuerte Apache.[8] The plan to use gendarmes as reinforcement in those parts of Greater Buenos Aires where the efforts of local police had failed was one of the last political wishes of President Néstor Kirchner. In December 2010, not long after Kirchner's sudden death, six thousand gendarmes were deployed to the nation's capital. To the relief of Horacio's family, his brother decided to resign from the unit and now leads a civilian life in Mendoza.

GEOGRAPHY OF CRIME

During the time I spent in Iguazú, I observed how often its residents marked the federal capital as the historical and geographical center of state violence and violent crime. On multiple occasions people shared with me their own experiences, referred to television news reports, and quoted official statistics to change the direction of the criminalizing gaze, which has since the 1990s implicated the Argentine Northeast as the frontera caliente. They did that by demonstrating the brutal reality on the streets of Buenos Aires, which was nothing like their quiet life on the border. This reversal of the center-periphery axis—along which blame for violence and crime in Argentina was assigned and to which the apparatus of security was applied—was exemplified in public discussions that started in 2011, when the fear of crime began circulating in Iguazú. Early on, rather than being autochthonous, assaults and robberies were framed as imports from the urban centers, allegedly brought to the tri-border region by migrants who were fleeing poverty and violence in the conurbano bonaerense.

The local press reported a series of violent episodes: two teenagers pointed a revolver at a bus driver and stole 200 pesos collected for tickets;[9] four brothers and a cousin were suspected of murdering a thirty-year-old resident in a family feud;[10] an ex-employee at a hostel armed with a knife tied up the receptionist and stole 23,000 pesos from inside a safe;[11] a neighbor threatened a seventy-two-year-old woman with a sharp weapon and stole a fan;[12] a six-year-old child was sexually abused and tortured by his mother;[13] a thirteen-year-old approached two teenagers while they were eating ice cream on a bench and, pointing a firearm, asked for their cell phones;[14] a man on a motor scooter was attacked with a machete when he refused to pay a toll in an illegal booth set up in a barrio;[15] a purse with money and documents was stolen from a tourist in a hotel restaurant and, though the suspect was identified on the street, he escaped due to a general power outage in town.[16] What attracted attention in these stories was the gradual *dis*-placement of violence from poorer outlying barrios such as Barrio Santa Rosa, Barrio Primavera, Villa Florida, or Ribera del Paraná, widely thought to be dangerous, and its *re*-placement in the most central streets of town. It was not so much crime per se, considered as a given in some areas, but rather instituting violence as an issue visible in the heart of Iguazú that alarmed residents, lending some legitimacy to the proposed installation of surveillance cameras. Crime was also intimately connected to alternative income-generating strategies and thrived under conditions of state abandonment and infrastructural deficiencies.

These and similar stories provoked fervent discussions among Iguazúenses. News publics began looking for culprits of crimes and solutions to insecurity, which they insisted was a new problem in the area. Scapegoats for troubles in Iguazú were traditionally found among the unauthorized peasant settlers from Paraguay or Brazil, but in 2011 attention turned to the alleged migrants from the *villas miseria* (shantytowns) in Buenos Aires, who were seen as importing an urban form of violence. It was rumored that Governor Closs had agreed to move some of the residents from the notorious Villa 31, a shantytown built along the port of Buenos Aires in Retiro, and resettle them in Misiones, primarily in Posadas, Oberá, and Iguazú. In the federal capital, Villa 31 was considered to be a source of insecurity, where original Italian and rural Argentine settlers and more recent immigrants from Bolivia, Paraguay, and Peru were locked in cycles of poverty and crime. Earlier attempts to relocate the population, including moving some of them to Fuerte Apache, had been unsuccessful, and the government continued to receive criticism for its inability to restore order in the capital. Iguazú media provided a platform to extend this national practice of vilifying the shantytown residents. Online news sources had sections for comments, which turned into a public arena for perpetuating xenophobic remarks and criminalizing poverty. New urban migrants, who were already targeted in the metropolitan media, were held accountable for bringing insecurity to Iguazú—a discursive practice that matched with the efforts of Iguazúenses to invert the geography of blame and to prove that the capital city was more violent than the alleged frontera caliente.

As elsewhere in Latin America, where governments have been failing to provide security and justice to the people (see, e.g., Dammert and Malone 2006; Goldstein 2004, 2012; Risør 2010; Sieder 2011), some Iguazúenses suggested dealing with rising crime by taking up arms. They embraced the dictum of the privatization of security, promoted by neoliberal reforms, which have eroded governmental safety nets, excused the state from its responsibility toward the economic and social well-being of its citizens, and surrendered its obligation to protect them from physical harm. In Iguazú, which has regional delegations of all federal security forces, fear of crime might seem to be unfounded. It seems counterintuitive that a hypersecuritized space targeted by governmental surveillance and law enforcement initiatives would be experienced as insecure. But it is not a paradox. As social science research in militarized communities in urban Brazil has demonstrated (Caldeira 2001; Holston 2009; Penglase 2009; Wacquant 2008), increased government enforcement can result in insecurity for local populations, which are first depicted as dangerous, producing fear among more privileged citizens, and consequently they are targeted by the state's repressive apparatus. These situations suggest the discrepancy between the broader scope of the global and national security regimes and local concerns with the lack of citizen security.

Incongruity between the scales of security-making also adds to insecurity in the border community in other ways. I showed in chapter 2 that Iguazú has a strong presence of federal forces, including the army, prefecture, gendarmerie, and federal police, but their jurisdiction is over

organized crime, primarily drug and human trafficking, money laundering, and contraband of illegalized goods, from cigarettes to expensive
electronics. It does not cover urban delinquency, such as assaults, robberies, or homicides, which create more immediate concerns for the
residents. In the meanwhile, local police in charge of common crime are
underequipped and underpaid, attracting widespread criticism for their
inability to protect the people. The following comments to several news
stories that *La Voz de Cataratas* published in March 2011 illustrate how
Iguazúenses' angry reaction to the present situation—their widespread
sense of insecurity in a formally securitized and militarized border
space—lays the ground for legitimating vigilantism. These comments
also reinforce the reversed geography of violence and crime in Argentina, with Buenos Aires as the source and the border town as the target:

> *Vecino de Iguazú:* Yes, they are from Villa 31. The robberies began when
> they came. Take action and send these people back home or send them to
> another less populated town. In a few months we will be like Buenos
> Aires: robberies, deaths and criminals. Let's save our city![17]

> *Vecinaa:* Every day Iguazú is getting full of these *chorros* [thieves], we are
> already similar to Buenos Aires. A time will come when we will not be
> able to walk peacefully in the streets.[18]

> *rumplenstiltskin:* I carry a friend, a 45mm caliber gun attached to my belt.
> The day when you'll see a news article about a chorrito who died at the
> door of a house or near a bank with a bullet hole in his head you will
> known who did it.[19]

> *Anónimo:* The police will not confront the chorros of Villa 31. It is a catas-
> trophe. Use arms to defend our families, neighbors![20]

> *Daniel Díaz Acuña:* I came from Buenos Aires to live in peace, but. . .
> Would I need to arm myself again to do so? Do we need to take a couple
> of these down so they stop fooling around?[21]

> *Vecino Enfafado:* It is true that all these dregs come from Buenos Aires
> because here we had never heard of motochorros. It is logical that it starts
> with armed robberies! God does not want me to meet one of them because
> for sure they would be floating in the Paraná. Be careful, neighbors! Arm
> yourselves![22]

People who leave comments in news forums often choose to sign as
"vecino" or "vecina" (neighbor, or resident). The term designates a
concerned citizen and by opting for it, readers indicate their belonging
to the local community and their stake in the problem of rising crime.
This term also creates distance between them, as the town's "proper"
residents, and the criminals, seen as outsiders. Similar trends of blaming

FIGURE 11. Reporter and cameraman waiting to interview the police superintendent in Villa Alta. Puerto Iguazú, June 2010.

the other have been observed by scholars who study the criminalization of immigration in Europe and the U.S., where undocumented foreigners are commonly accused of bringing both crime and disease across international borders (e.g., Chacón 2008; Chavez 2013; de Genova 2002; Dowling and Inda 2013; Ngai 2004). In contrast, in urban centers across Latin America the talk of crime is often directed at the rural migrants from the interior of the country, who are seen as dangerous, which Caldeira (2001) shows with the category of *nordestino* in São Paulo. In Iguazú, unauthorized settlers from nearby rural areas of Paraguay and Brazil were habitually pinpointed as culprits of the town's social problems, such as land occupation and drug dealing. However, in 2011 the fear of crime was directed at metropolitan Argentines, whose otherness was not a matter of their citizenship as much as their urban background and social class—purportedly these were extremely poor residents and squatters from the city. Certainly not all Iguazúenses agreed with the criminalization of porteño migrants. Instead of blaming the newcomers, real or imaginary, others, albeit fewer in numbers, suggested the perpetrators of violence were local:

> *Vecina:* In the very center of Iguazú you cannot walk after 10pm. All the *vagos* [idlers] meet there, drinking and selling *falopa* [drugs]. And you say

you don't know who they are? Please! Enough hypocrisy. Villa Florida is full of these criminals.[23]

Manuel: I suggested paying someone to take me to a home that belongs to someone who used to live in Villa 31. Months after I published my request, I have not received a response and have come to a conclusion that there is nobody from the villas of Buenos Aires in Iguazú. Chorros are from here! Stop lying![24]

Despite disagreements about the origin of the criminals, residents saw Iguazú as being on the verge of an era of violence and insecurity. Curiously, crime became a worrisome issue in the beginning of the twenty-first century, as opposed to the 1990s, when contraband in the border area thrived, laying the foundation for the discourse of the frontera caliente. Fifteen years had to pass after Hernán López Echagüe's adventures with corrupt gendarmes and prefects, recounted in the previous chapter, before security would become publicly considered a diminishing resource. One resident expressed his disappointment in the following comment:

Renato: Security was the added value that Iguazú always had. It is losing it. Recently the sirens of firefighters are heard more often, the problems of parking began, neighbors are almost unable to sit outside. We are losing the spirit of the town.[25]

Rising concerns about insecurity drew from the same polarization of the national space, opposing Buenos Aires and Iguazú, as illustrated by Horacio's story. His personal disenchantment with the capital and his decision to move back to Misiones contrasted the danger in the city, where assaults and robberies were random, with a peaceful life in the Argentine Northeast, where violence was subtly disguised in social structures and did not erratically threaten residents. Many Misioneros articulate this juxtaposition as they reflect on their travels between the capital and the border: the first is a faraway anonymous location, a place of uncertainty and insecurity, while the latter is home, familiar and safe for those who respect the rules of complicity and convivencia and do not meddle in the business of others. When at the beginning of 2011 Iguazúenses became concerned with security disappearing from their hometown, they continued to project violence onto the national capital. Rather than being a marker of a distant place, it was now considered as a characteristic of those who lived in the crime-ridden areas. Associated with people rather than place, crime was seen as mobile, something that could be imported to Iguazú by newcomers such as the migrants from Villa 31. It was a threat from the outside, potentially harmful to the local ways of life, widely talked about in the media and in the wider Iguazú community.

MILITARY TOWN

The relationship between Iguazú journalists and Argentine security forces in the tri-border area is tight. If a stranger shows doubts about safety, Iguazúenses are likely to say: "Iguazú is safe because *todas las fuerzas* [all the armed forces] imaginable are stationed here." These include an infantry regiment of the army, the naval prefecture, and the national gendarmerie, as well as federal and regional police delegations (see chapter 2). Considering the town's history and the continual presence of multiple security forces, it is not surprising that many Iguazúenses have developed personal connections to them through family members, neighbors, or friends who serve in the military or work in law enforcement. Nor is it surprising that a significant part of the local news deals with the activities of the fuerzas: successful operations of intercepted trafficking, confiscations of contraband, anniversary ceremonies, training exercises, and recruitment campaigns.

Local media heavily rely on the military and law enforcement when covering crime; news is almost exclusively based on institutional press releases. Prefect Héctor Vera summed up the symbiotic relationship between the security forces and the media in Iguazú when he told me: "We are always in contact. They need news. We need our work to be publicized. And people are interested in what we are doing for them."[26] There is a comparable appreciation on behalf of the journalists. One radio director admitted that among all government agencies, the police, the prefecture, and the gendarmerie "are the institutions that have the most *aceitado* [lubricated] contact with the media."[27] A young reporter who frequently visited the fuerzas expressed a similar attitude: "Relationships with gendarmerie, prefecture, and police are very good. Every time I ask for information they always give it to me. They have always opened the doors for me. They have always asked whether I needed anything else. They have always given me the correct information. They have never told me what I can and what I cannot say."[28]

These symbiotic ties between the security forces and the media have positive and negative effects on news-making. An important example of the latter is that the status of Iguazú as a military town limits public discussion of state violence in Argentina's recent past. During the dicta-

FIGURE 12. Cameraman of the local TV channel filming the civic-military parade during the two-hundredth anniversary of the Argentine Naval Prefecture. Puerto Iguazú, June 2010.

torship of 1976–1983 the government widely used its military and police apparatuses to repress the population, implicating the fuerzas in grave human rights violations, but in Iguazú, people are hesitant to condemn the regime. According to the 1984 report of the Argentine National Commission on the Disappeared, known as *Nunca más (Never Again)*, there were five secret detention centers in Misiones: the Eighth Squadron, "Alto Uruguay," of the gendarmerie; the Casita close to the Posadas Rowing Club; the Provincial Police Information Service; Police Station No. 1; and the Federal Police Office.[29] These were not as big as the detention centers situated in the historical seats of state power, such as Córdoba, Rosario, and Buenos Aires; sometimes they were merely used as transit stops for prisoners on their way to the neighboring provinces. Emphasizing that Misiones was peripheral to the state terror campaign, some who lived in Iguazú during the 1970s and 1980s say that during the Dirty War "life went on here as usual." "Misiones is very young politically," one journalist commented, explaining that the educated militarized youth that were targeted by the regime lived in the central provinces, far away from the tri-border area.[30] Referring to "el proceso," people often use the same contrast between Iguazú and Buenos Aires that they make when commenting on current claims about danger in the Triple Frontier: even during the military dictatorship, on the remote border there was peace, and in the urban centers—insecurity and violence.

During el proceso and the regime's persecution of the independent press, many of those who work in the Iguazú media today were only children; others were not even born. Therefore, their knowledge of the Dirty War waged on the border has been largely handed down through memories from their parents and grandparents. When we talked about the military regime, younger reporters often explained to me that people who were kidnapped and tortured by the state apparatus were Peronist youth militants, some of them members of the Misiones Agrarian Movement (MAM, Movimiento Agrario Misionero), not random Iguazúenses. Others, however, spoke about arbitrary disappearances. For example, the mother of one journalist told me how a local electrician's entire family disappeared overnight, the authorities saying that they had been "transferred."[31] "They've traveled," was a common answer government officials would give to inquisitive people.[32] When I asked about their experiences during the dictatorship, locals often said, "Se tapaba mucho" (It was covered up well). In the context of the pervasive distrust and public silence that characterized life during the Dirty War, when people did everything to avoid attracting attention, some remember how the terror of the regime reached deep into their own home. An Iguazú journalist born in the south of the province told me how one day in 1976 gendarmes arrested her father and brothers, who were involved in radical militancy, releasing them a few weeks later. Meanwhile, another brother of hers was doing mandatory military service in Rosario, where opposition to the regime was strong. When he came back home, to the horror of the family, he shared stories from his military service, including how they would climb onto the roofs to kill "leftists."[33] For this family, their home could not provide a safe place to talk about the atrocious practices of the regime and unequivocally condemn state violence. The terror coerced people into silence, which extended from the most intimate setting of a family home to the public sphere.

During el proceso historiador Villalba, who hosts a program about the region's past on Radio Cataratas, lived in Iguazú and worked in the media. Until the coup in 1976, Villalba was the town's democratically elected mayor, but when the military took over he had to leave his post. Under the dictatorship he continued to work as a correspondent for the provincial newspaper *El Territorio*. Although there was heightened control and the military regime was vigilant when Iguazúenses crossed the borders to Brazil and Paraguay, where they were not allowed to make announcements in foreign media, Villalba says he never had problems with the junta.[34] In contrast, another Iguazú journalist, at that time a beginning reporter elsewhere in the country, had a markedly different experience with the military regime. Mariquita, who was appointed in 2009 to be the director of the Iguazú branch of the Argentine national radio, recalls that starting her career in the media during the dictatorship had a profound impact on her professional formation. "I knew what it meant to work in the media when there were *desaparecidos* [the disappeared], there were dead, there were political prisoners, and we could not talk about them," she remembers.[35] Then living in Posadas, the young reporter had a relationship with a political activist who was imprisoned in Buenos Aires. Because of this connection, her editor at *El Territorio* wanted to assign Mariquita to work in the archives rather than allowing her to do reporting, where she could potentially criticize the government. Unwilling to compromise, she quit. But Mariquita was not afraid of the regime: she used her severance package to start a bimonthly publication, *La Pizarra* (Slate), which was critical of Argentina's involvement in the Malvinas-Falklands War, and during the last year of the junta's rule she engaged in human rights activism, demanding the release of political prisoners.

Compared to the country's urban centers, the military regime's efforts at eradicating "subversion" were less intense in remote and rural Misiones. Here, people's experiences during the dictatorship were varied, but overall fewer of the region's current journalists and their families were directly impacted by the government's repressive policies. Since the collective memory of state repression was thus less articulated in local public discourse, Iguazúenses could more confidently speak up in support of the military as a panacea to solve the problems of social disorder. In 2010, for instance, there was widespread agreement, shared by both officials in the security forces and common residents—including high school teachers, students, and their parents—in support of the mandatory military service, which Argentina suspended in 1995. Many said that the return of "la colimba" would teach youth discipline and values, thus saving them from engaging in deviant behaviors and preventing them from becoming criminals.[36] To a large extent, this proposition should be understood within the broader context of the fear of crime, rising insecurity, and concerns about youth unemployment. But such strong belief in the moral power of the military also draws from the comparatively mild experiences of state repression that Iguazúenses had during el proceso and in its aftermath. For these reasons, to this day the official discourse of the military junta—

according to which the opponents of the regime were "subversives," individuals who threatened to destabilize the country and thus had to be persecuted—still holds some legitimacy in Iguazú. I was surprised to hear several people suggest reviving the official narrative of the dictatorship, which blamed violence on armed leftist guerilla groups such as the Montoneros, and absolving the government. Such revisionist voices are still audible in private conversations, even as many Iguazúenses publicly acknowledge and denounce the atrocities committed by the junta. Because there is no consensus about the role of the armed forces—in the country's past and in its future—public discussions about it in this military town are extremely rare.

ON THE SIDE OF THE GUILTY

Silence on the subject of state terror during the military regime is interrupted by loud voices of those Iguazúenses who despite their family connections to the fuerzas unambiguously oppose the idea that the Dirty War was justified to maintain national security and disagree with the proposition that mandatory military service would be an effective means of restoring order. One journalist said about the matter:

> My father was a gendarme, so I grew up within the environment. When the military took over the government, my father was beginning his studies in the gendarmerie. He did not have problems during the dictatorship because he was still studying. But I have a stance with regard to what happened in those times. I wouldn't have enjoyed living then because I would have been one of the people killed. I like the freedom of the press. I defend my rights. I think I would have been one of the first ones to be kidnapped—not for throwing bombs or anything like that, not for terrorism—but because I would have fought for what I need. I love doing journalism, but it is an unconditional fight.[37]

The journalist's name is Jorgelina Bonetto. When I met her in 2010, this cheerful twenty-eight-year-old fan of rock music and motorcycles liked to tie her blond hair into a ponytail, radiating an easygoing confidence whether she walked down the street or talked on a radio show. She was born in the province of Córdoba, in the *sierra* of Central Argentina. Although her family is originally from Mendoza, Jorgelina's father worked for the national gendarmerie, and every three to five years he was transferred to a new location. Jorgelina had her first experiences of working in the media when she was very young. A year after arriving in Iguazú at the age of nine she conducted a radio program called *Chicos*

de Hoy (Children of today). When she graduated from secondary
school, Jorgelina briefly moved back to Mendoza to study law, but,
disappointed with the program, she quit and returned to Iguazú. Resuming her career in the media, she worked for the morning news program
on Canal 5. Everything went well until at the age of twenty-two Jorgelina became seriously ill. She was diagnosed with a large uterine fibroid,
and after her surgery, at the plea of her parents, decided to stay with
them in Mendoza. While recovering, she enrolled in a social communications program at the Universidad Nacional de Cuyo. At the bus stop
the day before leaving for an exchange program in Rosario, Jorgelina
met Sebastian, her future husband, and, despite doctors' predictions,
soon became pregnant with her first daughter. Jorgelina dropped out of
school once again, got married, and decided to relocate to Iguazú,
where at the time we got to know each other she was raising two daughters and working as a reporter for *La Voz de Cataratas* and as co-host
of a radio program on Radio Yguazú.

Jorgelina lists the advantages of living in a border area, where each
neighboring town provides different opportunities: Puerto Iguazú is a
safe place, where residents "don't have to live in fear of being assaulted
when they walk in the streets"; Foz do Iguaçu has "impressive infrastructure"; and Ciudad del Este has flourishing commerce. Only here, in
the proximity to the border, can residents afford to purchase furniture
and electronics, among other things, which cost three times more in
other parts of the country. "I am in love with the Triple Frontier, with
what Iguazú has," she said, smiling.

In her explanation of why she preferred Iguazú to Mendoza, Jorgelina adamantly rejected the discursive stigmatization of the area:

> I don't feel danger here. This is why I came to Iguazú. I want my daughters
> to grow up in Iguazú, where they are free to meet with neighbors, free to
> walk peacefully down the street. Things happen here, like in any other place.
> However, it is nothing in comparison with the big cities. Mendoza is a very
> dangerous city. There are robberies every day. On my birthday last year the
> door to my house was broken and everything was stolen. Such a thing has
> never happened to me in Iguazú during all the years I lived here. The only
> thing they have ever stolen was the laundry left outside to dry. I live here, I
> live peacefully, but when I go to other places they tell me Iguazú is danger-
> ous. My mother calls me on the phone and says: "Careful with the girls.
> They will kidnap them." "But mother, during all the years you lived here,
> how many times was a girl kidnapped?" I ask. She is paranoid. The little I
> can do in my job with the media is to transmit the truth. I want everyone to
> know the truth: I am here because I feel peaceful.

But another, not less significant, reason Jorgelina left Mendoza was a family tragedy. "I have a murderer for a father," she laughs. For a moment this eerie yet sincere laugh condenses the contradictory feelings Jorgelina has been coping with. Then she explains: After her father retired from the gendarmerie, he murdered the mother of her youngest brother and is now serving a prison sentence in Mendoza. "What happened to my father made me wish to return to Iguazú. A thing like this would never have happened here," says Jorgelina. This family tragedy did more than urge her to relocate—it was an important lesson in how the press should handle crime stories. Like the majority of Iguazúenses who worked for the media, Jorgelina did not have a diploma; she argued that the most important quality for a journalist is lived experience.[38] In particular, her father's story became a powerful template that she used when reporting on violence. During the morning news program on the radio she had to read excerpts from graphic crime narratives published by the Brazilian daily *Gazeta do Foz* from Foz do Iguaçu and the Paraguayan *Vanguardia* from Ciudad del Este, which she criticized for the way they portrayed violent crime:

> *Vanguardia* sensationalizes the news. Today, for example, I read that a crack trafficker was shot dead, and there was a picture showing him with three gunshot wounds. This is shocking. I think that we can inform without falling into sensationalism. Apart from being an assassin or a trafficker, good or bad, he has a mother, a father, children, who are not guilty for his choice of life. This is a question of respect for the person's relatives. I am saying this because it has happened to me. My father is a murderer, but I am not guilty for that. Therefore, I respect people who for whatever reason end up like this. I don't think it is appropriate to show a dismembered person on the front page.

This sensibility about what is appropriate for news stories did not come from formal training in the ethics of journalism. It was the result of Jorgelina's personal encounter with the media, from the other side of the frontlines:

> When it happened to my father, all the media chased after us. They tapped our phones. They would not move away from my mother's doorstep. It was a terrible week. The news was all over the media. It was a popular topic because they were a normal educated couple; he was from the military force; she was a young girl, an accountant; they had twenty years of age difference. . . I had never thought something like this would happen to me. It taught me to keep in mind that there are other perspectives. When it happened to my father, I was on the side of the guilty. It hurt. [. . .] I could not understand. I felt judged by society, though it was not my fault. [. . .] It

FIGURE 13. Jorgelina Bonetto reporting from the 25 de Mayo parade. Puerto Iguazú, May 2010.

helped me to reconsider journalism as a means of informing. My job is to provide information, and I am trying to do it without giving my opinion of whether it is good or bad. People can make their own conclusions.

Jorgelina's striving for objectivity comes from a tragic personal experience, but it blends with general tendencies in the coverage of military and law enforcement activities in the Iguazú media. Historically formed symbiotic relationships between the people and the military discourage journalists from pursuing stories further than they are invited to. Jorgelina's reporting on the fuerzas is mediated by her father's life trajectory—first as a young gendarme during the dictatorship, then as a convicted murderer—which shows that family ties have a significant effect on the news journalists make. This effect can be cumulative. Although Jorgelina's biography is exceptional, in this military town many journalists are directly or indirectly related to the security forces. Since it is not uncommon for residents to change professions, some Iguazúenses have even served in the military or were members of the police intermittently during their careers in journalism, and their experiences, as I will show, continue to affect their work in the media. It explains why reporting on the fuerzas consists of cautiously circulating authorized narratives.

COPY AND PASTE

When making news, journalists stitch together their lived experiences of violence, personal and professional ties to law enforcement, and available discourses of crime in the tri-border area. They weigh the possible outcomes of the representations they create against their own security. The local media in Iguazú cannot simply be seen as entrepreneurs who manage narratives of violence as business. For them, news has other uses. In comparison to professional reporters who cover crime for the mass media, who often look for sensational and graphic accounts, they are more implicated in the stories they tell. Aware of the inferior, potentially unlawful, subject position to which the global security discourse assigns all border residents, Iguazú journalists avoid collaborating with the state in constructing "an oppressive faux cartography" (Briggs 2007) of the orderly state and its criminal margins.

For Iguazú journalists, the production of news about crime is *tactical* (de Certeau 1984).[39] In their stories, in order to prevent further securitization and militarization of the area and to "cuidar el destino" (to protect the destination), they portray the security forces as effective government agents who successfully control the border. Local media tactics include careful consideration in the choosing of names and categories to describe the place (as, for example, when instead of the negatively charged "Triple Frontier" they use "Tres Fronteras"; see introduction), and selecting how much coverage to give to the region's security problems. In most situations, journalists rely on press releases from the military and law enforcement and short interviews with top officials. They do not conduct in-depth investigations, which could put them in dangerous situations; moreover, if the fear of crime in Iguazú spread on the national scale and impacted the flow of visitors to the falls, the tourism-based economy could be negatively affected.

Reporting on crime in the Iguazú media generally follows a straightforward outline. News stories publicize the achievements of federal security forces in their fight against drug trafficking, human smuggling, and contraband, and the successes of the regional police at capturing local delinquents, without asking further questions to situate particular crimes or law enforcement operations within larger frameworks or offering social, economic, or political analysis. This tendency is noticeable in the descriptive and repetitive titles of crime news, such as "Raid on Drug Trafficking," "Seven Tons of Marijuana Captured," "Fight against Drug Trafficking: Prefecture Confiscated Crack and Detained

Two People," "A Blow to Drug Trafficking," "Cocaine Confiscated," and so forth.[40] Published by *La Voz de Cataratas* on February 22, 2013, the following article, "Cocaine Paste Confiscated and a Person Detained," is typical:

> Iguazú (LVC_Prefecture) On February 2, at night, personnel from the Iguazú Prefecture, patrolling their jurisdiction as part of the "Operation Northern Shield," conducted by the National Ministry of Security, detained a man who was trying to get into the country through an unauthorized passage with a hundred and ninety three (193) doses of cocaine paste, packaged into small bundles for retail.
>
> The operation took place close to the riverside; more specifically, in the vicinity of an area known as "The Old Dumpster Stop," near Barrio 1ero de Mayo.
>
> The detained, of Argentine nationality, is currently being held by the Iguazú Prefecture, at the disposition of Federal Court in Eldorado, which is in charge of the legal proceedings of the case.[41]

The structure of these news stories varies little. Usually a "copy and paste" of the press release by the fuerzas, such a story consists of a brief description of a successful intervention to stop criminal activities, which includes confiscating illegal merchandise or detaining suspects, or both. When a reporter is assigned to cover the event, the narrative may also quote a high-ranking official from the agency that conducted the operation. Absent from local coverage of organized crime is any analysis of what relevance the occurrence has in the broader context: Is 7 MT of marijuana a large or a small shipment? What about 103 doses of cocaine paste? How much is caught annually and what percentage of all drug trafficking that is estimated to pass through the borders in Misiones does it make up? Where do the drugs come from and what is their intended destination? Most importantly, what conditions make this border vulnerable to drug trafficking? There is no discussion of how drug trafficking and other forms of organized crime are rooted in regional social structures, how they relate to economic inequality, and how they are enabled by governmental and police corruption and impunity. Media accounts are heavily focused on the act of capturing the outlawed merchandise by the federal security forces. News coverage becomes a ritualistic performance in which the media provide the stage for the government's symbolic enactment of border control (see Andreas 2000).

There can be exceptions. Sometimes journalists are tipped off about a story by a trustworthy source and, if they are able to verify the information, they write original and newsbreaking articles. Though the format of these pieces is not much different from that of the press releases sent out by the security forces, such *primicias* (breaking news) are addressed to the local audience, who are able to use their familiarity with Iguazú to read between the lines and stitch up the remainder of the narrative. This form of extending crime stories through collaboration between reporters and their publics is most visible in the comments sections, where anonymous readers add pertinent details to complement short news reports posted online. Here, the threads of the story are also extended to address broader social issues. On one such occasion, *La Voz de Cataratas* published an article about how the gendarmerie confiscated marijuana and cocaine in a counterfeit ambulance with rescue logos, detaining a former high-ranking officer of the Iguazú volunteer fire department (Jusionyte 2015). Although the original publication did not include the officer's name, in their comments newsreaders quickly identified the suspect as the town's ex–fire chief.

In addition to applauding successful operations, journalists in Iguazú report on anniversaries, trainings, and meetings, establishing security forces as proactive state agents in the tri-border area. This is their answer to the accusations of lawlessness and to the claims about the region's allegedly porous and insecure borders. News titles are performative in that they serve as proof of effective law enforcement presence and a confirmation that no further securitization and militarization is necessary: "We Will Rescue Misioneras Wherever They May Be," "United against Trafficking," "Inscription into Gendarmerie," and so forth.[42] These narratives, too, are brief, based on press releases sent by the fuerzas, and often include a short history of the agency, an outline of its jurisdiction and achievements, and photographs of commemorative ceremonies or other formal events.

Officials of the fuerzas maintain cordial relationships with journalists, inviting them to observe training exercises and partake in celebrations, and even offering occasional rides on patrol boats, planes, and helicopters for exclusive reports. In exchange, news stories that appear in the media generally abstain from criticizing the security forces. Because federal agencies rotate their chief regional officers every few years, when a new person is appointed, that person has to establish relationships of trust with the Iguazú media community. Invitations and favors to local journalists become a regular practice, through which symbiotic ties are established and revamped on a regular basis. On the one hand, this connection between journalists and the fuerzas works as a control mechanism—complicity and convivencia result in the media's uncritical reliance on official news sources and hinder their ability to investigate crime. On the other hand, these practices serve as an effective means of protection for local journalists. Most of the people who work in the Iguazú media lack formal training in investigative reporting, often do not have resources or access to enable them to verify information that is handed down to them, and many are entangled in personal or patronage relationships with the military and law enforcement. In this small-town scenario, the monotonous copy-and-paste style of publishing of crime news, first sketched and authorized by the fuerzas, can be understood as a tactic that journalists use to balance their potentially risky profession with the need to ensure their own safety.

WE ARE ALL NEIGHBORS

In the 2010 trinational meeting of journalists of the Triple Frontier (see chapter 3), Mariana Ladaga, correspondent for the Paraguayan daily *La Nación* in Ciudad del Este, summed up the reasons why many events in the border area are not reported.[43] First of all, she said, there is censorship, which results from the economic interests of media companies. Owners want to protect their business and continue to receive advertising money from public institutions and commercial establishments. There is also self-censorship, guided by the interests of individual journalists. Add the lack of resources; and, finally, the issue of security. "In a small city, where it is easy to be recognized, it is very important to take security into consideration," said Ladaga. At least two of these factors—self-censorship and concern about security without the guarantee of anonymity—are at work in the story of what happened to Yanina Faria, then a twenty-three-year-old reporter for *La Voz de Cataratas*. My field-notes provide a glimpse into the predicament of small-town journalism, showing how the media, when they withhold news affecting reporters and their families, by extension abstain from covering crimes in their neighborhoods, making them appear less violent than they often are.

On an evening in June 2009 Yanina was taking photographs of a federal police intervention in an alleged drug case in her neighborhood when family members of the suspect started threatening her. The morning following the incident I accompanied Yanina to the federal police headquarters in Iguazú, located on San Lorenzo Avenue, in a residential neighborhood not far from the Tancredo Neves International Bridge. After waiting for a half an hour in the hallway, decorated with advocacy posters against human trafficking and profiles of wanted criminals, with monetary rewards for information about them, Oscar Fenocchio, the chief of the Iguazú division, invited us into his office and offered coffee; he was prepared to listen to Yanina's account. Rather than a formal procedure for filing a complaint, the meeting was a benevolent gesture on the part of the official, who was on good terms with Kelly, the director of *La Voz de Cataratas*.

Here is an excerpt from the conversation:

Yanina Faria: I am a journalist. Last night I was on a public bus with my mother. We were going to get off at the next stop, when I saw something happening on the corner of las Calandrias and J. Silveira . . .

Oscar Fenocchio: Don't tell me the names of the streets because I don't know them. They don't matter.

YF: I am telling you so that you could understand. It was on the corner near a house next to a building where my father's lottery agency is located, by the bus stop. I was planning to get off at the next stop because I was on my way to my editor's office. But since I saw a lot of people and cars I decided to get off earlier and see what was going on. So I got off and saw that the police had detained my neighbor, who lives in the house behind ours. His family is known in the barrio to be very problematic. The father is well known for talking bad. The sister of the detained was my classmate in secondary school. She was there and she shouted at me: "Yanina, what are you doing here? You shouldn't be here! Go away!" They know I am a journalist. I approached the police officers and introduced myself: "I am Yanina Faria, I work for *La Voz de Cataratas*. Could you explain to me what this is all about?" One of the officers was about to give me an explanation, when the father of the suspect approached and said: "What is this girl doing here? She shouldn't be here! She doesn't have anything to do with it." Since I did not want to make the father angry I thanked the police officers and retreated to take pictures.

OF: You took pictures?

YF: Yes, I took pictures, but not of the suspect.

OF: Is the suspect known to be a consumer or distributor?

YF: Yes, he is known. And so I retreat, take pictures (I have them here, if you want to see), and the sister shouts at me: "Go away, go away!" "Tell your daughter to leave"—she yells at my mother—"I will get her when she is alone."

OF: Alright, so you went to the local police and filed a complaint about the threat?

YF: Yes. Later, when I was going to the police station, my dad called me, telling me that the mother of the suspect approached him at work in the lottery agency and threatened him: "Faria, sos boleta [Faria, you are dead]! You denounced my son."

OF: When he was being apprehended, the suspect had dropped the bag with marijuana, there was no concrete evidence against him . . . [Fenocchio paused] Generally, if they threaten to kill, they don't do it.

YF: Sure [Yanina did not sound relieved].

OF: When they tell you they will kill you, they don't do anything. But your father should file a complaint with the local police. And regarding the issue of drugs in the barrio, there is nothing to be added. We know that there is activity, that drugs are sold, but we don't know yet who distributes in the barrio.

YF: What was it?

OF: Marijuana . . .

YF: We are not going to publish this story. We took this decision with my editor last night. We are all neighbors.[44]

"We are all neighbors" was the main reason why the news did not appear in the press. It was also the point on which Yanina and Fennochio did not understand each other. For her, providing the names of the streets was essential in order to explain what happened. Vicinity, or the fact that Yanina, her family, the suspect's family, and even her editor all lived near each other was the reason why the threat mattered. For the police chief, location was not significant as his agency's jurisdiction was federal crimes, which by definition transcend any single barrio. It was a clash between the world of local journalism, meticulously grounded in a particular social space and embedded in the cultural intimacy of neighborhood relationships, and the world of an armed branch of the federal state, too standardized and universal to appreciate the nuances of everyday life in the community.

Soon after the incident Yanina received an invitation to work for the police. Law enforcement officers were impressed by her diplomatic coverage of a road blockade that teachers organized on the highway at the entrance to Iguazú. Instead of uncritically siding with the protestors, who complained of being beaten by the police, in her reports for the radio Yanina also interviewed law enforcement officers and included their explanation of the events. The commissary liked it and invited her to work at the new headquarters of the regional police delegation. He wanted to hire a journalist—as someone who was familiar with the other end of communications—to be in charge of the press office. At first going through a period of disillusionment with the media and excited about the new opportunity, Yanina accepted the offer and went to the police academy in Posadas for training. But when she returned to

FIGURE 14. A boy riding his bike in front of the neighborhood mall on Las Calandrias Avenue. Puerto Iguazú, June 2009.

Iguazú, she did not stay with the institution for long. At the press office of the Misiones police she could not cope with the merger of the two worlds. "I did not feel like *policía*. I felt very limited. As a police spokesperson, I could only say what my boss ordered," she said. Yanina left the police and went back to work for the media. A year from that evening in June, working at Radio Cataratas, just a few blocks away from her house and the street corner where the incident with her neighbor took place, she continued to run into his family on a regular basis.

At a media workshop on handling dangerous assignments that took place in Ciudad del Este in 2010, Colombian press freedom activist Adriana Blanco defined *amenaza* (threat) as "direct intimidation with an announcement or insinuation to provoke serious harm to the journalist or their family." It is "a restriction to make the journalist do, tolerate, or omit certain conduct in their work." Journalists in Iguazú have received threats in connection to their coverage of political issues, but when they talk about such incidents, they often downplay the risks. Several reporters told me that even in potentially dangerous situations they successfully avoided being seriously hurt because they knew the accepted code of behavior and respected its rules. This local knowledge of how to be a reporter under conditions of convivencia is passed on from senior, more experienced journalists to their junior colleagues. Immediately after the incident involving Yanina and her neighbors, Kelly shared with Yanina her own experiences with managing threats. The editor of *La Voz de Cataratas* recalled how once her children picked up the phone at home to hear somebody threaten to set their house on fire. Another time Kelly was hit by a car while biking on an empty street. In such situations, though she claims not to be intimidated, Kelly does not publish sensitive information. "In order not to fan the flames," she explains. Due to her experience working for the radio she has become good at recognizing voices. Once, as soon as the anonymous caller hung up the phone, she immediately knew whom to call back, and, to his great surprise and embarrassment, she asked whether the individual who had just threatened her would agree to speak live on air.

Local journalists criticize the *amenazas* they occasionally receive as attempts to kill the messenger in order to drown the message. A newspaper correspondent who in 2010 worked for a provincial daily was frustrated about being threatened while covering a story of alleged illegal appropriation of government money by local officials: "What was my sin? To inform about the robbery? Who stole: Those people or I? Who is the bad guy? It is the one who informs. They kill the messenger. It has always been this way. The messenger is the guilty one." He received threatening calls on his cell phone and at the home of his ex-wife and children, but, like Kelly, well trained in what he called the "gymnastics of journalism," he knew what to do: "I was absolutely sure where the threats were coming from, so I sent them a message through a friend of mine and through a high-ranking official in the security forces. I told them they could beat me up if they wanted to, but if I received one more threat to my children's home, I would hit them with the car."[45] Family is an important factor for many journalists, who, in defense of their parents, spouses, and especially children, do not hesitate to deploy the same discourse of violence that circulates in response to the state's failure to ensure citizen security. When the messenger's family becomes the target, taking law enforcement into private hands is seen as legitimate—at least hypothetically, for there have been no situations where a journalist retaliated against threats; and fortunately, the threats rarely translated into actions. In the workshop on security measures a disagreement broke out among the participants as to how much information they should reveal to their families regarding their whereabouts and the details of investigations. Though some suggested the more the better, because information can help families find the journalist in case of trouble, many were opposed to this position, arguing that it is better to leave the families unaware of the specifics of their work in order to protect them.

Personal safety in terms of protection from bodily harm is not the same as security. The latter is a much broader concept and, in addition to physical well-being, is predicated upon trust in social networks and economic guarantees, such as continued employment. Threats to the media that are more common, subtler, and that go beyond silencing a particular journalist take the form of blackmailing to withdraw advertising—the primary source of revenue for the privately owned media in Iguazú. Near absolute dependency on money from publicity is the reason why issues regarding, for example, the tourism industry rarely make it to the headlines, although everybody knows that a considerable number of employees in hotels, restaurants, and travel bureaus work without contracts, are paid under the table, have no social benefits, and no union rights. In Iguazú, business is tightly connected to politics, politics has partnered with the media, and the media depends on business, forming a triangle of complicity. As one entrepreneur who directs a local media outlet put it, the main threat to journalists in Iguazú is not an assassination, but a warning to pull out advertisement. It was easy to see how this mechanism worked: several important companies with business interests in Iguazú, despite not needing any more publicity, regularly paid for their share of ads in all of Iguazú media. It was a covert form of blackmail against the press. Others, turning it upside down, called this "journalism of extortion" because sometimes owners of media institutions were the ones who initiated the deal, asking for ad money as a subtle request for a bribe in exchange for not reporting on certain issues. This is how one journalist explained the mechanism of extortion:

> Advertising in Iguazú is a favor. Businesses here do not need to make themselves known because there is little competition. [. . .] In this town commerce is concentrated in the area of five square blocks. If you need to buy something, you either find it on Avenida Brasil, or Avenida Victoria Aguirre, or República Argentina, or Misiones. Businesses don't need advertising. Hence the media must use resources to get advertising. Criticism is their resource. Those who find out the secrets of business owners have the most advertising. When I talk about secrets, I refer to the invasion of business owners' privacy, of getting to know the management of the company, which for the daily means obtaining advertising.[46]

This code of complicity, which local media, businessmen, and politicians respect and rely on, is likely the reason why there have been so few assaults against the press in Iguazú. Although skirmishes occur, temporarily destabilizing the productive equilibrium established between journalists and the primary news sources, these are rare—as when, in October 2009, at a nightclub the town mayor Claudio Filippa grabbed Vivi Villar, the reporter and news anchor of the local television channel, by her hair. During the confrontation that ensued, the Iguazú press association publicly condemned the battery, and other media expressed solidarity with their colleague. More often, however, journalists that disregard the established codes are subjected to slander, which discredits them and has proven an effective form of controlling the press. Whether it is a physical or a verbal attack, disagreements usually deescalate after a few days and rebellious journalists end up resuming their routine work and accepting the rules of the game of hide-and-seek played by neighbors in a small town.

POSITIVE INTERVENTIONS

It may seem that under such circumstances reporting on crime is hardly possible or, at least, very unlikely. Nevertheless, local journalists can maneuver around the constraints imposed on them and occasionally they make their voices heard. Their input is usually limited to issues that are not the primary focus of the fuerzas and that do not directly encroach on the business-political interests of Iguazú entrepreneurs, maintaining with them the silent and productive convivencia. The choice of themes is tied to journalist's personal interests and concerns. For example, Mario Antonowicz, the director and owner of Radio Yguazú, has been documenting unauthorized broadcasting by Brazilian radios set up on private property around town. Radio Yguazú has been strongly affected by foreign airwaves that interfere with Argentine radio and television frequencies; therefore, in addition to talking about the issue on his radio show, Mario sent a petition to Gabriel Mariotto, the president of the AFSCA, the Federal Authority of Audiovisual Communication Services, asking for the government to intervene. During the same time, Oscar Perrone and Juancho Montejano, two of the cofounders and CEOs of local cable television company C.V.I., were active in municipal politics, supporting the opposition and participating in forthcoming elections. In 2010–2011 they often used airtime to expose governmental neglect of the remote border town, which resulted in a shortage of water, late salaries for teachers, and failing infrastructure, all of which compound the effects of structural violence.

Another notable issue—and one not motivated by political or business ambitions—was violence against women. Among the journalists in

Iguazú, Kelly has been particularly vocal when it comes to this problem. Her personal stake in the matter led her to develop a close relationship with the director of the municipal program Luz de Infancia (Light of Childhood), dedicated to helping survivors of domestic abuse and trafficking. She was also invited to attend so-called *talleres de prostitutas* (prostitute workshops) organized at the Center of Prevention and Treatment of Women in Situations of Violence, where behind closed doors survivors of abuse shared their stories. Even though information obtained through these unofficial channels was off the record, these personal encounters provided Kelly with the needed background knowledge and motivated her to publish stories and opinion pieces on the subject.

Violence against women at home and women trafficking is not a visible and easily quantifiable form of crime, so it often goes unreported and remains excluded from statistics. However, cases of femicide—its most extreme form—are counted more accurately and can hint to the broader prevalence of domestic violence. During half a year between January 1 and June 30, 2011, 151 women were killed in Argentina.[47] In 119 cases, murders were committed by people who were close to the victims—husbands, partners, or boyfriends, present and former. Misiones, where during this period ten women were murdered, is one of the provinces with the highest rate of femicide in the country. Although media attention to murders and other types of violence against women is desirable, the main problem becomes the adequate representation of the victim and the perpetrator. Journalists from the metropolitan media organizations come to the border area to film interviews with survivors of human trafficking and promise not to reveal their names, but too often in sensationalized coverage they end up disclosing women's personal information. Such irresponsible handling of their stories makes survivors reluctant to seek media attention. Unfortunately, their desire for privacy has negative consequences because less media exposure results in diminishing public awareness about domestic violence and human trafficking.

Reporting on violence against women and human trafficking is difficult, and journalists often find themselves in a complicated position vis-à-vis survivors as well as law enforcement. Because of the potential ramifications of bad coverage, which can disrupt police operations and negatively affect the survivors, human rights groups actively engage both journalists and law enforcement personnel in order to clarify their respective roles and teach the ethics of dealing with these types of crime. To this end, in 2010, the Trinational Network against Human Trafficking, working under the auspices of the International Organization for

Migration, organized a series of workshops for local actors in the tri-border area.

As part of this initiative, three parallel events for the personnel of the Argentine, Brazilian, and Paraguayan security forces were simultaneously held in Puerto Iguazú, Foz do Iguaçu and Ciudad del Este. Cynthia Bendlin, recipient of the 2008 U.S. State Department's Women of Courage Award for her work to end human slavery, spoke at the seminar in Iguazú. In her address to the representatives of different fuerzas, including the gendarmerie, federal and local police, airport security, the prefecture, and migration control, she explained that the United Nations Palermo Protocol defined "trafficking in persons" as "the recruitment, transportation, transfer, harbouring or receipt of persons, by means of the threat or use of force or other forms of coercion, of abduction, of fraud, of deception, of the abuse of power or of a position of vulnerability or of the giving or receiving of payments or benefits to achieve the consent of a person having control over another person, for the purpose of exploitation."[48] She discussed the logistics of human trafficking in the tri-border area and reviewed cultural factors that contributed to naturalizing this crime in Argentina. Bendlin's voice echoed loud in the large auditorium when she asked her audience: "Do you know what victimization is?" When nobody volunteered an answer, she said: "Making the victim tell her story is a form of re-victimization. And they are forced to do it again and again to different authorities, to the police, the judge, the psychologist. They come back with a label of prostitute. They are victims, not perpetrators. This is a cultural understanding that needs a lot of work in order to be corrected."[49] That day Bendlin's talk was tailored to security forces personnel, who often were the first to encounter survivors of human trafficking, but they were not the only culprits guilty of revictimizing these women. In the search for a sensational angle to cover a story, the media were also contributing. Given their crucial role as mediators, a separate seminar was organized for local journalists, instructing them how to be responsible when reporting on human trafficking and human slavery.

This issue also brought the fuerzas and the media together. In June 2010 representatives of the Argentine, Brazilian, and Paraguayan security forces and journalists from all three countries attended a joint workshop, which the International Organization for Migration held in the conference center of Itaipú Binacional, in Paraguay. At the workshop, Teresa Martínez from the Special Unit of Human Trafficking in the attorney general's office in Paraguay said that the press always wants to know the victim's background, but the story told in the media can be very harmful both to the survivor and to the investigation. Journalists tend to sensationalize the details surrounding the woman, converting her into a double victim of abuse, while they ignore the identity of the perpetrator. Martínez advised the media not to disclose too much in order to avoid violating survivors' rights to privacy. Neither should journalists provide insight into law enforcement operations against traffickers; identifying the time or place of police raids might enable the perpetrators to escape, ruining month-long investigations. The prosecutor suggested that instead of focusing on the details of specific cases, the media could help in prevention stage by informing the community about human trafficking. This mandate is reflected in the guidelines for journalists published by the International Labor Organization as part of the Program of Prevention and Eradication of Commercial Sexual Exploitation among Girls, Boys and Adolescents in the Triple Frontier. According to the document, the role of journalists is as follows: to expose the topic, provide the broader context, include multiple voices and perspectives so that readers can recognize the perpetrator of crime just as easily as the victim, discuss possible solutions, and follow up on the cases.[50]

Prevention is what the Iguazú media can and does do. Unable to investigate the larger drama of international human trafficking that links the tri-border area as the supply region to urban centers in Argentina, Brazil, and Europe, local journalists are raising awareness about the broader issue of violence that starts in the family. They are vocal about violence against women as a crime that might not be perceived as such in communities where machismo is engrained in their behavioral norms. In their print, radio, and video reports with straightforward titles such as "Denounce Human Trafficking" or "Denounce, Don't Be Silent,"[51] some local journalists encourage women to file complaints instead of living in constant fear and allowing their silence to contribute to naturalizing this type of violence.

In an editorial entitled "Attention: The Violator Might Be at Home," provoked by an incident she was told about and which, like many others, went unreported, Kelly drew attention to sexual abuse within families: "The majority of these acts remain under impunity because this topic forms part of the taboo. Ignorance and lack of understanding within the family, culture, judicial system, which often blames the victim and hides or excuses the violator, prevents the individual from complaining about the act, making the abuse into a secret. There are millions of secret survivors that carry the load of an abuse, never shared."[52] According to

Marcelina Antúnez, the former director of Luz de Infancia, in 2010 there were only two official complaints of domestic violence filed in Iguazú. Survivors' fear of being publicly exposed in the media was among the reasons for such a low level of reporting. Iguazúenses learned about the risk that women take when they report abuse and the absence of protection available to them when in 2010 Mariela García, who worked as transit inspector, was murdered at the women's police substation while she was filing a complaint.[53] Accused of domestic abuse, her former partner—police sergeant Mario Muga—shot her in front of other female officers. In this case, residents were outraged, and the story was extensively covered in the local media.

Despite their limited resources and other constraints on openly talking about crime, dedicated journalists participate in public education campaigns, raise awareness about domestic violence, and encourage women to speak up.

PERFORMING SECURITY

Media can be a powerful tool for spreading the sense of insecurity. Unless someone directly experiences violence or hears about it from family members or acquaintances, daily news is the main source that Iguazúenses turn to in order to become informed about crime in their town and around the country. But the press provides more than information. In addition to circulating bare facts about who, what, when, where, why, and how, which add to the discourse of crime, the media open up a space for public discussion. The comments sections of local dailies and call-in shows on the radio and television become the vehicle for rumors to circulate. In these public forums residents voice at times impatient and angry concerns about rising crime, pointing to its alleged culprits and, in defiance of the state's monopoly on violence, threaten to take justice into their own hands.

In terms of security, reporting in Iguazú is both pragmatic and performative. As this chapter has shown, how journalists cover violence and crime depends less on their commitment to challenge the larger framework of criminalization that the border area is subjected to and more on their lived experiences and local knowledge of complicity and convivencia. Denied the veil of anonymity, facing limited resources and even fewer reliable sources, Iguazú journalists avoid taking risks that would result in danger to themselves and their families. Weak private media companies, linked to business and political interests, further impede their independent investigations. Therefore, even when concerns about common crime began rising, Iguazú media continued to reprint press releases from the fuerzas, conveying the sense of a secure border community, effectively protected by the prefecture, the gendarmerie, and the police. While residents expressed their doubts about the direction in which the town was moving, journalists still held on to their belief that—compared to metropolitan areas such as Buenos Aires— Iguazú was a safer place to live. Complicity and convivencia, more than mechanisms of media censorship and control, worked as modes of protection from harm for journalists, physical as well as economic. Because with rare exceptions journalists stayed within the permissible boundaries of what could be addressed in the media, there have been very few assaults against the press.[54] Coverage of organized crime in Iguazú might be described as thin, but journalists compensate by focusing their attention on such problems as domestic violence, where their intervention is more likely to yield positive, albeit comparatively less publicly noticeable, results.

Security is a performative project, one that journalists actively participate in, negotiating their own insecurity with their aim to make Iguazú into a safer place, an attractive venue for raising a family, and welcoming to the visitors whose money fuels the local economy. Journalists are well aware of how living and working in a town where everybody knows everybody constrains their coverage of crime. They are trained in the "gymnastics of journalism" required for a life in a "pueblo chico," which can turn into "infierno grande." However, more than being powerless victims within a network of complicity, constantly forced to keep quiet about the delinquency and injustice they witness, the media knowingly and willingly function within the local moral-legal regime, which redraws the boundary between law and crime. As the next chapter will show, part of the reason why illegal activities in the tri-border area are not reported in the local media is because in a remote, neglected corner of the state, legality and legitimacy are understood differently. An alternative moral economy affects when and whether contraband is newsworthy. Sometimes smuggling is not covered in the media not because it would be a dangerous assignment, compromising the safety of the journalist, but because it is not seen as a threat to security in the community. Some practices may be illegal, that is, but not illegitimate.

5

On and Off the Record

If you make a denuncia, [. . .] you will take away the work of
these Paraguayans. It will make me neither richer nor poorer.

—Javier Villegas

JOURNALIST WITH A CAMERA

Zooming in on a landmass across the Paraná River, the camera moves
past an abandoned convention center and focuses on a green-and-
yellow landmark, a monumental version of the border demarcation
signs found throughout Latin America, its colors blending with Brazil's
surrounding subtropical jungle. As the camera swiftly turns in a clock-
wise direction, it pans over the Iguazú River and, amidst lush vegetation, barely spots another marker: painted in *celeste y blanco,* sky blue
and white, an obelisk built in 1903 celebrates Argentine national sovereignty. Finally, as the camera glides further to the right and returns
across the Paraná, it captures a red, white, and blue Paraguayan sign-
post, rising tall above the river port. "We will share the experience of
crossing by boat from the port of Presidente Franco, Paraguay to Puerto
Iguazú, Argentina," comments a journalist's voice behind the camera.
The three of us—two journalists and myself—present our documents to
a man in a checkered shirt sitting on the rocks by the river. Though he
does not look like a border official, he confidently and authoritatively
acts like one. We gather our fares, which can be paid for in any combination of Argentine pesos, Brazilian reais, and Paraguayan guaraníes,
and board the ferry.

   The journalist with the camera is recording the trip. But as soon as
she notices an acquaintance, she briefly turns off the device and
approaches him: "Esteche! What are you doing here? *Contrabandeando*

FIGURE 15. Argentine boundary landmark in Iguazú under reconstruction, March 2014.

algo [smuggling something]? *Pirateando* [pirating]?" Both laugh. The ferry is full of vehicles with Argentine registration numbers whose owners are returning from shopping centers in Paraguay. After she is done talking with her acquaintance, the journalist turns the camera back on and interviews a couple of German tourists she has just met on the boat. "What do you think of the Triple Frontier? Is it dangerous?" she asks. "No, no!" answers a man wearing a safari vest. "It's very nice. I enjoy the nature." As the ferry traverses the river and slowly approaches Puerto Iguazú, passengers notice a long line of minivans with tinted windows, waiting to get back to Paraguay. As on the previous occasions when I travelled across the border with Argentine or Paraguayan journalists, my companions don't pay attention to the vehicles in the recognized contraband circuit. The camera does not focus on the vans, nor does the voice behind it acknowledge their presence.

In this case the journalist used the camera as a lens to tell a particular story about the Triple Frontier *for the record*. Celebrating the uniqueness of the border-crossing experience, the natural beauty and safety of the area, the story was circulated by a local media outlet. But by the time this selective border narrative was made public, another story—

about the origin of the camera itself—had been obscured. This same camera had been brought into Iguazú six months earlier. We were then visiting the duty free shop, colloquially referred to as "El Duty," located outside the Argentine border checkpoint, and one of the store managers gave this camera as a gift to the journalist whom I was accompanying. I recall how during that trip the journalist driving the car tensed up as we returned past the customs control. At the checkpoint, she stopped at a designated spot and a female officer approached the vehicle. The journalist lowered the window and greeted the woman by her first name. Though the officer threw a glance at the bags with "Puerto Iguazú Duty Free Shop" logos on the back seat, which contained, among other things, a new handheld video camera, she did not inquire about their content. The journalist closed the tinted window and, as we drove away from the border post into the town, said: "Iguazú residents are not allowed to make purchases either in Paraguay or in el Duty at the border with Brazil. We still do it. Contraband. They know who I am and they don't check me at customs."[1]

This chapter examines how Iguazú journalists—who occupy a multifaceted and seemingly contradictory position in the community as members and participants in the informal border trade and producers of representations about the area—maneuver the boundaries of the formal law and social norms in their daily personal and professional lives. The tri-border area is a particularly interesting place to question the role of media in establishing and maintaining the distinction between legality and illegality. As I showed in chapter 2, a significant number of articles about Misiones in the Argentine mass media focus on different forms of criminal activities, including drug trafficking, contraband, and government corruption. This coverage represents a trend in the press to depict the border as a haven for organized crime. However, as discussed in chapter 4, local journalists reject such negative representations and emphasize that Iguazú has less crime than most metropolitan areas in Argentina. Here, I will show that this disjuncture between how Buenos Aires–based media and border journalists interpret breaking the law is not arbitrary. Practices are never "legal" or "illegal" in and of themselves; rather, they become such through complex processes of labeling in which both governmental discourse and news-making play a role. Iguazú journalists create stories *for, on,* and *off the record* to (re)produce a locally meaningful boundary between law and crime.

Managing the mismatch between law and social legitimacy has long been problematic for the Iguazú media. Often, border residents see legality and illegality as a continuum: depending on how justifiable certain practices are, they are considered as more or less severe violations of the law. Consequently, the media treats them as either newsworthy or not. As the conversation on the ferry reveals, for Iguazúenses, *contrabandear* (to engage in contraband) or *piratear* (to engage in pirating) are ironic terms that they invoke to refer to the common sense of participating in formally banned—but widely practiced, justified, and socially legitimate—economic exchanges. Residents use the border space to their own interest by creatively maneuvering the law in their everyday routines. When journalists choose whether to cover stories of crime, in addition to official legal criteria they draw on their knowledge and experience as local residents. Conscious of the way the media is capable of reproducing legal effects, such as enforcing the policing of goods and people classified as "illegal," journalists use the public sphere tactically. They refuse to squeeze lived situations into generic, state-centered schemes of law and crime common in mass media representations. They depict some illegalities and obscure others, participating in legitimating both legal and illegalized activities. When the media categorize practices from the point of view of the state, employing the official vocabulary and the binary discourse of law and crime, they produce *legality*. But when they avoid, or speak around, illegalities that are commonly accepted by the community, the local media also (re)produce *social legitimacy, or licitness.* In this complex sociolegal situation on the border, Iguazú journalists juggle between news stories that they intentionally frame *(for the record)* with evidence cited from official sources *(on the record),* and those that ought to remain excluded from public discussion *(off the record).* This way, journalists partake in keeping informal economic practices, illegalized yet licit, officially illegible.

BORDER TRADE REGIME

For decades, neighboring economies in the tri-border region were separated by different currency values, tax rates, labor regulations, and tariffs. Residents and visitors benefited from relatively lax controls, looking for better prices by easily moving across international borders between Argentina, Brazil, and Paraguay (see chapter 3). People and goods swiftly changed directions in response to legislative advances in each country, until the creation of the Southern Common Market, MERCOSUR, in 1995 instituted new conditions for the regional economy, prohibiting unrestricted cross-border exchanges commonly practiced by local residents. MERCOSUR had a significant impact on border markets because it only allowed circulation considered legal by the states (Grimson 2002b:167). As with other regional trade agreements, for example, NAFTA and CAFTA in North and Central America, it activated integration from above, allowing large-scale commerce to disregard the existence of borders while creating new barriers between the people who live in border zones, exacerbating social inequality (see, for example, Galemba 2012). Not only were local consumers disadvantaged when compared to multinational corporations and other large businesses, but there was discrepancy between residents of the border region and those from central areas of Argentina: when in 1998 the Federal Authority for Public Income began limiting how much Argentine residents could purchase abroad, Iguazúenses were given smaller quotas compared to people who did not live close to the border.

The latest iteration of this legislation, Regimen de Tráfico Fronterizo (RTF, Border Trade Regime), outlined in the General Resolution of the Federal Administration of Public Income No. 1116/2001, establishes that Argentine citizens and foreign residents who live less than one hundred kilometers from the border have a US$50 monthly quota for shopping in Brazil or Paraguay.[2] People must prove their residency in the area by presenting their birth certificate or national identity card. They are allowed to purchase nonperishable food items and nondurable goods such as clothes or shoes manufactured in the neighboring country, for personal use, in quantities that do not suggest commercial ends. Due to the fear of foot-and-mouth disease and other sanitary considerations, the importation of fresh food—primarily meat, fruit, and vegetables—has been strictly prohibited since 1999, which is when what Alejandro Grimson (2002b) referred to as "hygiene wars" between the neighboring countries broke out. Argentina was the first to ban imports of certain categories of produce from Brazil, on the pretext of guaranteeing that its national territory would be free of foot-and-mouth disease. When in 2001 the government admitted that despite its measures, there were outbreaks in the country, this time Brazil closed its border with Argentina, adding phytosanitary checks as a measure to prevent diseases. At the time of my fieldwork, these regulations prohibiting the import of animal and plant products, including seeds, were still in place.

Iguazúenses criticize limitations imposed on shopping in the neighboring states because historically borders were more permeable to small-scale traders and consumers, but they are especially angry that prices of food products in local convenience stores in Iguazú are very high in comparison to those in the central regions of Argentina. By the time the merchandise reaches this remote border town, located more than a thousand kilometers away from the capital city, freight costs increase its price. Other factors are also at stake. In 2010 and 2011, when frequent protests, fuel shortages, and skyrocketing fuel prices caused delays in ground transportation, prompting the Kirchner government to renationalize the energy company Yacimientos Petrolíferos Fiscales (YPF), the price of basic commodities in Iguazú rose sharply. Since the 1990s, regulations limiting what border residents could purchase in the neighboring countries have been partly designed to protect such a costly internal market from international competitors in Brazil and Paraguay. Restricted to buying their day-to-day necessities in expensive local stores, Iguazúenses complain that the lack of competition allows vendors to inflate prices at will. Given these circumstances, many people in Iguazú have been taking advantage of the greater variety of cheaper products across the border, even though bringing them into the country means breaking the law.

Local residents commonly engage in and broadly tolerate this thriving informal market, and the Iguazú media, balancing between legality and legitimacy, have crafted particular ways of reporting on contraband: they show some and hide other prohibited exchanges based on whether activities are justified by the common sense of living on the border. When they make news stories, journalists tactically maneuver between legibility and illegibility. To understand this, it is critical to situate reporters as local Iguazúenses who eschew the negative images in the mass media that depict the Triple Frontier as a place of crime and violence. Journalists seek to "cuidar el destino," ensuring that tourists keep coming to the national park to see the waterfalls and spending their money, which fuels the local economy. This agenda means that they do not pursue stories that play into the narrative of the porous, notoriously insecure border. But in addition to this strategic rationale, another factor that determines whether journalists cover small-scale contraband is the extent to which they, too, participate in the informal economy. In the tri-border area, the media operate by different standards of newsworthiness, grounded in the disjuncture between socially justified local practices and formal state laws.

CLANDESTINE BANANAS

I remember the first time I saw Estela. It was early afternoon on a chilly day in June, and everybody was getting ready for siesta, when Kelly called me to the front door. A middle-aged woman, accompanied by a little boy, had stopped in front of the house with a cart full of fruit. Kelly went out to the street to greet her. "They didn't catch you today, señora?" she teased, and bought a few bananas: two-dozen of them cost half the price of those in the supermarket. When the first heavy drops of the winter rain caught them all outside, Kelly invited Estela and her son to hide under her roof. She then went back into the house and brought a blanket, which she offered to Estela and the boy to keep them warm. The rain stopped as abruptly as it had started, and soon the woman and her young companion were on their way further down the street, selling cheap smuggled fruit to other residents of the neighborhood.

Before long I became used to seeing this woman, coming at different times of the day and, standing in front of locked front gates of our neighbors' houses, clapping her hands to announce her arrival. Sometimes she would come alone; other times with more children. Sometimes she would not come at all, possibly caught by the prefecture while crossing the river through one of the piques—the trails that Paraguayan food smugglers like her shared with traffickers in cigarettes and drugs. The presence of these women was common knowledge in Iguazú, where they were known as *cuperas*. "It could be because they carry more things than is allowed by the *cupo* [quota]," one journalist speculated on the origins of the name. Down the river in Posadas they are called *"paseras"* (ferrywomen) and on the Brazilian border in eastern Misiones—*"pasadores"* (courier-smugglers). Some cuperas use a wheel cart that they push through residential neighborhoods; others set up stands with their produce at busy intersections in the center of the town. Appreciating lower prices than in local stores, Iguazúenses readily purchase fruits and vegetables from these smugglers.

The following example from my fieldnotes shows that cuperas are so commonly tolerated that even the security forces are not strict about catching them as they cross the border. In June 2009, I accompanied Yanina, a reporter for *La Voz de Cataratas,* as she interviewed a high-ranking official of the naval prefecture. When Yanina asked about the types of merchandise captured on the river, the official admitted:

> I am less interested in confiscating a kilo of lettuce than a kilo of marijuana. The truth is that with marijuana and cigarettes they send vegetables, so if a cupera brings in vegetables, it means there is no control. So what do we do? To me it doesn't matter that vegetables get across, while cigarettes and drugs do matter. Yet I have to confiscate vegetables because there is a law that says that. It is like a cat-and-mouse game.[3]

The prefect explained in detail how illegalized commodity flows intertwined as they crossed the international border, so that illicit goods such as drugs were brought in the same canoes that were transporting licit but banned foreign items, including food. But he warned Yanina: his acknowledgment that the prefecture had little interest in capturing food smugglers was to remain "off the record."

Later that week Kelly and I boarded one of the prefecture's powerboats. On the condition that the invitation would remain informal, we were offered the chance to observe the routine of patrolling the river. As we sped up and down the Iguazú and later the Paraná, we spotted numerous piques: the narrow sandy openings on the shore and trails leading up into the forest. Both the prefect and Kelly knew the names of these clandestine crossing points: Pique Ferreyra, Pique Galeano, Pique Armoa, Pique Hito Tres Fronteras . . . When during our lively conversation on the patrol boat Kelly admitted that she was buying fruit from a cupera, the officer was not surprised by her confession. On the contrary, in defense of his own role of policing, he explained that the prefecture does not search for food smugglers *intentionally*, but rather, might "happen to find them" on the river. Cuperas are often detained when the prefecture is conducting operations to intercept drug traffickers or cigarette contraband, or "when there is nothing else to do." Once they are stripped of their merchandise, the prefect said, cuperas are always let go and the following day they are back on the river, trying their luck again and perhaps crossing undetected. This repetitive ritual of capture and release of the cuperas makes up the routine of law enforcement and food smuggling on the border. When a little before noon Kelly and I got off the patrol boat and returned home, Estela, this time accompanied by three kids, was in the neighborhood selling bananas. "I just met the prefect and saw the places you will pass through to get back home in the evening," joked Kelly, and both women laughed.

The story published in *La Voz de Cataratas* following Yanina's interviews with officials of the prefecture focused on the procedures of handling contraband products that were intercepted on the river. "The prefect reported that when food products are confiscated they are handed over to the National Food Safety and Quality Service, SENASA (Servicio Nacional de Sanidad y Calidad Agroalimentaria), which is responsible for destroying them, 'because sales and consumption within the country are completely prohibited,'"[4] noted the article. The text also included a quote from the prefect in charge of the Iguazú delegation: "Although we understand the need to have cheaper vegetables and

FIGURE 16. Prefect patrolling the Río Paraná, which marks the border between Argentina and Paraguay, June 2009.

other food items in our town, our job is to implement sanitary laws which prohibit contraband and consumption of fresh produce." Then the story shifted to drug trafficking, which the prefect called "an issue that worries us most." The publication reiterated official information that collapses the categories of illegalized goods, licit and illicit, so that bringing in bananas and drugs across the border is equally unlawful, even if the latter are assigned a higher priority on the agency's to-do list. Both the media and the security forces accept food smuggling as an unavoidable side effect of structural inequalities created by the border, but they only do so off the record. Although the article cast a hint of social legitimacy over smuggled food, especially in comparison to drug trafficking, it remained implied.

Among Iguazúenses, rumors about what happened with the confiscated produce were not assuaged by the prefect's formulaic explanation of the existing rules. People speculated that SENASA officers divided the food they received from the prefecture and the gendarmerie among themselves. Motivated by readers' comments in response to Yanina's article, *La Voz de Cataratas* decided to further probe into the fate of confiscated goods. With this goal, Yanina and I went to the SENASA office at the border checkpoint near the Tancredo Neves International Bridge. Marcelo Andrés Gorgo, food safety and quality inspector, told us that SENASA was responsible for sorting out the merchandise they received from the fuerzas into plant and animal products. He explained how the produce was sprayed with disinfectant and kept in air-conditioned storage rooms until another agency picked it up and took it to the town

FIGURE 17. A grocery store sign in Villa Florida, March 2011.

of Montecarlo, where it was destroyed. Yanina asked whether we could see the storage facilities, so Gorgo led us to a small locked closet behind the customs office. Peeking inside, we found that apart from an empty box or two, the closet was vacant. Struggling to find an explanation, the inspector told us that it was Wednesday morning, which meant that earlier that day the merchandize had been collected for destruction. At *La Voz de Cataratas* none of the journalists believed this story, but they did not pursue it any further.

Food also moves the opposite way—from Argentina to Brazil and Paraguay. Trade agreements permit Brazilians and Paraguayans to spend up to 300 pesos (about US$70) on Argentine products without being taxed on the border. However, this purchase quota excludes products that are subsidized by the Argentine government and labeled exclusively for consumption in the domestic market. During my fieldwork, the most frequently smuggled Argentine commodity was subsidized cooking oil. Foreigners purchased oil in large quantities without receipts, avoiding implicating particular stores, and hid it in vehicles with double interior walls or under the seats. Journalists who lived in neighborhoods close to the Paraná also told me about boxes of oil unloaded from trucks and taken across the river to Paraguay through the same piques that smugglers used to bring cheap vegetables, poultry, and cigarettes into Argentina. In 2010, speaking off the record, an Iguazú customs administrator acknowledged to *La Voz de Cataratas* reporter Jorgelina Bonetto that their work practices diverged from what was prescribed by the law. In order to minimize commercial disruptions and to appease both consumers and distributors, customs officers used their discretion to allow Para-

FIGURE 18. Bottles of subsidized cooking oil found in a vehicle with hidden compartments. Courtesy of Aduana Argentina and *La Voz de Cataratas.*

guayans to take bottles of subsidized oil out of the country as long as the quantity did not surpass "ten or twenty liters."[5] When contraband exceeded what this vague informal quota permitted, the customs office registered it as an infringement of the law.

Journalists in Iguazú did not investigate petty food smuggling. Their news coverage on these border violations was limited to formal statements made by the officers in the security forces and other government agencies responsible for upholding the law, usually when they confiscated significant loads of contraband. Everyday food smuggling, which was widely tolerated by residents and given low priority by the security forces, was not very newsworthy, and the presence of cuperas in Iguazú was a public secret. But the media were even less likely to report on corruption that accompanied and facilitated large-scale contraband and was part of the broader issue of organized crime (see chapter 4). Though reasons were different, small and socially legitimate smuggling, on the one hand, and major flows of contraband, on the other, fell into the local media's blindspot.

When *La Voz de Cataratas* published an investigative report on corruption at the port of Presidente Franco that had been conducted by the large Paraguayan newspaper *ABC Color,* readers in Iguazú welcomed it as an accurate portrayal of crime, which implicated state officials on the border. They congratulated the journalists in the neighboring country for taking on a subject that their local press was both reluctant and largely unable to investigate. Yet they also admitted taking part in these law violations. "I'm not from Misiones, but I've lived in Iguazú for a while. We've all gone to Ciudad del Este and brought unauthorized merchandize. Let's stop lying to ourselves!" wrote one reader, who signed as "citizen"; similar comments followed his.[6] Among them was "Raul": "There is not a single person who does not bring stuff from Paraguay and Brazil, hidden in some compartment of their vehicle. Let's stop blaming these starving Paraguayans who come here to avoid hunger." "Rodrigo Rivero," however, noted that there is a line between illegal practices that are socially legitimate and those that are not: "We all bring stuff from Paraguay, but these are *boludeces* [small, unimportant things]. This article is about large-scale contraband of products that are subsidized by the government for the poor people from here." This comment shows that the functioning of the informal economy on the border is not predicated on a public consensus about the extent of its legitimacy. Rather, these markets are wrought with ambiguities, both legal and moral. Although many Iguazúenses engage in smuggling items for personal consumption and consider the two-directional flow of goods across the border to be a balanced form of exchange, others see the contraband of subsidized commodities out of Argentina as both illegal and illegitimate, treating it as stealing from the state and its citizens.

State laws such as import prohibitions ban people's access to goods, whereas others, such as subsidies, facilitate access to goods. This situation gives rise to complex moral economies, where the same practice can be justified or criticized depending on the direction of contraband flows and on the social status of the people who participate in it. Because the boundary between the licit and the illicit is relative and shifting, smuggling rarely becomes the focus of the local media. Journalists are reluctant to put forward their position on an issue that lacks social consensus and that is unlikely to form one in the near future. Moreover, reporters in Iguazú are also actors in the informal economy, which for them is not only a source of more affordable produce for the household, but also an important supply of tools necessary for engaging in media production—a precondition of their journalistic work.

TOOLS OF MEDIA PRODUCTION

One day in March 2011 I was with Kelly when her cell phone rang. She answered the call: it was her contact from the customs office on the Tancredo Neves International Bridge. They had just captured a van full of smuggled electronics that was destined for Argentina and the official wanted *La Voz de Cataratas* to get the scoop. After she hung up, Kelly got into her car and drove to the border post. Although obtaining permission to photograph the checkpoint area is a cumbersome bureaucratic procedure—which I learned on a previous visit with another reporter—Kelly was immediately allowed to take pictures of the electronics, neatly arranged for display on a table outside of the customs booth. Had she been too busy to come, her contact would have sent her pictures of lined-up cell phones, photo and video cameras, DVD players, USB memory sticks, GPS devices, and other confiscated equipment via e-mail. To demonstrate the efficacy of their work, the customs office regularly issued press releases with photographs of their booty, willingly providing such information to the public.

But this smooth collaboration between customs and the media obscures an important issue. As the story in the beginning of this chapter hinted, journalists on the border are directly bound to the informal economy by the very nature of their profession. In Iguazú, they often access the means of media production—cameras, computers, digital voice recorders, and microphones—through illegalized routes. Commercial venues in Iguazú have only a limited selection of expensive equipment, so media organizations make major purchases like radio antennas, transmission stations, and professional video cameras in Buenos Aires. But the most popular, and the nearest, destination for purchasing smaller electronics, both for personal and professional use, is across the border in Paraguay. Ciudad del Este is a shopping metropolis with a much greater variety of goods than Brazilian or Argentine border towns. As discussed in chapter 3, taxes on consumer electronics are significantly lower in Paraguay than in Argentina, making it an attractive place for Iguazú journalists to buy many of their day-to-day necessities such as cassettes, memory cards, batteries, and cables. For example, in 2010, a MiniDV cassette for a video camera in Ciudad del Este was three times cheaper than in Iguazú.[7]

Significant price differences for electronics between Iguazú and Ciudad del Este explain the rationale for smuggling. Savings from purchasing cameras or computers in Paraguay could amount to hundreds or even thousands of dollars per item—meaningful sums of money for owners of small private media companies, who have limited budgets formed by mixing personal and business income. Savings were even more substantial for individual reporters, who earned as little as 1,200 pesos (about US$300) per month. Owning a digital voice recorder and a camera with photo and video capabilities relieved journalists of the burden of borrowing company equipment and allowed them to pursue freelance work. For some, it was a matter of economic survival.

In chapter 3, I described the routine of going from Puerto Iguazú to Ciudad del Este—the identity checks on the Argentina-Brazil border, regular traffic congestion on Puente del Amistad, and flexible migrations and customs controls in Paraguay. The most complicated part of shopping in Ciudad del Este is not getting there or protecting yourself from pickpocketing while shopping in the crowded malls, but passing through the Argentine customs control on the way back. To avoid detection, one needs practical knowledge about crossing the border, which the locals have learned and perfected through experience. Resenting the rigid controls implemented since the creation of MERCOSUR in the 1990s and strengthened in the early 2000s, when following 9/11 the surveillance and policing of the border were increased, locals have invented ingenious ways of bringing electronics into the country. Iguazúenses refer to this practice as passing the merchandise *"por izquierda"*—literally "by the left," but in this context meaning "outside of the law." The following example illustrates how creative Iguazúenses can be in avoiding border control. When a news editor bought a portable computer in Ciudad del Este, he explained to me how he hid smaller items, such as cables and the power adaptor, in an empty thermos used for preparing mate, while his wife sat on the new laptop in the passenger seat as they crossed the checkpoint on the Argentine border, where inspection is most rigorous. Larger desktop computers are often brought in disassembled, on multiple trips. Usually people discard original packages in Paraguay not only because they are bulky but also to convince Argentine customs that these items are not new purchases. This tactic is especially easy with cameras. When my digital SLR camera was stolen, a friendly reporter gave me advice on how to purchase a new one in Ciudad del Este: "Throw out the box, take a few pictures with it, and then carry it across the border as your own already-used camera."

Other commodities, such as flat-screen TVs, might seem too big to be smuggled stealthily. Yet, I heard from reporters in Iguazú that shops in Paraguay offer transportation services; for an extra fee they will take the responsibility of delivering the purchase across the border. Alternatively, for a small surcharge Argentine smugglers can carry products through checkpoints by exploiting their personal connections. Those who have lived in Iguazú for many years usually know customs officers well—unlike the federal security forces, customs authorities do not rotate their personnel—so their vehicles are rarely inspected. Even if they are stopped, they undergo a rather superficial, symbolic act of state control, as seen in the beginning of this chapter, where I recounted how a journalist easily passed through the checkpoint with a new video camera. As happens in border areas worldwide, state agents in charge of supervising them go through the motions to show that they are doing their job, while largely allowing cross-border flows to proceed (see, for example. McMurray 2003, Reeves 2014).

There is another important link between Iguazú media and law evasion. In the introduction I explained that many local radios in Iguazú, known as *"truchas"* or *"piratas,"* historically did not have licenses to operate. Although the new Argentine media law invited all media organizations on the border to register with the federal audiovisual communication agency, AFSCA, the advantages of *blanquearse* (going "legit") have been limited by a number of requirements that legalized media have to meet. One of these requirements involves transparent purchasing policies. All media equipment has to be bought legally, with receipts—that is, in Argentina. This rule discourages registration among border media, which—for some more than others—depend on the electronics supply from Paraguay. "The requirements are very strict and include purchasing authorized equipment, so you cannot bring it *del otro lado* [from the other side]," one media entrepreneur said.[8] Because the price of legalizing is high, some were considering deferring registration in order to maintain access to cheaper, if illegal, equipment.

Kelly was invited to see the confiscated goods at the customs office during a period of sharply intensified control on the bridge. In the early months of 2011, news stories about smugglers caught with illegal electronics hit the media at least once or twice a week, and sometimes every day. The publications conveyed only minimal information from a press release, including the kind of vehicle intercepted, as well as the quantity and price of merchandize confiscated. Around that time, over the course of three days, *La Voz de Cataratas* reported that "customs arrested a tourist from Córdoba who was riding an international bus line between Ciudad del Este and Iguazú, and confiscated latest generation cell phones for an estimated value of 10,000 pesos (US$2,481)"[9]; "customs officers implemented checks of vehicles circulating across Tancredo Neves Bridge and found merchandize from Ciudad del Este for a value of 84,000 pesos (US$20,847)"[10]; "Iguazú Customs stopped two tourist buses and confiscated electronics worth 20,000 pesos (US$4,963). Passengers had placed merchandise in luggage for clothes."[11] There

FIGURE 19. Kelly Ferreyra covering the 2009 urban waste recycling campaign organized by *La Voz de Cataratas* in support of a local recycling cooperative, Cooperativa de Recicladores Cataratas.

were also a few stories about women who taped cell phones to their thighs and waists under bulky clothing to pass the checkpoints without being detected. When Kelly published the story about the buses, I commented that both of them belonged to long-distance tour companies. "They don't catch the ones from here because they have it all arranged with customs," she said.[12] Although intended as a joke, her response quite accurately depicted the situation. Despite strengthened control, illegal electronics were being brought from Ciudad del Este to Iguazú, where they were resold in local variety stores and through informal channels.

In order to publicize its competence, the customs office habitually informs Iguazú journalists when illegal merchandize is captured. Nevertheless, they are wary of disclosing too much and making border control transparent via the media. When on behalf of *La Voz de Cataratas* I requested data on the number of searches and confiscations the customs performed annually, the office was not able to provide us with this information. After some delay, the data was apparently collected; but the head of the Iguazú customs office did not authorize its release to the media. Kelly's contact advised me to call the director and reason with him about how publishing this information would improve the image of the institution. But it was futile. As of 2011, Argentina did not have laws that committed government agencies to hand over public information to the media, and Iguazú journalists rarely if ever challenged the authorities to claim their right to receive it.

Besides performing their public courtship, which results in media publications on exclusively successful law enforcement practices, border control officers and journalists also meet on the backstage of the formal state, where more deals are forged on the basis of trust and reciprocity between friends, neighbors, and fellow residents of a small town. It is on this backstage that the boundary between the legal and the illegal is flexed to allow journalists to bring in untaxed media equipment from Paraguay, as their vehicles are not checked as thoroughly. Rather than being passive receivers of benefits, when possible, journalists contribute what they can—usually, information—to nurture rapport with law enforcement. For example, once a reader of *La Voz de Cataratas* posted the following comment to an online news article about electronics contraband: "Why doesn't anybody touch the cab that brings electronics from shops in Paraguay [. . .] There is a gray Renault with polarized windows that always loads merchandize at X [a shop in the border zone on the Brazilian side]. It is a hideout of contraband, authorized by some in Iguazú." As soon as Kelly saw it, she removed the comment from the online forum and forwarded it to her contact at the customs.

Like food, electronics form part of outlawed but licit cross-border commodity flows. From the everyday lives of journalists who prefer buying certain food items from Paraguayan cuperas to their professional news production facilitated by illegally acquired equipment, media practices along the border are embedded in the local informal economy. Journalists choose not to report such activities, especially if the people involved are other Iguazúenses rather than foreigners or Argentines from remote regions, as long as it benefits their community. These tactics of silence serve to maintain the feasibility and social legitimacy of the informal economy in the tri-border region. But this moral economy, based on social norms and obligations (Thompson 1971:79), is only valid for locals. When smugglers take the merchandise *out* of Iguazú, local residents, including journalists, are more likely to see these actions as illegal and illegitimate practices, and are less hesitant to make their capture into a news event. Newsworthiness of contraband depends on whether the actors involved—smugglers, law enforcement agents, as well as journalists—are outsiders, with no stake in the well-being of the community, or whether, as Iguazúenses, they partake in relationships of convivencia in the border town. The following stories—Javier's and Silvia's—demonstrate how the common sense of living together on the margins of the state determines and limits what illegal practices journalists report on in the media.

ABOUT COMMON SENSE

When we met in 2010, Javier Villegas worked for Radio Yguazú. He was a *movilero,* as street reporters that served as conduits between news sources—the town's residents, its officials, public service employees, and business representatives—and program hosts who conducted the shows in television and radio studios, were known. Before Javier settled on being a journalist, for two decades his career oscillated between working for the media and the Argentine Army. Javier was born in the federal capital in 1973 and lived there, growing up with his father, until his mother's family invited him, by then a teenager, to visit Iguazú Falls. What was initially planned to be a two-week trip became prolonged: Javier started secondary school and decided to stay with his mother in Misiones. Though he knew nothing about the media, his interest in music and his dreams of working in radio motivated him to learn. Javier took on any and all jobs related to the career he desired, from installing television cables to answering phone calls in the studio, before he was taught how to play vinyl records live on air and became a radio operator.

In 1992, Javier was called to do the colimba, mandatory military service. After his time in the army, he moved to Buenos Aires, at first working for a small community radio station and, when it closed, at a shopping center. But Javier did not remain in the federal capital for long. "I was already tired of Buenos Aires. In that period, in 1994, it was very dangerous. Once again I decided to return to Iguazú." He became a movilero for FM Libre, where for four years he conducted interviews on the street. Then, in 1998, he reversed the trajectory of his career and again entered the military, this time joining the Regimiento de Patricios (the Regiment of Patricians), one of the oldest and most prestigious infantry regiments of the Argentine Army. "In primary school patricians and grenadiers are mentioned in all patriotic acts, such as 25 de Mayo and 9 de Julio: patricians defended against the British; patricians defended the Cabildo.[13] When we were kids we wanted to be patricians. I was young and I wanted to try. I wanted to know the taste of being patricio," he said.

FIGURE 20. Javier Villegas reporting from the center of Iguazú after Argentina's successful soccer match in the 2010 World Cup.

But Javier did not continue in the army for long. In 1999, he left the Regimiento de Patricios in Buenos Aires and returned to Misiones to resume his radio reporting full time. With his wife and three children Javier now lives in Ribera del Paraná, a neighborhood on the banks of the Paraná River, through which most of the contraband to and from Paraguay passes. Despite his former career in the armed forces and his present one in the media, neither of these professional mandates circumscribes what he thinks about food smuggling and other contraband, nor can they explain why he does not talk about these practices *for the record*. As an ex-member of the security apparatus, he might be expected to view contraband from the purely legalistic perspective, formally separating the legal from the illegal, where the latter is considered to be a threat to the state, prompting him to report clandestine activities to law enforcement. On the other hand, as a journalist, Javier could use his intimate knowledge of living on a smuggling route to make breaking news stories, translating his experience of residency on the border into financial and symbolic capital; into money and public acknowledgment. Javier does neither. Rather than a function of ideologies underlying his professions—legalism and populism—his position is informed by his role as a resident of the community and a consumer

in the informal economy. Here is how he explained his take on contraband:

> I see working people, Paraguayans from the other side, who bring their veg-
> etables and their fruit to sell them here. If you make a *denuncia* [complaint],
> some will find a new pique, but you will take away the work from these
> Paraguayans. It will make me neither richer nor poorer. On the contrary,
> today it suits me because when I buy from them I pay much less. For exam-
> ple, for the cost of one kilo of onions [in Argentina] I can buy three kilos of
> onions [from Paraguay]. I see these things and try not to meddle in them. I
> am not sure I did well selecting the profession of journalism. One needs to
> have a lot of common sense.[14]

Javier's comment that he might not be a good journalist speaks to the
notion that reporters should be watchdogs over criminal and illegal
activities and are obliged to denounce them in the public sphere. He
contrasts this monitoring mission to "common sense," the rational
behavior that those living on the border have developed in relation to
informal trade and other illegal activities.[15] The Iguazú media also use
such local notions of common sense in their journalistic practices. Javier's work as a reporter depends on, and is powerfully shaped by, his
residency at the border. The acknowledgment that covering smugglers'
activities would make him neither richer nor poorer—if anything, more
likely the latter, as he would have to purchase produce in expensive
grocery stores—is an important reason why journalists maintain public
secrets. For a reporter, to look the other way is to show solidarity with
neighbors and complicity with the majority of Iguazúenses, who benefit
from the status quo of informal markets. While national mass media
usually assume a black-and-white view of legality and illegality, the
practices of those living in Iguazú reveal the farce of such an artificial,
and stark, divide.

Rather than being a spokesperson for the security state, Javier
chooses the convivencia of the local community. "The army taught me
companionship [compañerismo]," he says, reflecting on the effects that
his experience in the military had on his work in the media. After a
pause, in a thick porteño accent that marks him as different from his
colleagues in Iguazú, Javier added: "I would like to cover more social
themes, be more *solidario*, to go to a barrio and ask: 'Señora, what is
happening? What do you need?' [. . .] People here don't like the press.
One takes out the recorder and asks why something is not working, and
then they run away. I would like to do journalism that is more commu-
nitarian."[16] This solidarity with the community, which draws from

Javier's socialization into the military code of compañerismo, builds into the convivencia and complicity that I discussed in chapter 4. Adherence to the local moral and social norms and commitment to fellow residents are powerful mechanisms through which media producers reconcile news-making with the common sense of living in the shared space of the border town.

In Iguazú residents often justify engaging in unlawful though licit economic exchanges by critiquing unfair policies dictated from the remote political center in Buenos Aires. As is common in other border areas, where state presence is often distorted, residents view the national law as limiting and criminalizing instead of enabling and protecting. Such "bad law" constrains habitual economic exchanges, renders the increasingly larger sector of the population that continues to engage in banned practices as illegal actors, and foments the growth of the informal economy (see Vásquez-León 1999). Consequently, in the eyes of people who feel neglected by the state in terms of inadequate social assistance and the absence of economic incentives while at the same time being subjected to intensified policing, the law loses legitimacy. Although Iguazúenses are proud to be Argentine citizens, they are annoyed by what they see as detached policy planning in the capital. Regulations that intimately affect their everyday lives, from free-trade agreements to policies circumscribing the work of the media, are formulated far away by politicians who are insensitive to their daily realities and their pressing needs. The geography of legality and legitimacy is mapped onto power inequality between the central commercial areas of the Argentine state and its peripheral, marginalized frontier. Faced with what they see as longstanding government injustice, Iguazú journalists use local common sense to justify their refusal to report on petty smuggling and other minor law infringements, thereby contesting the state-centered communicative cartographies that underlie the mass media's coverage of law and crime.

PEOPLE JUST LIKE US

Silvia Martínez, one of the few journalists born and raised in Iguazú and a good friend of Javier's, also invokes local common sense, contrasting it to the legal norms deployed by state institutions. She grew up in Barrio Almirante Brown, a neighborhood close to the Paraná, not too far from where Javier now lives. After five years of studying law at the Universidad Católica in Posadas, and a few more working in the tourism sector in Iguazú, Silvia discovered her passion for journalism by

FIGURE 21. Silvia Martínez recording an interview with Iguazú volunteer firefighters, June 2010.

chance. "My mother is always looking for opportunities to do community service, so when I read in *La Voz de Cataratas* that there was a *comedor* (canteen) in Barrio Primavera that distributed milk to children, I wrote to the editor asking for their contact information." At that time Silvia was still working in the casino, but later, when unwilling to tolerate what she described as the company's mistreatment of its employees, Silvia quit her job and asked Kelly whether she needed help with the daily. "I had always liked writing, so I wanted to collaborate. She invited me to talk over mate and with the four pesos that I had in my pocket I bought some pastries. When I met Kelly, I told her my story. I said that I had no idea what a journalist did."

Silvia began going out to gather news with another reporter for *La Voz de Cataratas,* and for a while worked without pay. She said she immediately liked the vocation. Interested in social issues in her community, she found journalism to be a productive form of paying attention to what people around her had to say and an efficient means of circulating their knowledge to the broader public. As a deeply committed Iguazúense, from the start Silvia had a special agenda: "I try to look for news in places that don't receive much attention, to see other things that are not daily news." But her story shows that news-making in Iguazú was not easy for reporters, who faced significant material and temporal obstacles. "I have my camera. As long as my camera works, everything is all right. If it breaks, I will need to buy a new one. Kelly would give me hers, but I would waste time going to her house [it takes about an hour one way on foot] to download pictures and videos." Silvia says that mobility is a big problem for her. "On the one hand, it is an advantage that I walk everywhere and don't miss anything that is happening on my way; on the other hand, it restricts my ability to go to the barrios. I love going to the barrios, talking to people in community health centers. But it takes many hours. The main problem is that in digital media you must make multiple news stories every day, not just a few, so I cannot sit and listen to the problems in the health centers, attending to pregnant twelve- or thirteen-year-old girls." These and other issues faced by the marginalized population are very important to investigate, she says:

> [In Iguazú media] the topic of poverty is always a critique of the government, but poverty does not depend only on the government. It is a social problem. [. . .] We all take part in creating this socioeconomic context. We are all guilty. Not because I vote or I don't vote, but because I can do something for my neighbor, but I don't do it. People disassociate from poverty. There are deprived barrios, humble barrios, and I don't want to take responsibility for them, so I blame the government. The media emphasize that poverty is the fault of the government. [. . .] But there are also nice things that are happening in the poor barrios and the media should disseminate this information—that there is somebody who teaches karate for free at a school. So if I am a math teacher I could also go there to teach. If I don't provide this information, I don't allow these people to find each other.[17]

Silvia sees the media as a social actor in the community, responsible for building ties of solidarity among residents that have been neglected by the state. Instead of being a watchdog over governmental activities, journalism for her entails a commitment to deploy information in order to produce positive effects for the town. Sometimes this involves generating news, such as writing about volunteer programs in the outlying neighborhoods; other times it means withholding news, such as maintaining public secrets related to the informal economy. The fact that she is local has not put Silvia in denial about crime in the area. However, based on her experience of growing up on the border, she has a deeper understanding of, and broader justification for, practices that transgress state law:

> As kids we used to go swimming in the Paraná. We saw how the boats came, how somebody signaled them that the prefects were not around. There was a certain sense of togetherness because we were witnesses to all of this. But we were little and we greeted them all, even the boats carrying prohibited merchandise. You see all the movement but don't say anything because you don't want to put yourself in the middle. You know it is bad, but you also know that people do this because they need to get by.

Part of the Argentine Northeast, Misiones is among the poorest provinces of the country. Poverty is perpetuated by inadequate governmental policies, leaving locals unable to pay inflated prices for food and other goods. Living across the river from Paraguay, with its cheaper alternatives, local residents have long pursued informal and illegalized routes to acquire commodities for their households and their workplaces. Emphasizing her local background, Silvia said: "People from other places learned to live here, but they don't have the same love for the town. For me the bad things that happen here really hurt. It's not just news. It hurts me." With these words Silvia acknowledged that news has the potential to criminalize those whose ways of life it represents (or misrepresents), and she explained why certain things are better left unsaid. As an Iguazúense, she embodies the multifaceted border identity, which cannot be summarized in oversimplified news stories about law and crime.

Iguazúenses have always found ways to respond to Argentine government policies that encroach on their common interests. Local economic practices dynamically adjusted to the changing rules of the state. In 2010, when I asked them, many residents in Iguazú did not even know what the allowed quota for shopping abroad was (some estimated it reached US$150 per month) because it mattered little in their daily lives. Iguazúenses' claim to the right to take advantage of price differences created by the border was so strong that, in November 2010, Luis Aranda, one of the leaders of the motoqueros—the biker-smugglers introduced at the beginning of this book—took the "citizen's bench" in the town council to demand that the old regime of minimally regulated cross-border trade be returned. Aranda presented a fifty-page-long document, signed by five thousand Iguazúenses, asking the legislators to support their plea for a new quota to legally import poultry and other food products. "O pasan todos o no pasa nadie" (Either everybody is allowed to pass or nobody is), he insisted.[18] The leader of the union of motoqueros pointed out that illegal fruits, vegetables, and poultry brought by bribe-paying entrepreneurs and smugglers from the neighboring countries were common in stores around Iguazú, but law-abiding citizens who obeyed the regulations were excluded from the market. In his speech Aranda reignited the old dispute that has long existed between licensed traders and smugglers, who evaded the tax system by organizing economic exchanges outside the control of the state. "I understand that the municipality cannot change the national laws of SENASA, but they can help us with the procedures that are necessary in order to mitigate the injustice. There are entrepreneurs whose pockets are full, while others are starving," claimed Aranda.

Aranda's public speech during the town council meeting was an ironic performance. On the one hand, though he presented himself as being an advocate for legitimate businesses and against contraband, motoqueros were active contrabandistas in informal trade; on the other hand, in Iguazú no clear-cut boundary existed between legally authorized entrepreneurship and illegal movement of goods across the border: they were tightly connected and dependent on each other. This was also not the activist's first performance. "Pájaro" Aranda was already known for organizing public manifestations in the 1990s, including a blockade of the Tancredo Neves International Bridge, demanding the removal of import prohibitions. His seemingly incongruous position encapsulates the situation in Iguazú, where small-scale local vendors, banned from selling foreign produce, both asked for changes to the restrictive trade regime and, their requests pending, were complacent with and collaborated in smuggling.

As a result of Aranda's speech, the following week the Iguazú town council approved a three-point communiqué responding to the dual problem presented by the motoquero performance: the need to change policies that disadvantage local business owners and the need to better control the extensive informal economy. First, the councillors asked the national government to investigate the possibility of raising quotas established by the Border Trade Regime. Second, they addressed the municipal government, requesting the executive to strengthen control to more effectively detect businesses that were selling foreign merchandise, both in public places and in authorized commercial venues. Finally, the councillors appealed to the customs authorities, SENASA, the gendarmerie, and the prefecture, asking them to intensify control at border checkpoints and other "vulnerable" areas, preventing the entry of merchandise into the country outside of the established regulations.[19]

While local legislators supported the motoquero cause against the national government, requesting an increase in quotas for the merchandise, circumscribed by the Border Trade Regime, they did not suggest adding food products such as poultry, fruits, and vegetables to the list, which was Aranda's main request. Instead, they called for tightened controls of the thriving informal market within the neighborhoods of Iguazú and along the borders with Paraguay and Brazil. From the choice the motoquero union leader gave the town council—"o pasan todos o no pasa nadie"—officially the authorities chose "no pasa nadie" (nobody passes). Still, "pasan todos" (everybody passes) remained the status quo. Bringing fresh food from neighboring Brazil and Paraguay was against the law. Yet chicken, fruits, and vegetables were continuously delivered to convenience stores or directly to residents' homes.

Journalists who have lived in Iguazú long enough to know what is happening and why are unlikely to investigate food or electronics contraband. But they also often overlook drugs. In the blindspots of the media, illegal but tolerated goods intertwine with illicit substances. Silvia said: "Here it is very easy to cross the puddle of the Paraná with a paddle and contraband anything. We know there are barrios that need to be investigated, but I don't want to get into it because it involves very humble families."[20] Silvia knows people who live on the banks of the Paraná who are drawn into the illegal drug trade. Teenagers often work for Paraguayan traffickers, who become *padrinos* (godfathers) of the family, sometimes replacing an absent parent. In order to support their families, smaller children become *mulitas* (little mules) for traffickers, carrying drugs across the border or distributing them in town. Silvia said that the children involved cannot complain because they do not want to compromise their family's source of income: "They can't say anything; even when they are threatened they need to shut up, because all their brothers live from this."

The unwillingness of Iguazú journalists to cover border crime is related to the deep interconnectedness of criminal activities with the region's economic struggles and marginality. Silvia justified such illegal flows by explaining that the smugglers are "people just like us, except they live off of something illegal." Although local residents consider smuggling drugs to be both illegal and illicit, compared to the licitness of food and electronics, even this border violation is partially justified by the local common sense: Silvia argued that traffickers do not choose their profession, but rather get involved in unlawful practices out of desperation. Her attention is on mulitas, the privates of contraband, not on the bosses of organized crime who are behind the trafficking operations. Engaged in smuggling, or being complicit in it, people violate the boundaries of law, not those of the moral code. Iguazú journalists watch the poor being criminalized, while MERCOSUR assists multinational corporations with the fast and easy transport of goods that the treaty has "legalized." Witnessing this injustice, by keeping practices that have widespread social legitimacy out of media coverage, Javier and Silvia, like their colleagues, contribute to the maintenance of the informal border economy and reproduction of illegal yet licit practices, which, in the absence of sufficient legal employment and social welfare, support their community.

PRACTICES OF (IL)LEGIBILITY

To rephrase Henri Lefebvre, as a social space, the border is *produced* before being *read,* and not in order to be represented, but rather to be lived by people in their own particular ways (1992[1974]:143). International and national media have designated the Triple Frontier as a violent place, but, as de Certeau wrote, "space is a practiced place" (1984:117). Local journalists in Iguazú are simultaneously architects and walkers, producers and users of the border. As users, they "make *(bricolent)* innumerable and infinitesimal transformations of and within the dominant cultural economy in order to adapt it to their own interests and their own rules" (de Certeau 1984:xiii–xiv), and it is precisely in relation to their role as users that journalists as producers operate. Representations they create not only depend on but also influence their routine on the border.

Concurring with Veena Das and Deborah Poole (2004) that the margins of the state are spaces of creativity, in this chapter I have shown how local journalists juggle the legibility and illegibility of illegalized border practices, depending on their social legitimacy and their own stake in the outcome. They use practical vision and common sense to decide what kinds of local knowledge will become public information. Although the rationale for avoiding certain topics includes journalists' personal safety, time, and financial constraints, in addition to their commitment to promoting tourism, such logistical difficulties are only a part of what limits news reporting in Iguazú. Living on the margins of the state and on the doorstep of alternative economic, political, and social regimes provides journalists with a particular understanding of what constitutes socially legitimate activities. This, in turn, powerfully shapes how local media determine what is newsworthy.

As we have seen, in Iguazú the letter of the law and local practices, as well as local social and moral regimes, often do not coincide, making it difficult for contentious topics to enter the news agenda. While the national media, which look for more sensational angles from which to cover regional stories, often discursively produce the border as a space of the illegal, local media produce the illegal as an illegible practical alternative to the formal economy. Iguazú residents, including border officials and journalists, tacitly agree that legality and illegality are two ends of a continuum, along which certain practices can be seen as more severe violations of the law than others; therefore, some of them go "on the record," while the rest remain "off the record." What happens when a contentious issue, which falls in the domain of public secrets, is unexpectedly exposed in the local media is the subject of the next chapter.

6

Blurred Boundaries

NOBODY TALKS ABOUT THIS

One evening when we sat down to take a break after a long day of traversing the town in search of news stories, I asked Jorgelina what issue, falling outside the purview of Iguazú media agenda, worried her the most. Without hesitating for a moment, she said: "When I was younger, people who lived on the banks of the Tacuara stream and had as many as ten children, would sell one. Ten months later, after they spent the money, they would complain that their child had been kidnapped."[1] But Jorgelina only initially referred to the past. "People from all over the world come to adopt children in Misiones. They don't even adopt—they buy babies from these eighteen-year-old girls who have eight or nine children. Nobody talks about this." Then, in her usual candid tone, with which she addressed the most serious questions, Jorgelina explained how she saw the dilemma: "There are many childless couples that want to have a baby. Why is there no institution that would arrange for it? 'You have ten children, señora, what do you want to do with them all? How will you feed them? Would you like to give them into adoption, señora?' This would help people who don't have children; it would also help those who don't have the means to support large families." Jorgelina was frustrated that adoption laws in Argentina were so strict. "It is very difficult to adopt now. There are people who have to wait fifteen years for a child, while here children are dying of hunger, malnourished. I don't understand. What is the problem? There is a lot of bureaucracy, a lot of paperwork, and here people continue to die." Later that year, when Javier and I were making the television program *Proximidad* (see chapter 1), I remembered this conversation with Jorgelina and we took on illegal adoptions and child trafficking as one of the topics for our investigation.

As a point of intersection between my anthropological research on security and journalism and my collaborative engagement with media production in Iguazú, this chapter examines the making of a news story about legally ambiguous practices from two different yet overlapping narrative genres: journalism and ethnography. Continuing the earlier themes of the book, I extend the analysis of how at the disjuncture between the formal laws and local norms, different social practices are constituted as threats, crimes, and public secrets, which complicates news production. In the early 2000s and during my fieldwork in Argentina between 2008 and 2011, the topic of irregular adoptions was contentious in Misiones. Sensational mainstream media coverage of the illegal "birth industry" and the global concern with child trafficking criminalized the border region, and increased security measures resulted in further uncertainty about common practices of informal fosterage, marginalizing poor residents and enabling, rather than disabling, conditions that facilitated the sale of children. Iguazú journalists found themselves lingering at the crossroads between newsworthy stories and their commitment to defend their community from faulty accusations from the national media and the government. They treated adoptions as a public secret, protected by the laws of silence. Journalists did not want to contribute to the circulation of discourses that too often ended up confusing informal fosterage, illegal adoptions, and child trafficking, making border residents fearful of potential legal consequences and their socioeconomic effects.

This chapter focuses on the process of investigation that underlies the relationship between ethnography and journalism. I relate my experience of making a story for the media by dividing the narrative into "takes." In cinematography, the concept of "take" refers to consecutive attempts to make a single continuous shot, and is used to denote the multiple stages of production involved in filmmaking. Here, it highlights the fragmentation, repetition, and unfinished quality of the story. This stylistic decision to organize the material into temporal and thematic segments captured on film tape emphasizes the distinct processes and forms of journalistic and ethnographic rendering of knowledge. As two modes of representation, the production of "takes" (filming) and the production of fieldnotes (writing) have different implications for the reporter/researcher and for the people in our stories. Often, in the narration of experiences of the illegal, the written form is preferred to the visual. Despite the availability of technologies to disguise identities, those who live navigating the line between the inside and the outside of the law are uncomfortable with video exposure: it is too immediate, public, and capable of reproducing legal and moral categories that criminalize them, accentuating racial, ethnic, and social inequalities on the margins of the state (see chapter 1).

Whereas media production usually requires finding sources that consent to going *on the record* and thrives on newsworthy statements from the actors involved, anthropological research is conducted on the backstage of this public performance, where, based on relationships of trust, information is gathered *off the record*. When journalists fail to elicit evidence to support the story, their reporting resembles a mosaic of jagged pieces—the "takes" that in this chapter edge uncomfortably onto each other, leaving the narrative fragmentary and inconclusive. The anthropologist, in contrast, stitches up ethnographic notes into a whole by filling in the gaps of recorded information with extensive local knowledge, acquired over prolonged periods of time. In an ethnographic account, truth is not a function of verification through public exposure, but is tested during the researcher's embeddedness within the community. My use of the structure of "takes" in this chapter juxtaposes the ruptured, incomplete mode of storytelling characteristic of video-making for the news media against the flow and the depth of the ethnographic narrative employed throughout the book, as complementary forms of knowledge production.

I trace the blurry yet meaningful boundary between journalism and ethnography as two genres of approaching and representing social reality. This boundary was particularly marked when, depending on whether they saw me as a reporter or an anthropologist, Iguazúenses judged the extent to which they could share public secrets with me. Considering the sensitive nature of the matter, unsurprisingly, most of what I learned about illegalized activities was either through lived experience or through conversations that were not video- or audio-recorded. These encounters and comments, written down in my fieldnotes, inform the ethnography of this book, but, as this chapter shows, they were insufficient evidence for a television program. The boundary between the two modes of knowledge production was also palpable—and more critical—to my work in another way. Although during the process of journalistic investigation for *Proximidad* and ethnographic research my two roles blended to the point where sometimes even I found it difficult to tell them apart,

I was acutely aware of which pieces of local knowledge could be included in the television program, and what, if made public, could increase people's sense of insecurity. Information that fell into the latter category was reserved for this book, where the length and the breadth of the account allow me to situate illegality within political, economic, and historical contexts, reducing the risk of reinforcing the discourse of criminalization. I suggest that the existence of the boundary between journalism and ethnography—permeable and negotiable, but producing real effects—is, therefore, not only methodological but also ethical and political. Media reporters and anthropologists have different commitments to the people who are their sources and their publics, and their stories serve distinct ends: while the former aim to inform by revealing hidden truths, the latter are more concerned with explaining the hiding of truth as social phenomena.

The following story of making the television program is reconstructed from entries in my reporter's journal and from my ethnographic field-notes. Some details of the account have been modified; the names of some of the people involved have been changed or left out, while others—recorded on tape and publicly broadcast on television—are real. Encounters during the program production are presented in the motion video format of consecutive "takes," eleven of which comprise the narrative. In order to avoid interrupting the flow of the story, the broader discussion of its main subject—illegal adoptions—precedes and follows it. In the next section I underscore the relevance of actions and statements later depicted in the "takes" by situating the issue of adoptions within Latin American and specifically Argentine media and legal discourses about the sale of children and child trafficking. In the end, however, my goal in this chapter is not to investigate adoption practices per se, but to focus on the process of media production. The television episode on illegal adoptions was our attempt to publicly articulate social and legal contexts that enabled the sale of children and child trafficking in the tri-border region; the difficulties we encountered in the course of making it showed that the community was wary of trespassing the fine line between security, provided by the status quo, and uncertainty, brought by the public exposure of illegal practices in the media. In the events described, my role as an anthropologist merged with that of a journalist in what turned out to be a professionally frustrating but analytically rewarding experience: it enabled me to understand the role that local reporters play in contributing to the security of their community, even when it goes against their mandate of making newsworthy stories; and it taught me to recognize the nuanced ethical and political boundary between journalistic and ethnographic knowledge production.

FOSTERAGE, ADOPTION, AND TRAFFICKING

Until the mid-twentieth century the institution of adoption did not legally exist in Argentina, even though diverse practices of fosterage were common. Without interference from public agencies, prosperous families would take in and raise the children of the poor, usually assigning them to an inferior status in their new home (Villalta 2010). These socioeconomically vertical adoptions were not unique to Argentina, and they are not a thing of the past. In contemporary Brazil, as Andréa Cardarello (2009) shows, children from the lower classes can be transformed into "abandoned children," perceived as potential threats to society (i.e., future criminals), justifying the termination of their family's parental rights and making them susceptible to adoption by the elite. This process of what she calls "legal child trafficking" has been validated by the discourse of "salvation," which defines both domestic and international adoption as "an act of generosity" (Cardarello 2009:143). But Latin America also has a long tradition of informal movement of children between houses of relatives and neighbors—practices of extralegal family-making that are legitimate within communities with fewer recourses. In the Argentine Northeast such informal fosterage is called *criadazgo*—from the term *"criar"* (to raise)—which refers to situations where families raise children who belong to their relatives or neighbors without going through the legal process of changing the adopted child's identity.

Because it overlaps with questions that have been at the core of anthropology as a discipline, including kinship, identity, and migration, ethnographers have productively intervened in discussions about adoption, examining the cultural and political economies undergirding shifts of caregiving and underscoring the issues of race and indigeneity entailed in the transnational movement of children (e.g., Kim 2010; Leinaweaver 2013; Seligmann 2013). Moreover, their attention to people's fluid subjectivities and tactical uses of agency has enabled anthropologists to compellingly deconstruct the taken-for-granted norms that stigmatize and criminalize certain "morally questionable" behaviors, and these deconstructions have important implications for understanding the informal and irregular transfers of children addressed in this chapter. Notably, in her work on human trafficking Kay B. Warren interrogates the moralizing dichotomy between vulnerable and innocent victims and evil perpetrators prominent in legal and media discourses, arguing that it reduces migrant women's subjectivity to the logic of coercion and violence, denying them agency (2012:117), at the same time that the machinery of international human rights law reorders heterogeneous reality, prepping it for interventions from the state and from human rights activists (see also Warren 2007). Under circumstances of extreme poverty in rural and urban Latin America, giving up children to adoptive families, which might appear as abandonment and, from the legal perspective, constitute a violation of human rights, could be understood as an act of maternal obligation and care on the part of parents who have no means to support their offspring (see Scheper-Hughes 1993).

As this chapter shows, the sale of babies in Misiones is generally interpreted from one of two perspectives: more vocal in the mainstream Argentine media is the position of moral righteousness, which criminalizes and stigmatizes both biological parents and intermediaries in the exchange; the less public approach validates difficult decisions by poor families who choose a better life for themselves and for their children over paternal obligations of care that they are unable to meet. Since there is no consensus regarding the social legitimacy of irregular adoptions and due to the high stakes of acknowledging being a witness to these practices—which, among other consequences, comes with media scrutiny and police investigation—as Jorgelina said, "nobody talks about this."

In their overview of adoption practices in Latin America, Jessaca B. Leinaweaver and Linda J. Seligmann aptly note, "What is defined as legal or illegal, formal or informal, public or private, is never straightforward but rather always colored by such concerns as the intervention of the state in intimate domains" (2009:7). In Argentina, the earliest law to regulate adoptions, passed in 1948, established what was called *adopción simple* (simple adoption), which allowed children to keep their biological parents' last names and did not give them any inheritance rights in the new family. In 1971, the military government strengthened the element of inequality characteristic of Argentina's adoption system by legalizing *adopción plena* (plenary adoption), which left biological parents of adopted children without any rights to intervene in the process. The child's ties with his or her birth family were severed and the biological family was left defenseless in the face of state institutions (Villalta 2010:344). But these legislative steps did not change how society understood adoption: in Argentina, as in Brazil, it was considered in terms of the ideology of salvation, an act of kindness and charity by the better-off bestowed upon children, the majority of whom lived in poverty.

The socioeconomic bias inherent in the country's adoption laws was partially corrected in the 1990s, when the plight of the Abuelas de la Plaza de Mayo—the grandmothers who mobilized in search of grandchildren appropriated by the military junta that murdered their parents—brought the question of adoptions to the forefront of public debates in Argentina.[2] Coming into effect in 1997, the new law ordered the creation of the Single Registry of Prospective Adoptive Parents (RUAA, Registro Único de Aspirantes a la Adopción), prohibited international adoptions, mandated adoptive families to inform their children about their "biological reality," and legalized simple adoption, which, in contrast to plenary adoption, does not require the child to completely cut off ties with his or her biological family or erase his or her personal history, and is considered an alternative that ensures better the protection of birth parents' rights (Villalta 2010:352).

This national debate, centered on the Abuelas' struggle to identify children who had been appropriated by the military, had only limited repercussions on adoption practices in Misiones. Here, extended families have long engaged in criadazgo, which was a legitimate, unofficial means of sharing childcare. Historically, the habit of giving away children of the poorest peasants to be raised by more affluent *colonos* (settlers) was even more common in Misiones than in other parts of the country (Tarducci 2006). Informal adoptions, whether socioeconomically horizontal or vertical, were popular, justified, and—due to the legal ease of obtaining guardianship—swift. As rumors about this situation spread, Misiones became an attractive destination for families from other parts of the country who were looking to adopt. But the flexibility of the law was not the only reason why prospective parents chose this province over others. Outsiders were drawn to the area by their racial preferences for "white" babies. During the last decades of the nineteenth century and in the beginning of the twentieth, large numbers of migrants from Poland and Ukraine arrived to Misiones, creating settler communities that were later joined by Germans, Swedes, Swiss, Italians, Russians, and others. Compared to other provinces, in Misiones light-skinned and blue-eyed children are more common, and studies have shown that adoptive parents generally give preference to these phenotypical characteristics (see Cardarello 2009; Tarducci 2006). Add widespread poverty and the fact that teenage pregnancy rates are among the highest in Argentina, and it becomes clear that Misiones would be a likely destination for both legal and illegal adoptions.

Human rights activists and scholars working in Argentina argue that it is important to distinguish between *irregular adoptions, sale of children,* and *child trafficking*. The International Organization for Migration, which in Iguazú regularly holds workshops on human trafficking for federal and local security forces personnel, human rights activists, and journalists (see chapter 4), distinguishes between the Spanish terms of *trata* and *tráfico:* while "trata" corresponds to English "trafficking" and refers to the violation of an individual's rights, including kidnapping and forced labor, "tráfico" violates the integrity of the country's borders and is a crime against the nation-state, which should be translated as "human smuggling." The international human rights community broadly uses the concept of "child trafficking," which blends these two terms. According to UNICEF, child trafficking is "the recruitment, transportation, transfer, harbouring or receipt of children for the purpose of exploitation,"[3] either domestically or across state borders. The determining feature is *the end*, defined as "the purpose of exploitation." Therefore, child trafficking is distinct from the sale of children, which, according to the United Nations Optional Protocol to the Convention on the Rights of the Child, is "any act or transaction whereby a child is transferred by any person or group of persons to another for remuneration or any other consideration"[4] without necessarily leading to exploitation. Finally, an irregular adoption implies a transgression of some part of the legal regulations of the adoption process, usually bypassing the courts and directly registering the child under the adoptive family's name, but it does not necessarily involve intermediaries or entail monetary compensation to the birth mother; nor does it imply exploitation. Argentina also adheres to the Inter-American Convention on International Traffic in Minors, which has a broader understanding of traffic as "the abduction, removal or retention, or attempted abduction, removal or retention, of a minor for unlawful purposes or by unlawful means."[5] Following this expanded definition, irregular adoptions fall into the category of trafficking because of the illegality of its means. Informal fosterage, or criadazgo, is not covered in any of these classification systems provided by international law; however, the lines that separate criadazgo from child trafficking, sale of children, or irregular adoptions are blurry and contextual: there are no guarantees that a child who is informally raised by relatives or neighbors would not be exploited or that there would be no monetary transactions involved.

The contradiction between international views of "trafficking," Argentine adoption laws, and local understandings of criadazgo in Misiones is problematic in terms of security and news-making. Since the mainstream media often conflate these terms in their reporting on the region, locals have become distrustful of how this inaccuracy and misrepresentation contributes to the criminalization of border residents and the securitization of the area. Jorgelina was right: although many Iguazúenses had, usually indirectly, encountered the sale of children or irregular adoptions, viewing at least some of these practices positively and fearing the consequences of more state intervention, they did not like to talk about it in public.

In part this silence was their response to the scars of alarmist and sensationalized coverage that the issue of adoptions in their province received from nationwide media. When a series of publications claimed that in northeastern Argentina the trade in babies was a profitable business, implicating legal and medical professionals, these accusations had negative effects for the local community. Migration control on the border became more rigorous. Mistrust of judges as potential accomplices and intermediaries spread. Residents and the media raised suspicion about mothers who gave their children into adoption, questioning whether they might have sold them, thereby subjecting these women to further marginalization. Meanwhile, families seeking to adopt became frustrated by the lengthy and unnecessarily complicated legal process, which made adoptions very difficult and rare, and pushed some into choosing the alternative route, bypassing the law. State intervention in the name of security—its legal and bureaucratic fight against child trafficking and the sale of children, complemented by strengthened law enforcement—was counterproductive. It only worsened the precarious living conditions and deepened the economic insecurity of the poor, which were the initial conditions that made irregular adoption practices, including the sale of children, possible.

BIRTH INDUSTRY

"More than once in these columns we discussed the highly irregular adoptions in the province of Misiones; it was suggested that there existed 'a birth industry' for the sale of children [. . .]. These children came from communities with the poorest resources, on the verge of total destitution," began the editorial of the Argentine daily *La Nación* on October 7, 2008.[6] By then, eight years had passed since December 2000, when Aída Araujo Vázquez de Moreira, the judge of the civil and commercial court of the southern Misiones town of Oberá, was dismissed after a broadly televised scandal. The scandal was caused by a media report that showed several lawyers providing children with falsified birth documents and selling them to people from other provinces and from abroad. Claudio Moreira, the judge's husband, was one of the lawyers implicated:

Canal 13 secretly filmed him asking a couple to make a deposit to the Moreiras's shared bank account, allegedly covering the expenses of an irregular adoption. It did not go unnoticed in the media that the previous year the court, presided over by Araujo Vázquez de Moreira, had approved over a hundred adoptions—an unusually high number. The judge was suspended, and a judicial investigation began.

But the numbers of irregular adoptions continued to grow. As the media later reported, an avalanche of people looking for easily adoptable babies descended on Misiones. In 2007, six courts in the province granted 262 plenary adoptions and 237 guardianships leading to adoption.[7] This did not include cases of "deleted identity," where a newborn was illegally directly registered under the name of adoptive parents. "Many cars would come and I could see they were not from here because *la tierra* [the dirt on their tires] was of a different color," said a resident of Oberá who accused her neighbors—a family of fifteen squeezed in a tiny wood shack—of selling four children.[8] In December 2008, the news agency DyN quoted another woman, a twenty-eight-year-old resident of Oberá, who confessed to having sold two newborn sons and two daughters for sums varying between 3,000 and 5,000 pesos (equivalent to US$714–1,190) over a period of eight years.[9] Ricardo Buiak, a member of the Misiones parliament and a former priest of Oberá, told *Clarín* how "in Oberá it is known which taxi drivers take the couples from other parts of the country to the poor barrios, which hotel owners provide them accommodation, which clinics administer childbirths. If only the nurses would talk . . . When I was a priest, I was told how they administered births, while adoptive parents were waiting in the adjacent room, with civil registry papers already in order."[10] Stories like these proliferated in the media, causing a public outcry.

Parliamentarian Sandra Montiel, who was actively promoting stricter legislation regarding adoptions in Misiones, argued that the problem stemmed from the law itself: when determining guardianship, judges tend to respect the choice of biological parents, giving rise to "economic intermediacy" used by groups who "negotiate in life and the reproductive situation of vulnerable mothers."[11] This arrangement facilitated the "birth industry," referred to in the above-quoted editorial in *La Nación*, creating a criminal network that includes "*busca panzas*" (literally, "those who look for bellies," but more accurately translated as "womb hunters")—doctors, lawyers, and even cab drivers who identify women as potential vendors and, through psychological means and financial promises, coerce them into selling their babies. Although the entire "operation" of adoption was estimated to cost at least 40,000 pesos (US$9,500), the biological mother would only receive about one-tenth of that amount.[12] Often the most important intermediaries, sometimes acting as busca panzas, are lawyers, who connect the pregnant woman or a woman who recently gave birth with a party interested in adoption, do the paperwork, and present the case in court (Tarducci 2006:51). Although Argentina has signed two major international documents prohibiting child trafficking—the Optional U.N. Protocol to the Convention on the Rights of the Child and the Inter-American Convention on International Traffic in Minors—in his article for *Clarín* Ernesto Azarkevich notes that as of 2008 the state had not passed laws criminalizing the mediation in the sale of children.[13]

Misiones used to be one of only two Argentine provinces allowing couples from the rest of the country to adopt local children. In 2008, 92 percent of the 794 candidates on the registry of applicants for adoption in Misiones were not local; most of them came from Buenos Aires, Córdoba, and other larger urban areas. "Misiones is a melting pot, and the mixture of *gringos* [whites] and *criollos* [Spanish descendents] results in 'a good product,'"[14] said parliamentarian Buiak, referring to a commonly held idea that the features of the German, Polish, and Ukrainian immigrants, with their blue eyes and light skin, attract many families to look for babies from this region. Among the reasons why illegal adoptions and the sale of children prospered in Misiones, class was as important as race. "Poverty justifies the loss of values," commented Sandra Giménez, a pediatrician and the vice-governor of the province, suggesting that there existed a direct link between precarious living conditions in the Argentine Northeast and child trafficking.[15]

Motivated into action by this wave of media scandals, the provincial government passed a law ensuring that couples from Misiones would receive priority in the waiting list for adoption. Furthermore, Governor Maurice Closs announced that in order to stop the "irregular adoption of babies based in poverty," a subsidy of 1,000 pesos (US$238) would be provided to ten thousand low-income pregnant women. To prevent fraud, the compensation was to be given over a period of time: starting with the sixth month of pregnancy women were entitled to receive three installments of 200 pesos and, when the child was inscribed in the civil registry, they would get 400 pesos more.[16] The provincial daily *El Territorio* noted that in 2009, compared to the previous year, the number of Argentines from other provinces inscribed in the list to adopt a child in Misiones fell eight times.[17] But, the paper suggested, the dramatic drop in legal cases does not prove the effectiveness of the government's actions—on the contrary, it could signal the upsurge of illegal practices enabling faster adoptions.

In an effort to explain the historical trajectories and multidimensional patterns of suffering among the poor, anthropologists have employed the concepts of *structural violence* and *violence of everyday life,* which refer to conditions that lead to the normalization of social abandonment. In a 1969 publication, Norwegian sociologist Johan Galtung introduced the term "structural violence"—distinguishing it from "direct" violence—to describe situations in which people are purportedly harmed by some social structure or institution that prevents them from meeting their basic needs. This idea was later picked up by medical anthropologist Paul Farmer (1992), working in Haiti, who used it to explain how political, social, and economic forces structure the risk for AIDS, tuberculosis, and other infectious diseases, as well as other forms of extreme suffering, including starvation and rape. Since then the concept has become one of the essential tools in anthropological studies of inequality and poverty, even though some scholars give it a different name. For example, in her book *Death without Weeping: The Violence of Everyday Life in Brazil* (1992), Nancy Scheper-Hughes writes about "violence of everyday life" for mothers in a poor area of northeastern Brazil who are forced to ration their care toward infants that have a better chance of survival, allowing the sickly ones to die. Both terms—*structural violence* and *violence of everyday life*—point to institutionalized brutalities that follow set patterns to unintentionally but disproportionately affect the poor. Their suffering, as Philippe Bourgois and Jeff Schonberg write in an ethnography about homeless heroin injectors, "is chronic and cumulative and is best understood as a politically structured phenomenon that encompasses multiple abusive relationships, both structural and personal" (Bourgois and Schonberg 2009). Rendered invisible by their routine pervasiveness, these harmful structural forces— political, economic, institutional and cultural—blame the victims, who end up in zones of social exclusion and social death (see Biehl 2005).

According to official government statistics presented by the National Institute of Statistics and Censuses (INDEC), 8.9 percent of the population in the Argentine Northeast, which includes Misiones, Corrientes, Formosa, and Chaco, lived below the poverty line in 2013.[18] However, these numbers, indicating a reported decrease in poverty rates in recent years, have been heavily criticized for inaccuracy. The investigation conducted by the Universidad Católica Argentina found persistence of poverty and social inequality that was actually worsening. Their data suggests that over 10 million people (or a quarter of Argentina's population) live under conditions of poverty—in precarious homes, without access to formal employment, quality education, and sufficient health services.[19] In 2008, 37.1 percent of Misiones residents were reportedly living below the poverty line,[20] and it is unlikely the numbers have changed as dramatically as the 2013 figure of 8.9 percent quoted above suggests. That precarious social and economic conditions are real and that they have disastrous effects for children was painfully brought to public attention in October 2010, when the mainstream media reported that children in rural Misiones were dying from malnutrition (see chapter 2). In some areas, seeing how the government's inadequate social policies perpetuate abject poverty, residents understand and justify the actions of families who, when they cannot support their children, give them away to be raised by others. This empathy does not mean that Misioneros actively engage in irregular adoptions, nor do they promote them. Any informal arrangements become less legitimate if they involve intermediaries who profit from their roles and if children are exchanged for money, household appliances, or other valuable things. Publicly, the sale of children is not tolerated, and committed local human rights activists work hard to give the issue more media exposure and assist the victims. Nevertheless, in the interstices of strict adoption laws, fear of criminalization caused by negative media portrayals, and poverty, which affects many families in Misiones, conditions for child trafficking persist and irregular adoptions continue to be practiced under the veil of public secrecy.

PROGRAM PRODUCTION

There was no easy way of approaching the topic in Iguazú. The law of silence that protected the public secret of irregular adoptions had political and ethical implications, but so did attempts to address it. This chapter looks at the backstage of a journalistic investigation into a contentious issue and, to emphasize the process of filming and the fragmentary structure of media representations, its narrative is presented as a series "takes." Each of the takes contains an encounter during the production of the television episode in September 2010 with people who had knowledge and experience of adoptions. The description of events blends information from my reporter's notebook with the narrative account from my ethnographic fieldnotes. The following outline of takes is edited—some story lines in our investigation are not included because they were cut short before becoming relevant on either the journalistic or ethnographic plane; multiple others were combined to avoid redundancy—but this narrative format highlights the splintered process of making news against the background of concerns over legality and security.

Take 1: The Hospital

I begin this Monday morning by going to the town's only public hospital, which carries the name of its former director, Marta Teodora Schwarz—an Argentine doctor whom the locals call the *"ángel de la selva"* (angel of the jungle). My objective is to find out whether there have been cases of women who, after delivery, did not want to keep their newborns and decided to give them into adoption. Ingeniero Raúl Zarza, who has been the director of Hospital Marta Schwarz since June 2009, when his predecessor, Doctor Roberto Arevalo, was elected to the town council, is standing at the reception window and, together with two assistants, registering patients. For months in 2010 and 2011, demanding higher wages, doctors and nurses participated in a strike, coordinated by the state workers union ATE (Asociación Trabajadores del Estado), officially in effect three out of five days of the week; therefore, on Mondays and Fridays, when the hospital was open to the public, the lines of patients, hoping to get appointments, seemed endless.

I wait for about half an hour until Zarza comes out to talk to me. He denies there have been any adoptions in the hospital. "All newborns receive *papel rosado* [pink paper] certifying that the baby was 'nacido vivo' [born alive], and all the women leave the institution with their own babies," he tells me. I ask whether he could repeat this information on the record, to which Zarza replies: "No problem." We agree to meet again early tomorrow morning.

When the following day Javier and I arrive at the hospital with our filming equipment, we see Zarza at the reception window. Despite the institution being on strike, there are patients who hope to be seen, and Zarza is talking to them. We wait, but he does not pay attention to us and does not come out to face the camera. About an hour later, tired of being ignored, we leave.

Take 2: The Activist

Marcelina Antúnez wanted to meet in a quiet, private place. "Find a location that cannot be easily identified," she warned me when we spoke over the phone. When we decided to film the interview in my temporary apartment in Villa Nueva, Marcelina specifically told me to make sure there were no pictures hanging on the walls. Javier and I were skeptical about taking such precautions: everybody in Iguazú knows that *Proximidad* is our independent production, and, if they wanted, it would not be difficult to track us down. But we listened to Marcelina's advice. When a car dropped her off in front of my house and as soon as she was inside, we locked the front doors.

Marcelina served as the director of the municipal program Luz de Infancia, which started back in 2004 under the auspices of the Ministry of Labor and Social Security, and was designed to help survivors of domestic violence and human trafficking. However, in July 2010, two months before our interview, the mayor of Iguazú refused to extend her contract. He cited financial difficulties as an excuse. Marcelina sent several press releases and spoke on the radio, reasoning that the program's four employees could not subsist on approximately 800 pesos (US$190) per month, but to no avail. When the mayor appointed a new person to lead the municipal program, Marcelina redirected her energy to the civil association Amigos del Programa Luz de Infancia (Friends of the Luz de Infancia Program). As other volunteers put it, she worked "in the empty spaces left by the official action." For months after being fired, Marcelina still held the keys to a white building on the corner of the block where the town's social service offices were located. Better known as "la casita de Marcelina" (Marcelina's cottage), it housed victims of sexual exploitation after their rescue from brothels in Buenos Aires or the Argentine South until they were ready to reintegrate into the community.

Seated on a chair in a small hallway, which also served as my living room, Marcelina thanks us for investigating "topics that society hides and keeps very well hidden."[21] In her hands she has a folder with documents of cases she has dealt with since Luz de Infancia was launched. "There are many cases of the *venta de bebes* [sale of children]. Rumors that in this area *se consigue* [you can get] spread mouth to mouth and people came," she said. "We have intervened in cases that involved very poor girls, brought from Paraguay, given accommodation in Puerto Iguazú, and for the duration of their pregnancy supported by the baby's future adoptive family [. . .]. But maintaining a pregnant woman with an intention to get her child is not legal." Although it is not impossible to make arrangements in the hospital, Marcelina explains that the girls usually give birth privately. At the civil registry, babies delivered at home can immediately obtain a national identity card with the adoptive parents' last names.

She talks about how widespread poverty perpetuates child trafficking in the province. A baby, according to Marcelina, costs between 70,000 and 100,000 pesos (US$16,000—23,800), a significant amount of money for a poor family struggling to get by. But not all the money goes to the mother. Marcelina says that it is a profitable business that starts with the people specialized in *localizar panzas* (finding bellies). "Then it begins. Maybe the pregnant girl does not want to give the baby up for adoption, but they exert continuous psychological pressure, so that she ends up agreeing." Marcelina emphasizes that *"gente de poder"* (powerful people) are involved in illegal adoptions in Iguazú: "These have to be professionals. Any common person would not be able to handle all the legal procedures involved in selling a baby." She recalls one case:

> We received a call from the criminal court asking us to look after a four-month old baby who was traveling with a nurse from Eldorado. The baby had all the visible characteristics of a boy, but the airport security personnel noticed that the documents belonged to a girl. So they began asking questions. The woman, rather elderly, became nervous. At first she said the baby was her daughter. Then she said it was her granddaughter. She was contradicting herself. So they checked the baby and confirmed that it was a boy. The documents were falsified. An investigation was opened and they left us in charge of the baby. [. . .] The strongest suspicion was that the baby was brought from Paraguay and was being taken to Buenos Aires. Since nobody claimed the child, a family in Eldorado adopted him. This is important: in all these cases nobody claims the children. Why? Because families get money.

Marcelina says there are many cases like this. She talks about another one in which five Paraguayan brothers and sisters were brought into Argentina across the Paraná by canoe. Their mother was disabled, and, before they were sold, the five siblings lived with their neighbors. When the court intervened and opened an investigation, nobody claimed the children, so they, too, were given up for adoption in Argentina. Marcelina suggests that in these situations no complaints are filed because people who sell their children do not want to confess to committing a crime. As a human rights activist with an unambiguous moral-legal agenda, she does not consider the possibility that biological parents do not want to or cannot look after their children. Instead of merely evading criminal prosecution, their reluctance to claim kids who are "rescued" from adoptive parents can be a sign that they view giving their offspring up for adoption—even through irregular channels, outside of the law—as an act of love. Though usually happening along the axis of extreme social inequality, transfer of care does not necessarily involve coercion. It can be a consensual agreement between biological and adoptive families, which moralizing and legalizing discourses of blame make into an issue of human rights and a domain for law enforcement.

Iguazú residents have relatives and friends *"en las dos orillas"* (on both banks of the river), in Brazil and in Paraguay, notes Marcelina. Used to moving back and forth, when they visit family across the river, they "don't consider it as crossing the border." This widespread practice and the mode of thinking that accompanies it are very conducive to child trafficking. Couples from Buenos Aires are lured to the tri-border area with promises that if nothing can be found in Misiones, there are many more options in Paraguay. But Marcelina also says that the efforts of human rights organizations such as the Red Trinacional de Combate a la Trata de Personas en la Triple Frontera (Trinational Network against Human Trafficking in the Triple Frontier), in which Luz de Infancia actively participates, have pushed the criminal business to change their modus operandi. "Home delivery," which means the pregnant girl accompanies the adoptive couple to Buenos Aires and delivers the baby there, is now their most popular tactic.

Marcelina blames the social conditions, further exacerbated by alcoholism, for making poor families susceptible to the idea of selling a child. "Asked whether they sold their children, people reply: 'No, no, I gave my child away to be raised by another woman because I couldn't.'" It is not clear whether this admission means that Marcelina, at least in part, justifies the actions of parents who have no resources to care for their children and thus give them up for adoption bypassing the legal route. A resident of Iguazú since the 1970s, Marcelina is well aware of the common practice of criadazgo. Many children in Misiones have been raised informally by their extended family or even neighbors: "When a girl goes to work to Buenos Aires, the child stays with the grandmother, or an aunt, or a cousin, or an elder sister. This is not adoption. There is nothing legal about it. Yet it is common. As long as there are no intermediaries profiting from it, it is better for the child to stay within the family," she reasons. Marcelina understands and justifies unofficial practices of sharing or transferring childcare, conditioned by the region's economic and social circumstances. But as a human rights activist she uses the uncompromising dichotomy between victims and perpetrators as the guiding principle in her work. From this legalist perspective, the determining factor between informal adoption and the sale of children is the presence of an intermediary who profits from arranging the exchange.

Take 3: The Courts

Like other government institutions in Iguazú, in the morning the courts are bustling with people who are looking for solutions to their legal problems in the universe of signatures, authorizations, hearings, rulings, appeals, and a web of fees and fines. When, after passing the line of residents waiting outside of the building, I enter the reception area of the *juzgado de paz* (justice of the peace), I hear the phrase that is already familiar to me: the judge is not available for an interview. But this time there is a hint of a change in the explanation repeatedly given to me by the excessively polite court receptionist: the judge is about to leave for a two-week vacation. Despite our persistent attempts to talk to the judge, we have not moved an inch closer. Javier and I agree that we can't postpone the program until she returns. After all, there is no guarantee the judge will be more inclined to talk to us after her vacation.

Our backup plan is the *juzgado civil, comercial, laboral, y de familia* (civil, commercial, labor, and family court), located only a few blocks up the street from the juzgado de paz. When we reach it, we find the reception area crowded and tense. I recognize resentment in peoples' faces: some argue and shout, demanding attention from the state, which appears to have turned away from their plights; others sit silent, giving in to occasional sobs or tears; some came with children; others are lonely. Lawyers rush past them to deliver documents, obtain stamps, and get paperwork pertinent to their cases. Here, too, we have no luck: the judge is "extremely busy," his assistant makes sure we understand.

We knock on another door, and the public defender's voice invites us to come in. Broadly smiling, he says he cannot talk to the press without an authorization. He asks us for a written questionnaire, which he wants to show to his superiors. But, he adds, he has little to do with adoptions. As the public defender, he says, he works on the cases of undocumented children, primarily those who are born at home and then have to be properly added to the civil registry. Since Marcelina said that home deliveries facilitate the sale of children, I am not convinced by his argument that his area of expertise is only vaguely related to our investigation. The public defender is also in charge of overseeing cases in which the guardianship of the child is granted to a family member of the biological parent. "These are the limits of my jurisdiction," he says and advises us to speak to the prosecutor.

One of the court secretaries comes in and leads us through the narrow corridors and up the stairs to the second floor of the labyrinthine building. There, formal and courteous, radiating self-confidence so characteristic of law professionals, the public prosecutor greets us in her office. We are offered two chairs in front of her desk. The prosecutor explains that recent modifications to the adoption law in Misiones allow biological parents to give their child to a couple of their own choosing. Her role as the public prosecutor is to supervise the process. But during a year and a half since the family court opened in Iguazú, enabling proceedings that used to be administered in Eldorado to be solved locally, she has had only three cases. She says that in the north of the province, unlike in Oberá and along Route 14, there have been no issues with irregular adoptions. In order to prevent a potential confrontation, Javier and I reassure the prosecutor that we are interested in the formal letter of the law—what it says, how it works, what requirements adoptive parents have to meet. We don't want to ruin our chance to get an interview by questioning her about illegal cases. But right at that moment the door opens and the public defender enters the office. He asks to have a word with the prosecutor, and she follows him outside. When she comes back in, the prosecutor requests us to provide a written questionnaire, which she needs in order to get authorization from her superiors, she says. We leave, promising to come back with the required paperwork.

Take 4: Luis

It is at least a half-an-hour walk from Villa Nueva, where I am renting a tiny one-bedroom apartment, to the C.V.I. television studio in Villa Alta. Having just left home, I am crossing Plaza San Martín, the town's central square, when a red car makes an abrupt stop next to me and a man, whom I don't recognize at first, calls my name. Cautiously I turn my head to face the driver, and I am relieved to see Luis.[22] He offers to give me a ride to the studio, which I gladly accept. This meeting is not a coincidence. I have been trying to get in touch with Luis for several days and have left him numerous messages on his voicemail, but he's ignored my calls. Maneuvering the traffic up the hill to Villa Alta, he explains why.

Luis and his wife have been trying to adopt a child for four years. Three times they were very close. But two of the women asked for money; and the third mother was a teenage orphan, which, they knew, meant the case was fraught with potential legal complications. Then they received a call from the hospital of Comandante Andresito informing them that there was a pregnant woman who wanted to give her child up for adoption. Sixty-five kilometers from Iguazú, Andresito is the youngest municipality in Misiones, where poverty is pervasive, and where, I heard people say, very low income women consider giving their babies up for adoption as the best solution for themselves and their children. It was already late evening when he answered the call, but Luis immediately drove to Andresito. He tells me they reached the hospital just in time: the woman was about to deliver the baby inside his car. Luis learned that the woman had eight children: one had died and the rest had all been adopted.

The boy now lives together with Luis and his wife in Iguazú, but every weekend they drive to Andresito to visit his biological mother. They bring her clothes and household items, but not money. "She never asked for money," he says. The legal adoption process is not over yet. They have to attend two court hearings before they can formally register the baby under their name. The judge set the first hearing for October, a month from now. Luis says he feels stuck: he is very happy, but he is anxious, too. Although the birth mother has never changed her mind about her other adoptions, she still has the right to do so. Following the judge's advice, Luis has deleted all photos of the baby from Facebook. He is reluctant to talk to the media until the adoption process is completed. Seeing my hesitation to step out of the car, now idling in front of the C.V.I. studio, Luis reassures me: "When it's all over, I'll pay you to do an interview with me. But not now."

Take 5: My Neighbor

While I am preparing coffee, my neighbor peeks through the window, left ajar to let in the fresh September morning air. She greets me and asks: "What is *Proximidad* investigating this week?" I tell her that we are working on a program about illegal adoptions and child trafficking. Nodding in agreement with the importance of the subject, my neighbor shares a story. Once when she was in Posadas with her husband and their two children, a couple from Buenos Aires approached them. Explaining that they had come to adopt a child and had paid 40,000 pesos (US$9,500), but that the biological mother backed out of the deal, the porteño couple asked my neighbor whether she and her husband would consider selling their blond and blue-eyed son. I know the boy very well: even when I don't see them, I hear him playing with his elder sister in the vicinity of the house. A smart, cheerful, and beautiful kid, he may be older, but he certainly fits the racial profile of what prospective parents look for. But then my neighbor tells me a story that

FIGURE 22. Children playing at the indigenous Guaraní community of Yriapú, July 2010.

contradicts the commonly held view that the sale of children only affects white children. She says that in the parking lot off Route 12 outside of Iguazú, where tour buses take visitors to buy souvenirs, her husband saw an indigenous Guaraní woman holding a newborn in her arms. "A car stopped, the woman got in the car, and then got out of the car without the baby," she recalls her husband's words.

Impressed by my neighbor's close encounters, I ask whether she could repeat these stories on the record. She instantly tightens up. "It is dangerous. The police would show up immediately and start to investigate." Reluctant to lose such opportunity, I try to reason with her. I explain that we could disguise her identity, leave her outside of the camera frame, even modify her voice. But my neighbor's determination is unwavering. "I don't want to meddle in this murky business," she says, and leaves.

Take 6: The Politician

The moment I step into the television studio, Claudio Alvarez, the CEO and major shareholder of the C.V.I. media company, calls me into his office. Between us, on the desk, I notice the newest issue of the provincial daily *El Territorio*. Its front page is dedicated to a story that "busca panzas" have found a way to avoid new, stricter, adoption laws in Misiones: months before giving birth, women from Posadas and Oberá change their residency to Santo Tomé, Corrientes. Since 2009, when the adoption law was modified, giving residents of the province absolute priority in the single registry of prospective adoptive parents in Misiones, as long as there are Misioneros on the list, couples from Buenos Aires, Córdoba, or other localities cannot become guardians of local children. The article quotes Sandra Montiel, who introduced the new law in the parliament, saying that the law "will reduce the 'renting of wombs' promoted by the intermediaries in the 'legal' circuit."[23] Yet women were bypassing this law by moving to the neighboring province, where it did not apply.

Alvarez, himself a former parliamentarian in Posadas, tells me that he participated in debates regarding this legislation. "Alto Uruguay will always be suspected as an area of high adoption rates," says the politician, citing deep poverty rates as the main cause of why some people decide to give their children into adoption: they think it is a way to make sure their offspring get a better education and other things, which biological parents would not be able to afford. Worried about not having enough material for our program, I complain that although people are telling me about their experiences with illegal adoptions, few agree to speak in front of the camera. The politician acknowledges my desperation and suggests that I interview him. On the record, Alvarez talks about the changes to the adoption law in Misiones and the debates that he, as a parliamentarian, participated in. He says there were concerns that children would be adopted for use in organ trafficking. He also explains the broader context of the adoption issue in Misiones: after what happened in Oberá a few years back, when the media secretly recorded a judge confessing to being an intermediary in the sale of children, adoption became a very complicated topic to address in public.

When we finish, he picks up the phone and calls a friend of his, Liliana Cuenca, who is in charge of the *registro de las personas* (civil registry) office in Iguazú.

Take 7: Liliana

Liliana is on sick leave because of recent surgery, but she promises Alvarez she will see me in her house in Santa Rosa. Santa Rosa is one of the outlying barrios, at the far outskirts of Iguazú, and Alvarez lends me his car with a driver so I can get there. Once we reach Santa Rosa, the driver hails someone on the street and asks where "the woman from registro" lives. We get a response and head straight to the house located on Block B. When standing at the gate I clap my hands—since few homes have doorbells, this is a standard signal to announce an arrival—the dogs in the yard begin barking loudly. I start to think we have the wrong address or that Liliana is not well, when a few long minutes later she comes to the window, sees me, and then goes to open the door. I follow her inside, where we sit down at a large wooden table in her living room. Liliana tells me I cannot film her because she is on leave, and she is not allowed to give official interviews from home. However, she has no problem if I use the voice recorder, which I turn on and put on the table between us.

Liliana explains that at birth in the hospital every child receives a document with an inscription "nacido vivo," or "born alive"; commonly called "papel rosado," the pink paper, it is the first official identification of the newborn. The baby is also added to the hospital's registry. However, if a woman delivers at home, she is required to go straight to the office of the civil registry to record the baby's birth. In the case of an adoption, the child's name in the registry is changed when this is so ordered by the judge. Liliana estimates that each year there are about ten plenary adoptions in Iguazú; she is not aware of any simple adoptions, in which the adopted child's ties with the birth family are not completely cut off. I thank her for the information and go back to the car.

Take 8: The Doctor

We return to the hospital, which is still on strike. At first we look for Ingeniero Zarza. We are told that the director is around, although nobody seems to be able to locate him—he is not in his office or at the reception desk. As we wait, somebody suggests that we might speak to the neurologist Silvia Osivka, the vice-director of the hospital. She greets us warmly, and when we explain that we are doing a program on child adoptions and that we would like to interview a representative of the hospital, she agrees. Osivka leads us to one of the empty examination rooms—because of the strike, the hospital staff only attend to emergencies, so few of the rooms are occupied—where we set up our equipment.

Comfortably facing the camera, the vice-director begins by explaining the administrative procedures that childbirth entails and then discusses the process of legal documentation in the hospital's registry. The birth certificate issued by the registry contains the mother's fingerprints, she notes. As we move on to discuss adoptions, Osivka says that extreme

FIGURE 23. Hospital Marta Teodora Schwarz. Puerto Iguazú, June 2010.

poverty and lack of education among young girls, often single mothers, are the main reasons why they give up their children for adoption. "They don't have the economic means to support their baby. We should carefully examine the social circumstances. Instead of judging, we should act on them," says Osivka. The doctor, who for many years lived in Canada and recently moved to Iguazú "to give more meaning to her work," says that, drawn by the mixture of nationalities in Misiones, people come from very far away to adopt local children. "Many people want kids with fair skin, light eyes, blond hair, so babies with traces of the Central and Eastern European immigrants in Misiones are attractive to them." During her rather short time working at Hospital Marta Schwarz, the vice-director does not recall any incident relating to the sale of children. Off the record, Osivka admits that the only confusing situation that she knows about happened when three women tried to register the same baby as theirs. The hospital personnel noticed that different women carried a baby, who was wearing the same clothes, and they intervened. However, Osivka explains that it was not an issue of child trafficking: the women were Paraguayans seeking to get Argentine citizenship. She is careful not to give out too many details about the occurrence because, she says, she's already run into troubles with the Paraguayan consul.

When we are done recording, Osivka offers to take us on a tour of the hospital. Because of the strike, the hallways are unusually empty, and we follow the vice-director to the labor and delivery section. She points to the new air-conditioning units, donated by the Duty Free Shop. As we go from room to room, one family in a maternity ward allows Javier to film their newborn. Then Osivka opens the door to another ward and greets a Guaraní girl who has recently delivered a baby, but we do not enter. The Guaraní community has requested separate maternity wards "to reduce interaction to a minimum," Osivka explains. Our tour ends when we reach the obstetrics and gynecology office. The doctor on guard today is named Sandra. She says she is not aware of any adoptions happening on the premises of the hospital. But, Sandra recalls, she once noticed that a woman tried to register her newborn in the name of another person. She explains that doctors are not allowed to ask patients for their identification and, thus, have to depend on their good will, in hopes they tell their real names. Yet, they are responsible for signing such important legal documents as birth certificates. Osivka nods and adds that the hospital registry can only later check their documents. I try to convince Sandra to speak on the record—her story of the woman who attempted to register her baby under somebody else's name is invaluable to our investigation—but she politely refuses. As I am gathering my thoughts on how to persuade her, Sandra rushes out of the office to assist in a delivery. No other OB/GYN doctor is available to talk to us: a few are absent because of the strike, one is on a work trip in Posadas; and when, after searching the entire hospital, we finally find the last one, he gives a short and definitive "no."

Take 9: The Judge

Almost a week has passed, but there is no news of authorizations from the court. We submitted the questionnaires and written requests for interviews, as instructed, but every time I go to inquire whether permissions have been granted, the court assistants tell me to come back in the afternoon; then the following morning; then the afternoon again; and so on. Today is not an exception. As I do every morning, in hopes of finally hearing some news, I start my day with a visit to the court, where I habitually take a seat in the waiting room. Apart from me, there are four other people—three women and one man—sitting in line next to the public defender's office. People in the waiting room pretend not to listen to the intimate dramas of their neighbors, but in the reception area all conversations are uncomfortably public.

After half an hour, as I am about to lose hope that anyone would pay attention to me, a man in a gray suit comes into the waiting room and asks to have a word with me. He invites me to follow him upstairs, opens the door to his office, and introduces himself, by name and rank. Before I have a chance to say anything, the judge begins by praising *Proximidad:* in the context of the "rudimentary journalism" in Iguazú, it is "a very good production." I listen intently, unsure where the conversation is going next. After this formal and courteous prologue the judge transitions to the question of adoptions. He says that the superior court in Posadas has ordered them not to talk to journalists. Although the scandalous illegal adoptions that were exposed in the media did happen in Oberá and along Route 14, the judge says he has to be careful about what he says in Iguazú. Stunned by this unexpected meeting, I do not dare to interrupt his monologue, and the judge goes on to say that the birth mother's right to select adoptive parents for the child is "a gray zone" of the law. So much so that in several adoption cases that fell under the jurisdiction of the Iguazú court, instead of signing the paperwork himself, the judge asked for the authorization from Eldorado. "In order to avoid trouble," he explains. In front of me, the judge goes through the motion of washing his hands, showing he has no intention of getting involved in complicated legal matters. Before letting me leave, he warns that this information is to be kept strictly between the two of us. I am not allowed to comment on anything he has told me on television. The judge assures me that his assistant will provide written answers to my questions.

She never does. The public defender and the public prosecutor, through their assistants, also decline to participate in the program.

Take 10: The Lawyer

Juan Carlos Nabac is one of the longest practicing lawyers in Iguazú. His office is in a prestigious part of town. Considering how difficult it was to recruit people for the program, I was surprised when he agreed to an interview. Javier and I wait in the lobby for about half an hour, listening to the heavy rain outside and observing the receptionist flipping through the day's papers, until the lawyer invites us to come into his spacious office. Nabac addresses us from behind a thick wooden desk. He is nervous, and does not hide it. We set up the equipment, ready to begin, but Nabac is anxiously moving back and forth in the leather chair, and Javier has to readjust the wireless microphone, which has fallen off his shirt. When he gathers himself, the lawyer begins: "Adoption is a *tema tabú* [taboo topic] in Misiones." He notes the significance of the institution and, like Jorgelina did when we spoke about the issue months ago, he goes on to explain it in terms of supply and demand: "Everyday we see kids who don't have the possibility to grow up, to have a decent life, and we see people who, for different reasons, are not able to have children."

Nabac says that people often get confused between the cultural and the legal, judicially sanctioned, aspects of the practice. "There is a bureaucratic process, which must be followed in order to give legality and legitimacy to an adoption," he explains. In his opinion, bureaucracy is necessary to ensure the seriousness of the procedure, but Nabac observes that requirements for couples who want to adopt a child are very strict. They have to be signed up with the Single Registry of Prospective Adoptive Parents for Misiones (RUAAM, Registro Único de Aspirantes a Adopción de Misiones), and undergo checks for criminal background, housing conditions, physical and psychological health, and economic situation, among other things. The lawyer emphasizes that such an exhaustive investigation is indispensable to ensure that in the adoptive family the child will have better living conditions than those provided by the biological parents. Although since 2009, when changes to the law were made, priority in RUAMM has been given to families from Misiones, according to Nabac, as long as the judge sanctions it, couples from other localities are not prohibited from applying for adoption in the province. He explains that the legal adoption process consists of two parts: the first court order grants guardianship for six months; the second court order completes the adoption. Only then does the civil registry issue the child a new D.N.I., the national identity document, with the adoptive parents' last name.

Nabac shows us photographs of several families with children he helped them adopt. There is a tone of pride in his voice when he says they become an integral part of their new homes. But, Nabac acknowledges, there are very few situations that meet all the legal conditions required for an adoption. Couples who want to adopt far outnumber available children. Once listed in RUAAM, they have to wait a long time. "As the old saying goes, *la espera desespera* [waiting makes you desperate]," quips the lawyer. Illegal adoption, he says, happens when the child's identity is changed without following the court process. He gives an example: "A couple X comes to adopt a child; they do not go to the court; instead they go to the civil registry and substitute the identity of the father." Yet Nabac says that Iguazúenses have long adopted children by circumventing the legal process. There are many cases where families have raised orphan nephews or grandchildren, or sheltered their neighbors' kids. The practice of criadazgo may not have the stamp of the law sanctioning it, but, like many other Iguazúenses, the lawyer, too, sees it as socially legitimate.

As we are preparing to leave, thanking Nabac for his time, he tells us to visit a woman whom he refers to as "Señora Alvarez." "You will see how adoptions in Iguazú really work," he says, without explaining more.

Take 11: Señora Alvarez

The block on Misiones Avenue down the hill from the main Iguazú bus terminal is known as 73 Viviendas. A maze of block buildings and identical apartments reminds me of Soviet architecture. Nabac did not tell us Alvarez's apartment number, so I start looking around for residents who might tell us where to go. But the yard in between the buildings is empty. I walk in circles, examining balconies and stairways, until I see a woman on the second floor and greet her. She descends and tells us she recognizes me from television. Fortunately for us, she happens to be a good friend of Señora Alvarez's, so Javier and I follow her to a clean, humble first-floor apartment. We find Señora Alvarez sitting in bed, in white underwear. "She has difficulty walking," says the woman who brought us here. At first Señora Alvarez ignores us, acting as if she is not aware of our presence. I notice that Javier is uncomfortable in this situation. Approaching Señora Alvarez, I explain that we are from *Proximidad* and that we want to talk about her adopted children. She agrees. When I begin looking around for a better place to do the interview, she insists we film her where she is, in bed, in her underwear. Javier turns on the camera.

Drifting away from my questions about adoptions, Señora Alvarez talks about the misfortunes she has faced during her difficult life. She complains about her poor health and then expresses gratefulness for still being alive. She is a person of faith, she repeats several times, and throughout her now waning life she has helped a lot of children. Señora Alvarez recalls how once a young woman stopped at her door, explained that she had gotten a new job in the city and could not travel with the baby, and left the child. The mother never came back, so the child grew up with Señora Alvarez. One of the other girls she adopted is now sleeping in the next room, she says. "She works night shifts, so she rests during the day." Two more girls are away; one of them is married and lives in Buenos Aires. Señora Alvarez also has an adopted son. The woman who showed us into the apartment says that he comes home with his friends and uses drugs inside. He has robbed Señora Alvarez to buy drugs, and he has beaten her. He is the only one who has her last name. All the other children have never been legally adopted. Señora Alvarez raised them without ever following the legal procedures and without changing their identity. But the children don't care about their adoptive mother, the women tell us. They never help around the house.

As Señora Alvarez continues talking, revisiting the same points, her stories permeated with sadness, Javier is getting increasingly uneasy. He turns the camera off and on again; he complains about poor lighting in the room. Seeing his dissatisfaction with the situation, I suggest we end the interview. We do it abruptly, telling the women that we will come back for a longer conversation. Then we collect our equipment and leave in a hurry. There was something very uncomfortable about being in the small room with Señora Alvarez, seeing her suffering through the lens of the camera. After all our attempts to find people who wanted to talk about their experiences on the record, we were finally facing the social reality of adoptions. But it turned out to be more painful and more difficult to comprehend compared to everything we had heard from human rights activists, lawyers, doctors, politicians, and bureaucrats. These professionals used the binary grammar of legal versus illegal, right versus wrong, even while they underscored the existence of the vast and murky in-between. At Señora Alvarez's apartment we found ourselves in the middle of this messy space of moral and legal ambiguity, where biological parents leave their children at the doorstep of their neighbors', where adopted kids turn against their caregivers, where legal ties and affectionate family relations scantily overlap. I felt frustration and helplessness realizing that the camera could not adequately capture the nuances of this social reality without establishing moral and legal categories that would distort it.

In the Editing Room

Proximidad was a weekly program, broadcast every Tuesday after the evening news; we could not afford to spend any more time on this topic. It had already been over two weeks since we began investigating child adoptions, and we had to start preparing the next episode. We decided to work with the material that we had. It was my job to browse through the footage and select what would be included and in what order. The main building blocks of the program were the interviews we conducted during the investigation, which were held together by my comments. This time I knew that my input was going to be more important than it had in previous episodes; in order to fill in the large gaps left between what the interviewees told us, I would need to summarize what we learned off the record. The best material we had were the videos with Marcelina Antunez, the former director of the Luz de Infancia program; Silvia Osivka, the neurologist and vice-director of Hospital Marta Schwarz; and Juan Carlos Nabac, the lawyer. The comments made by Claudio Alvarez, parliamentarian and the major shareholder of C.V.I., the footage of Señora Alvarez, and the poor-quality voice recording of my conversation with Liliana Cuenca from the registry office were less helpful for making a good media story.

But the biggest problem was that we could not use any accounts of the close encounters with illegal adoptions: Sandra's—about how she saw a woman at the hospital trying to register her newborn in another person's name; Luis's—about his attempts to adopt a baby, including two situations in which birth mothers asked for money, and the current attempt, still under way; my neighbor's—about a porteño couple offering her money in exchange for her son. We also didn't have anything from the courts, not even official statistics. The public defender, the public prosecutor, and the judge had all refused to participate in the program, and even though they met with us and shared some relevant information, we were not authorized to use any of it in the program. Hence, the challenge was how to put the words of Marcelina, Osivka, and Nabac together to build tension and foreground the missing parts of the story, where necessary, teasing them out through my commentaries.

I had to address the question of why, facing a problem that lacks consensus with regard to its legality and legitimacy, the community preferred silence to public discussion. Maintaining objective tone and avoiding moralization or judgment was essential, but I wanted to leave a hint of frustration with this investigation because that was the key to the story. The off-screen commentary did not have all five Ws of journalism—who, what, when, where, why; it lacked names of people and places. Instead, my concise narrative interventions focused on where we had failed to elicit local voices—the long waiting and the closed doors of the courts, the problematic position of doctors who cannot check their patients' identity documents, the insecurity of the town's residents, who refuse to talk publicly about what they know and what they see to avoid being entangled in police investigations and followed by the media. The point was less to reveal the hidden facts than to draw attention to public silence. The program was constructed as a question rather than an answer.

When the outline was ready, I gave the footage and my commentaries to Javier, who put the episode together. It was aired on October 5, 2010. Unfortunately, it was the same week as the Latin American Studies Association meeting in Toronto, where I was presenting a paper and organizing a panel on media and power in the Latin American public sphere, so I was not in Iguazú to hear people's immediate reactions to the program. However, unlike with all previous episodes—on mandatory military service, same-sex marriages, or municipal waste recycling—the following morning after the program on illegal adoptions was broadcast, there was not a mention of it in the other media. When about a week later I came back to Iguazú, expecting to hear criticism, but also hoping for some acknowledgment for addressing a complicated issue, I was soon disappointed. The episode did not seem to have any repercussions among the town's residents: positive or negative. Nobody mentioned anything to me and I was hesitant to ask. Despite our attempts to break the code of silence, irregular adoptions and the sale of children remained a "tema tabú" in Iguazú, a subject that was not to be publicly exposed, even as it continued in practice.

FINAL NOTES ON ADOPTIONS

According to data compiled by the United Nations and published in the *Global Report on Trafficking in Persons,* between 2007 and 2010 in Latin America 1,600 children were victims of human trafficking, accounting for about 27 percent of the trafficking in the region.[24] The majority of trafficking victims, both adult and child, were females. Child trafficking was more prominent in Central America and the northern part of South America compared to the Southern Cone countries, including Argentina, where the share of victims who were children was slightly under 20 percent. The most frequently reported were cases of trafficking for reasons of sexual exploitation. Although the document mentions "cases of trafficking for illegal adoption and selling of babies," particularly in the Andean countries, these are not discussed in any detail.

A footnote explains that "illegal adoption is to be considered as a purpose of trafficking where this amounts to a practice similar to slavery as defined in the Supplementary Convention on the Abolition of Slavery, the Slave Trade and Institutions and Practices Similar to Slavery." Most of informal adoption practices and the sale of children in Misiones discussed in this chapter—performed with consent of biological families, who weigh their limited resources against the best outcomes for their kids—would not be considered cases of trafficking: many adoptive babies receive care and affection from their new parents and are not forced to work under exploitative conditions. In comparison, the Inter-American Convention on International Traffic in Minors, to which Argentina also adheres, has a broader definition of illegal adoptions in which the legality of the means is equally important to that of the ends. We need to recognize the existence of such divergences in the legal categories, just as we must be cautious with official statistical data regarding the number of trafficking victims. But we cannot ignore the effects that these concerns with global organized crime and human rights violations have when they are applied in particular social and economic contexts. Governments, in conjunction with the mainstream media, eagerly deploy the grammar of international law and the vocabulary of criminal threats in ways that have mixed consequences for communities targeted by these discourses.

This ethnographic story of a journalistic investigation into illegal adoptions shows the fissures between the official definitions of child trafficking, Argentina's rigid adoption laws, and the informal fosterage practices that are common and legitimate in Misiones. The disjuncture between multiple legal and moral regimes points to the difficulty in reconciling universalizing discourses of crime and people's experiences of security on the local level. The government's concern with alarmist media allegations about widespread child trafficking on Argentina's borders resulted in tighter control over adoption processes, which had negative effects on the very people it was aimed at protecting: mothers who were giving their children into adoption because they could not afford to raise them were often suspected—by their neighbors, by the media—of seeking profits and, thus, were further marginalized; law professionals, anxious about potential accusations of promoting and legally mediating the sale of children, slowed down or put adoption processes to a halt; and families who were looking to adopt children were subjected to lengthy and complicated legal and bureaucratic procedures that disillusioned them and pushed the most desperate to resort to illegal routes of adoption.

Although some legislative initiatives in Misiones, primarily financial support for mothers living in poverty, helped alleviate the social conditions that enable the sale of children and child trafficking, other government interventions had mixed results. For example, in some situations, updated adoption laws aimed at reducing the opportunities of illegal intermediaries paradoxically had an opposite effect. "La espera desespera," said the lawyer during the filming of the television program, concerned that long waiting times can lead some families to look for faster routes to adopt. Drastically reduced numbers of couples listed in the Misiones registry of adoptions added to suspicions that instead of preventing the problem, state intervention might have exacerbated it. Rather than helping those whose precarious social conditions made the sale of children possible, new adoption laws only further increased their legal insecurity. Under the circumstances, Iguazúenses were reluctant to discuss the question of adoptions in the public realm. Their experiences had taught them that addressing this contentious issue may give more incentive for the government to reinforce the loop of criminalization, regulation, and enforcement, which—through more media exposure, police investigations, and legal restrictions—had already produced negative effects for their community.

Of all the programs we made for *Proximidad,* the one on illegal adoptions caused the least reaction from Iguazúenses. While other episodes opened up the public sphere and facilitated conversations about neglected topics, our attempts to break the code of silence regarding irregular adoptions and child trafficking failed. Nevertheless, the story of probing a tema tabú is important in and of itself—it shows the predicament of the media in situations where concerns about legality, publicity, and security are at odds. People's refusals to go on the record, as documented in various "takes" we did for the program, reveal their distrust of public exposure. To them, the visibility provided by the media had the potential of drawing attention from law enforcement: my neighbor was afraid that if she shared her story about an encounter with the couple from Buenos Aires, the police would open an investigation, dragging her into a long and complicated legal process; Luis was concerned that his adoption case might be denied if the biological mother changed her mind, which media interest in the case could precipitate; court officials were wary of interacting with journalists after what had happened to their colleague in another part of the province, where journalistic investigation resulted in the suspension of a judge. In terms of maintaining the status quo, invisibility, which they all chose, was a guarantor of security.

Iguazú residents acknowledged the existence of the problem—the gap between poverty and law, the discrepancy between crime and informal legitimate practices—that contributed to the sale of children and child trafficking; however, they did not want to bear the consequences of being the whistleblowers. This tactical choice of invisibility, which was so evident in the production of the television program, is not limited to the question of adoptions, but extends to other legally ambiguous economic exchanges, such as contraband of food and electronics across the borders, which I described in the previous chapter. Where the boundary between the law and informal practices is contested in terms of legitimacy, for the local people, the benefits of obscuring it outweigh the importance of its public exposure in the media.

ETHICS AND THE POLITICS OF REPRESENTATION

This chapter has wound along the blurry boundary separating journalism from ethnography. Where the media narrative, unraveling on the ambiguous terrain between law and crime, could not proceed, anthropology proved to be uniquely equipped to tell the remainder of the story. Journalistic accounts are generally limited to sources that agree to go on the public record, whereas ethnographic writing is premised on a standard of protected identities. While the television program on illegal adoptions included several interviews—with the vice-director of the hospital, the lawyer, and the former municipal employee—the rest of the failed "takes" could not be made public. They were not useful for telling a media story. In contrast, in this ethnographic account, disguising the identity of people encountered during the investigation, I could show the negotiations and insecurities behind the scenes of news production and explain people's concerns with drawing a line between public secret and public knowledge.

Depending on the circumstances, the boundary between ethnography and journalism can be thin. Both professions entail interacting with the social world in order to gather information and then share it with wider audiences. Although there are slight differences in methodology and the temporality of ethnographic and journalistic storytelling (see chapter 1), it is equally important to distinguish their divergent ethics and politics of representation. During the making of the television program, the boundary between media reporting and anthropological research was established and tested in my encounters with Iguazúenses, which took place on unstable grounds, making each of us constantly negotiate trust and security. The town's residents and government officials had to evaluate my roles as a scholar and a journalist, deciding how much information to share with me: public exposure of a common informal practice—one that was illegal and lacked social consensus regarding its legitimacy—was considered to be a threat to the status quo of the community, concerned about potential police and legal investigations, which made people reluctant to speak on the record. Anthropological research, by contrast, was based on creating long-term relationships of accountability, and elicited more confidence from Iguazúenses.

Simultaneously producing two stories—one journalistic and one ethnographic—I had to judge what information could go into either one. My responsibility as an anthropologist was to protect the people who had shared their knowledge with me, and I was committed to giving back to the community. *Proximidad,* as a collaborative research project, accomplished my objectives on two levels: as a journalistic narrative, the program encouraged public discussion of complex local scenarios, even if in the case of illegal adoptions, with limited success; as an ethnographic story included in this book, the making of that *Proximidad* episode demonstrates the deeper social tensions over economic and legal insecurity in Misiones, which need to be addressed in order to improve the policies aimed at preventing child trafficking and the sale of children.

It is not easy to capture this legally murky social reality on camera. Most often, drawing on their previous experiences of the state, people are wary of being filmed engaging in or talking about outlawed practices. But even on those rare occasions when they agree to go on the record, as was the case with Señora Alvarez, the media proves incapable of grasping the nuances of their life stories. Too often journalists, like their sources, fall back on the dichotomous vocabulary that juxtaposes morality with impropriety and law with illegality, contesting legitimacy of practices that are in between. In their representations, some tones and inconsistencies are lost in the interest of telling a coherent story, uncovering hidden truth, or sketching a narrative that has the potential of leading to action and transforming the conditions that give rise to social problems addressed by the media.

But it is just as difficult to write about illegal practices that are intertwined with economic insecurities in an ethnographic book. Anthropologists cannot escape from questions about the politics of representation. Portraying people who take part in informal activities and justifying their defiance of state laws in an authoritative voice of social science, which is backed by direct experience during field research, risks contributing to the discourse of criminalization that results in further marginalization and securitization of those we work with. Alternatively, editing and censoring our ethnographic narratives to remove parts that fit uncomfortably with the positive image of the community that we consciously align with takes us dangerously close to propaganda, which not only compromises the efforts of conducing fair research, but has no real benefits to the community. Throughout this book I have sought to explain why certain illegalized activities persist as socially legitimate by situating them within the broader historical and political context of distorted state presence, economic inequality, and the common sense of living on the border. I have also carefully disguised the individual identities of people who shared their experiences with me in order to protect them from possible interrogation by law enforcement and the mainstream press. An ethnographic account allows for the time and space to address the nuances of social reality lived across the terrain of il/legality, and thus it is less likely than media stories to be co-opted and used by the security apparatus.

As happened to other texts that I described in earlier chapters, parts of this book may be misappropriated and reinterpreted within the framework of the national or global security regime. However, I anticipate that instead of becoming another piece of the puzzle, this ethnographic narrative will help deconstruct discourses and practices of securitization targeting the tri-border area. The risk of the text being used against the intentions of its author fades against the risk of leaving illegalized activities in the ethnographic blindspot and thereby participating in complicity with political structures and powerful actors that perpetuate conditions of insecurity under which Iguazúenses live. The background story of the television episode told in this chapter juxtaposed information that circulates *on the record* and knowledge that remains *off the record,* which required exposing illegal practices that people refuse to publicly address. But it did so in order to explain how public secrecy is enforced by powerful structures of the security regime that thrive on restrictive government policies and laws and that draw from criminalizing discourses of the mass media.

Conclusion

Ethnography of In/visibility

Ultimately, what I believe defines an intellectual as a social
actor is less a specific inheritance or social positionality, less
a functional position in a division of labor, and less a
formalized set of competences than a particular orientation
to, and consciousness of, knowledge.

—Dominic Boyer, *Spirit and System*

Four years have passed since I left Puerto Iguazú. I have stayed in touch
with the people whose lives make up the fabric of *Savage Frontier*—
Kelly, Silvia, Jorgelina, Horacio, Javier, Yanina, Mario, Andrés, Mariquita, and others—and in 2014 I returned to the field to visit them. Most
of the journalists that I met in the tri-border region between 2008 and
2011 still work for the local media, though several have since quit and
moved away. For those who remain, little, if anything, has changed.
Their concerns with the negative effects of the discourses of lawlessness
and danger on the border, coupled with their responsibility and interests
in protecting the informal economy and promoting the image of their
hometown as a safe place, still motivate their editorial decisions about
newsworthiness of local events. In Iguazú news-making continues to be
intricately related to security-making. An important goal of this book has
been to show that people interpret security in specific contexts of their
daily lives, where it acquires meanings and consequences that are different from its global and national forms. Which events in the tri-border
area become news depends on multiple deflections of security discourse,
translated between scales, and on the lived experiences of its effects.

Savage Frontier is written across fissures. I first noticed these fissures
in the change of tone during interviews that journalists conducted with

officials in the security forces; in the pause and transition—sometimes signaled, other times implied—between the limited information provided *on the record* and details and qualifications added *off the record*. These fissures mark the difference between public knowledge and public secret. They are invoked by the slash of the in/formal and il/legal, asserting the interdependence of the two parts of the economy, one authorized by the state, another—at least publicly, outlawed. Fissures are spaces of choice. During interactions between the media and the fuerzas, news and security are entangled in the split of in/visibility. In *Savage Frontier* a fissure also runs through the permeable boundary between ethnography and journalism. Because fissures are situational, those who maneuver across the fractured social terrain rely on local knowledge and the guidance of experience. Slippages can cause misunderstandings and confrontations.

"You came looking for danger on the border, but what did you really find?" journalists in Iguazú repeatedly asked me. Whether I was in a radio studio observing the production of the morning news show or I arrived for interviews with media directors and program hosts, they used my presence as an opportunity to invert our relationship. Without a prior warning, from behind the scenes I was suddenly put on the front stage, speaking live on air. They introduced me as a Lithuanian anthropologist from the United States who came to study the tri-border region. Then they would inquire: "What do you think about Puerto Iguazú and the Triple Frontier? Are the stories true?" The first time I was caught unprepared, so I justified my lack of knowledge by admitting that those were the very questions I sought to answer. But soon I began to accept these spontaneous interviews for what they were: a public performance. Each time I responded the same way: drawn by sensational narratives about this border area—a reported haven for traffickers—what I found instead was a peaceful, hardworking community. Nobody challenged this formulaic answer, despite their awareness that this was only a partial truth.

Before I ever set foot in the region where Argentina, Brazil, and Paraguay meet, it caught my attention as a highly mediated place. Articles published by the international press focused on the porosity of its borders: the ease of crossing them without legal documentation, the thriving market of pirated commodities, and alleged links between local commerce and the financing of terrorism. Iguazú Falls, decorating tourist brochures and featured in weekend travel supplements of the mainstream Argentine press, looked like a precious façade covering up informal and illegal transactions. In communicative cartographies, produced and circulated by the global and national media, the tri-border region was assigned a specific role—that of a violent, lawless frontier. Threats on this allegedly permeable Argentine border ranged from foreign cultural influences to mosquito-borne tropical diseases to organized crime. In the beginning my research was motivated by the absence of these stories in the local press. Iguazú journalists, who had a seemingly contradictory role of being residents in a community where illegalized practices were common, and also cultural producers, their vocation predicated on publishing news about life on the border, presented a curious ethnographic case.

With the image of the savage frontier impressed on me by the media, I was surprised by what I saw when I first arrived in Iguazú. I found a small town surrounded by lush green jungle, situated at the intersection of two rivers that separate Argentina from Brazil, to the north, and Paraguay, to the west. There were numerous souvenir shops, restaurants, and hostels catering to tourists, even though most of the million-plus visitors who come each year to see the waterfalls never make a stop downtown, their route leading straight from the airport to the national park. There were also small convenience stores selling local and imported products, from food to clothes to home appliances, frequented by Iguazúenses, many of whom earned their living by providing services to tourists. In addition to legal businesses, there were shops known for selling smuggled goods. Large storehouses were reminiscent of the era when Iguazú played a significant role in transnational commerce. Today, trucks carrying merchandise in and out of the country rarely stop in this town. Pointing to abandoned storehouses, residents recall the golden years of cross-border trade, and blame Menem's neoliberal policies of the 1990s for the irreversible damage to the local economy.

But these visibilities were complemented by invisibilities. What I did not see in Iguazú was as important as what I saw. Despite reported danger on the border, I did not see the police and armed forces patrolling the streets. There were no private security guards, no gated communities, no grates on windows. Often, residents would not bother locking their doors at night. I did not hear people complaining about crime. Instead, they told me that safety was the main attribute of this place. "When they talk about the Triple Frontier, they talk about traffickers of drugs, of arms, of children. [. . .] But I live in Iguazú and I see that people here are peaceful. I don't see armed traffickers around the corner, as they imagine. They think that here, in Iguazú, we live in trenches," Jorgelina once said to me. Rather than indicating the absence of the informal economy of illegalized commodities or its end, this tranquility was a sign that convivencia was an integral part of everyday life on the border. As such, it was not newsworthy. The persisting legitimacy of practices that had been criminalized by changing governmental policies was a public secret, shared by the town's residents, its media, and even the security forces; and it was protected by the law of silence.

Iguazúenses remember with pride how in the late 1990s the entire community united to protest against new trade regulations on the border. Back then the government wanted to impose customs taxes on *bicicleteros*— later they changed their bicycles for motor scooters and became known as *motoqueros*—a humble sector of workers who lived from reselling goods that they were bringing from Brazil. When in opposition to government plans Iguazúenses blocked the international bridge, the gendarmerie unit in Iguazú received orders to break up the blockade on the national route. "The gendarmes came and looked at us: how could they suppress the protest? They were our neighbors," remembered Silvia. Since the local commander refused to intervene, the government dispatched gendarmes from Corrientes. Residents recall how the late bishop of Iguazú, Joaquín Piña, a highly respected public figure, was the first to pick up a stick in his hand and stand in front of the people, facing the armed forces. Iguazúenses united to protect their way of life, which was threatened by detached policies made in Buenos Aires. Theirs was the common sense of the border.

"There are two Iguazú," one journalist said, picking up on a cliché to mark another fissure as we were talking shortly after I arrived in Argentina. "There is the Iguazú of the five-star hotels and then there is that other Iguazú, where children don't go to school and where many have not even seen the famous waterfalls." Throughout my fieldwork, I observed how journalists mediate between these two interdependent sides of Iguazú, easily trespassing social barriers to weave news stories from multiple voices in the community. Often, their narratives are ordinary, focusing on the minute details of everyday life: a school anniversary, a textile workshop for women, a new medical procedure available at the hospital. These small foci of grassroots state-building make up the largest share of local media content. Journalists also use the news to mediate the historically entrenched political and economic gap between Iguazú and the rest of the country. Confronted by the narrative of the frontera caliente, they are tasked with mitigating the criminalization of the area. They translate discourses of global and national security defining the Triple Frontier as a threat, and reconstitute security as a valid concern in the local context. In this endeavor, they make news *tactically*—by reporting on some but not other events in order to represent the border as secure; and *performatively*—by preventing further state intervention and anticipating positive social effects of selective news-making.

It was through a combination of ethnographic research and my own, at times frustrating, experiences of engaging in collaborative media production that I learned why issues that the frontera caliente discourse focuses on—particularly drug trafficking, human trafficking, contraband, and corruption—scarcely appeared in the local news. On the one hand, media institutions in Iguazú are weak: journalists lack professional training, while the small private companies they work for do not have sufficient resources. Struggling to produce multiple news stories every day, reporters have no time to pursue thorough investigations. On the other hand, often the media does not want to focus on illegal activities. Living in Iguazú, I saw how embeddedness in the local community, rather than being a resource, was an obstacle to discussing certain matters. In what Horacio called "pueblo chico, infierno grande," people were constrained by the rules of convivencia and complicity. For them, legality and legitimacy did not neatly correspond: resentful of the Argentine government, which has neglected the region and treated it as a backward corner of the state, people were complicit in justifying and engaging in illegalized economic exchanges. In this context, social intimacy ensured that the public secret remained *off the record*. As increased flows of tourists began bringing more opportunities to Iguazú, the media filtered negative news ever more rigorously, safety becoming the main emphasis in their narrative about the tri-border region.

Due to their ability to move stories from the domain of invisibility to that of visibility, from *off the record* to *on the record*, journalists occupy a unique position in the community. Like other residents, they participate in the informal market of illegalized commodities and are supportive of keeping it officially illegible. Yet their vocation is predicated on visibility, and, provided they wanted to, they could use the media to expose unlawful practices. This vulnerability that journalists present to the local status quo becomes evident when their relation to the media serves as a motive for denying them access to the informal economy. Usually, the perception of the journalist as a traitor and a threat to the community's way of life is directed at correspondents from the national media, who, in search of scandalous stories, come to "muddy the playing field." Iguazú journalists are unlikely to challenge the law of silence and reveal public secrets: first, because an exposure of law violations that are common and legitimate would imply tearing apart the social consensus, and second, because anonymity in the local press is nearly impossible. Mishandling knowledge would be both morally problematic and personally dangerous.

Still, suspicion persists. A journalist once told me how her profession had become an obstacle to partaking in an illegalized practice. When her car broke down, she wanted to take it to a mechanic in Foz do Iguaçu where both the spare parts and the repair service were comparatively cheaper. Although the law does not allow Iguazúenses to tow their vehicles to Brazil, there were rumors that for a bribe of 5,000 Argentine pesos (at the time corresponding to approximately US$1,400), these regulations could be overlooked. But the authorities on the border checkpoint were reluctant to accept a bribe from a journalist, fearing it was a setup. Concern about potential exposure in the media threatened to undermine the relationship of mutual dependence and trust established between the community and the government structures on the border. It was a standoff: both sides knew the informal protocol, but the journalist did not want to give a bribe, which was very high considering her income, while the officers on the bridge did not want to accept it. Unsure what else to do, this journalist talked to a higher ranking official, telling him that she knew about the existence of widespread irregularities on the border and she was aware that she had to give a bribe and to whom, but that nobody wanted to accept it. When she openly asked him for advice on what to do, to resolve the impasse the official gave her formal permission to take the vehicle to Brazil.

Reporting on crime and law enforcement pushes journalists to the frontlines of state efforts at security-making, where neither side completely trusts the other. The fuerzas eagerly share information about their activities, especially the capture of illegalized drugs, and the media willingly circulate this news to the public. Such cooperation is the symbolic performance of effective border control and contributes to the security agenda of the Argentine government. However, Iguazú journalists also obey and maintain the boundary between visible and invisible practices. They avoid covering organized crime and they look away from corruption in the fuerzas. They criticize the narrative of the frontera caliente, deliberately portraying Iguazú as a secure place. Concerned with their own safety and invested in mitigating economic precariousness in a remote, neglected region, dependent on the flow of tourists, they are using news-making as a tool in making security.

In a talk he gave at a university in Misiones, Andrés Colman Gutiérrez said that "those who are doing investigative journalism do it because they are passionate about working on a difficult terrain, [. . .] at times putting their own security or life in danger. [. . .] It is the type of journalism that wants to bring to the surface something hidden, something that the powers want to maintain hidden."[1] In Paraguay, employed by strong media organizations, professional journalists like Andrés are able to take on such in-depth investigations. Across the border, in Iguazú, they are hardly possible. Where crime is largely a function of unjust state policies, and as long as it does not threaten the town's residents, local common sense protects it from exposure in the media. Advantages of invisibility and illegibility of the informal economy are considered to outweigh the benefits of sensational news stories about smuggling and corruption, as the latter would only legitimate further ineffective government interventions. Tactical use of the media is a form of making security on the local scale, where its meanings and consequences are deflected from national and global security paradigms.

Only recently have residents in Iguazú become more concerned with urban insecurity. In 2014 a former reporter recounted her confusion when two visitors asked her for directions to get from the town's center to the border landmark. When she explained the itinerary, the visitors inquired: "Is it a safe walk?" The journalist paused. She did not want to lie, so she said that she did not know. "To my surprise, I realized that I never reflected on my usual response, 'go without worries, Iguazú is very safe'; it may be changing." Initially, rising crime was explained as an import of the urban form of delinquency. According to this inverted geography of blame, Buenos Aires and other cities were more dangerous when compared to Iguazú. This reasoning aligned with the local determination to counteract criminalization and securitization of the border town. It was also supported by personal experiences: journalists, who have encountered assaults and break-ins while living in metropolitan areas, saw security to be a resource found in Iguazú.

But if crime continues to rise, it may become more difficult for journalists to maintain the boundary between public stories and silenced local knowledge, which they use to challenge the narrative of the savage frontier. Urban crime is a different type of threat to the community and to the regional tourism economy: thefts and assaults, when compared to drug trafficking and contraband, directly affect common people, both locals and visitors. In this situation, the media will have to reconsider how to use the news to acknowledge concerns with citizen security, all the while remaining critical of global and national agendas targeting other threats conjured up in the border region. In this book I have laid the groundwork for understanding how, embedded in their communities, local journalists negotiate the boundary between events newsworthy of crime stories and violations of the law, which are seen as legitimate and which the media further legitimates. As this boundary shifts, news-making tactics will inevitably change.

Savage Frontier has explored concerns with security through their effects on journalism. In many ways, both journalism and ethnography are parallel modes of knowledge production. However, where the law of silence, imposed on certain activities, constrains the work of news media, ethnographic research provides the means to explain the reasons behind these limits. Due to its attentive methodology and ethical responsibility, anthropology is uniquely equipped to tell stories from marginal and unstable terrains where law and crime, security and insecurity blend into each other. In order to mitigate their social and economic uncertainties, stigmatized communities protect the vague boundaries of the il/legal, rendering them illegible to the state even when the latter has no interest in policing them. In Iguazú, as elsewhere, people consider media exposure, which may result in more rigorous government control and regulations, to be a potential threat to their livelihoods. Whereas mainstream media seek to make the invisible visible, ethnography aims at explaining that the boundary between these two domains is socially embedded and flexible. In writing alongside each other and, when possible, writing together, journalists and ethnographers can show that both public knowledge and public secret, separated by a faint line, are equally important for understanding complex issues of the contemporary society, such as security.

Savage Frontier goes beyond examining how news *is* made to understanding how and why news *is not* made. Careful documentation of news production—from the epistemic qualities of information to the logistics of cooperation between journalists, their sources, and their publics, from mainstream press rooms to community media in outlying urban neighborhoods—remains an important task for anthropologists, who have fairly recently developed an interest in news media and still have much to contribute to the subject, which has been dominated by sociology and cultural studies. I argue that it is critical to investigate the social conditions and circumstances that determine fissures in news-making and explain why some events do not become news. It is commonly held that, within their political and economic agendas, the mass media chase after popular headlines, while community media organizations have a social program oriented at improving the conditions of people's everyday lives. *Savage Frontier* explores how these divergent goals frame interactions between national and local news production in the tri-border area. But the book also shows that journalists use common sense of living on the margins of the state to differentiate between circulating public knowledge and keeping public secrets. As a social practice, news-making is laid across a terrain fractured by structural inequalities and reconstituted by local alliances, which hold the media accountable to the rules of maneuvering between shared stories *on the record* and practical knowledge *off the record.*

An important guidepost for news journalists navigating the fissure of in/visibility is security. The anthropology of security is an expanding field of inquiry. It includes in-depth analyses of the political logic and bureaucratic and legal processes of making security on the global and national levels; documentation of social and cultural effects that security discourses and practices have on targeted communities; and ethnographic case studies that have uncoupled security from the state and reframed it as a concern of its citizens, who struggle with the same dilemma of weighing rights against protection as do their governments. In *Savage Frontier,* these directions intersect at the interface between security and the news. I examined how security discourse works through the media, where it is renegotiated based on journalists' personal encounters with crime, violence, economic precariousness, and social insecurity. Yet the opposition between global and local security is deceiving. Security works as a Möbius strip: even though it appears to have a starting point and an outside, following its progression reveals that it makes a continuous loop with only one side. Ethnography is an effective method for studying the news media as the nodal point between the global and the local scales of making security, where the two blend into each other and cannot be split apart. This book joins the body of ethnographic scholarship that explores other interfaces of security: security and human rights, security and economic precariousness, security and science, among others. Moving forward, we need more ethnographically grounded studies of these intersectional qualities of security, tracing it through other, multiple domains of people's lives. In pursuing this work, our focus should be not only on how people are affected by and react to various forms of security-making, but also on how the meanings of security change through these interfaces.

In *Savage Frontier* the relation between security and news-making is not straightforward. For Iguazúenses, security is an imposed agenda that reaches this remote border town through the frameworks of global mobilization against potential threats, Argentine government policies, and sensational mass media narratives. At the same time, it is an embedded project, enacted in response to the expanding security apparatus and reconfigured within the parameters of daily concerns shared by residents on the border. The effects of convergence between these counterpoints of security-making are uncertain. Journalists may use news as tactics to maneuver the fissures of in/visibility, circulating public information, while respecting the laws of silence regarding public secrets, thereby extending legitimacy to the status quo. Still, the role of the media in terms of security remains unclear. On the one hand, by demonstrating that the fuerzas effectively control the border and by limiting their coverage of crime, the media perform security; on the other hand, they are complicit in obstructing the discussion of some dire social problems. Their silence with regard to corruption and the sale of children, for example, makes insecurity illegible and impedes justice, which does not necessarily enhance security. Selective media production, predicated on this constant renegotiation of in/visibility, is controversial, resulting in both security and insecurity effects in the community. Ethnography brings us closer to understanding that the relationship between making news and making security is fraught with such inconsistencies.

This book also contributes to the broader conversation about the ethnography of illegality. As a text that focuses on journalists who do not report on illegalized practices and even engage in some outlawed activities, it raises critical questions about the politics and ethics of ethnographic representation of crime. What becomes news in Iguazú and what does not is tightly linked to concerns over security. But how do such considerations affect ethnography? Inescapably, the narrative in this book includes descriptions of how Iguazúenses violated laws, for example, when they smuggled food or electronics. It could therefore be seen as contrary to the efforts of local journalists, who avoid writing about border crime. To prevent further securitization and militarization of the Triple Frontier, they challenge foreign and national mass media depictions of the region as a haven of criminality. Instead, they circulate an image of Iguazú as a safe tourist destination. By showing the presence of contraband and trafficking, the book may appear to side with the popular press, justifying increased surveillance, control, and other security initiatives on the border.

Every anthropologist writing about crime and violence faces the risk of our ethnographic narrative being misinterpreted and misappropriated, with deleterious effects to the communities we study. No matter the nuances of our analysis, which carefully situates unlawful practices within frameworks of structural inequality and social legitimacy, it might be inserted into the political agenda of the security state. It is a risk, however, which I prefer to its alternative of hiding inconvenient truths. Failure to mention existing illegalities would mean engaging in complicity with powerful actors, from government institutions to private businesses to corrupt border officials, who profit from violating laws, while their impunity is guaranteed by the code of silence. After all, everyday illegalities that Iguazúenses participate in—such as clandestinely bringing household appliances or toys across border checkpoints or purchasing contraband fruit and vegetables—are secondary to these larger wrongdoings, which deserve critique. The kinds of transgressions of the law that characterize daily life in Iguazú, as in many other border towns across Latin America and beyond, largely result from disjunctures between faulty government policies and the common sense of getting by on the margins of the state.

Rather than focusing on the presence of crime on the border, this ethnography has examined *why* local journalists avoid covering it. Anthropologists who study law and crime have argued that things and practices are never legal or illegal in and of themselves, but are legalized or illegalized through deliberate government action. News media also play an important role in processes of justification and criminalization, exposing some activities while leaving others in the blindspots of the public sphere. Exploring why such diverse practices—from smuggling to illegal adoptions—become public secrets, this book invites its readers to consider how the politics of news production intersects with its social circumstances. By doing so, the book also reveals the absurdity of mass media discourses that target the area as a "savage frontier" and critically points to their uses in advancing global and national security agendas.

In northern Argentina, the boundary between alarmist narratives of disorder and complicity under the code of silence is thick and layered. This ethnography addresses the political, ethical, and practical considerations involved in navigating these layers between public secret and public knowledge—for journalists as for anthropologists. My hope is that this conversation continues beyond it.

Notes

All translations from Spanish are mine.

1. Many journalists explicitly asked me to use their real names in any publications that result from my work. Unlike in anthropology, the practice of changing names is not common in the world of journalism, which mandates attribution of sources and strict limits on anonymity (see Bishara 2012; Vesperi 2010). Still, I complied with their requests only partially. Out of respect for the rules of the profession, I did not create any pseudonyms; instead—when it was necessary to protect confidentiality of journalists or other people I encountered—I erased their names. Throughout this book, I maintain the true identity of journalists when they act as public figures, that is, when they sign their articles or appear on radio and television programs. I also leave names to demonstrate crucial connections between journalists' personal experiences and their work in the media, but only where these connections are already publicly known. When information was shared with me off the record, particularly in discussions regarding illegalized activities, I ensure everyone's anonymity.

2. "Ronnie Arias y tres productores, presos en la frontera de Misiones," *Página/12*, August 25, 2007.

3. "Motoqueros y periodistas presos por acción ilegal en la frontera," *Territorio Digital*, August 25, 2007.

4. *Página/12*, August 25, 2007.

5. "Detuvieron a Ronnie Arias en el cruce El Pique," *La Voz de Cataratas*, August 24, 2007.

6. *Territorio Digital*, August 25, 2007.

7. INDEC (Instituto Nacional de Estadística y Censos), Censo Nacional de Población, Hogares y Viviendas 2010. Available online at http://www.censo2010.indec.gov.ar.

8. In his ethnography of urban policing in the banlieues of Paris, Didier Fassin notes how the language that calls residents of the housing projects "savages" living in neighborhoods described as "jungle" works to justify the deployment of police (Fassin 2013a). For another comparative case see Coronil and Skurski (2006).

9. Bourgois and Schonberg acknowledge that their book about homeless heroin addicts in San Francisco is vulnerable to ideological projections, but they write that "silencing, censoring, and sanitizing photo-ethnographic critiques of suffering and inequality are not productive alternatives" (2009:15).

10. "Re-export" trade in the tri-border region consists of merchants in Paraguay importing cigarettes, clothing, electronics, and other luxury items from the U.S., Europe, and Asia and selling them in Ciudad del Este to commercial Brazilian buyers known as *sacoleiros,* who take the products across the river into Brazil and resell them in street markets of Rio de Janeiro, Sao Paulo, and other major cities.

11. Larry Rother, "Terrorists Are Sought in Latin Smugglers' Haven," *New York Times,* September 27, 2001.

12. Michel Foucault defines governmentality as "the ensemble formed by the institutions, procedures, analyses and reflections, the calculations and tactics that allow the exercise of this very specific albeit complex form of power, which has as its target population, as its principal form of knowledge political economy, and as its essential technical means apparatuses of security" (1991:102).

13. Holbraad and Pedersen (2012) suggest this definition as an anthropological extension of the Copenhagen School theory of securitization. They further discuss convergences between anthropological work on security and security studies within international relations in the introduction to the edited volume *Times of Security: Ethnographies of Fear, Protest and the Future* (2013).

14. In his 2012 article on the semiotics of security, Carlo Caduff writes about a parallel issue in the context of infectious disease research, where scientific information becomes treated as a security threat and scientists working with sensitive data are subjected to government oversight. Also see Gusterson (1996) and Masco (2006).

15. As debates surrounding Wikileaks and NSA surveillance programs revealed, the U.S. government is highly concerned about the implications that news coverage based on leaked information has for national security. Like Daniel Ellsberg, who leaked the Pentagon Papers on U.S. involvement in Vietnam in 1971 and was castigated as a traitor for harming America's security, Glenn Greenwald of the *Guardian,* after publishing documents provided by Edward Snowden showing the extent of U.S. intelligence gathering in the name of national security, has been called a criminal. In February 2014 U.S. House Intelligence Committee chairman Republican Mike Rodgers told journalists that Greenwald was a "thief" because he was "selling stolen material" (see *Politico,* February 4, 2014; http://www.politico.com /story/2014/02/intelligence-chairman-argues-selling-snowden-docs-a-crime-103100.html#ixzz3MtZX27KZ).

16. Human Rights Watch *World Report 2014* also discusses how, in Argentina, the right to freely publish information of public interest can be undermined: in 2013, when a group of economists released unofficial inflation statistics

challenging the accuracy of official ones, they were subjected to high fines and criminal investigations. Electronic document, http://www.hrw.org/sites/default /files/wr2014_web_0.pdf (pp. 204–210).

17. From Oxford Dictionaries, available online at http://www .oxforddictionaries.com/definition/english/crime.

18. The United Nations Convention against Transnational Organized Crime and its three supplemental protocols (on human trafficking, migrant smuggling, and firearms trafficking) can be accessed at https://www.unodc.org/documents /treaties/UNTOC/Publications/TOC Convention/TOCebook-e.pdf.

19. In an overview of the anthropology of crime and criminalization, Jane Schneider and Peter Schneider suggest that the other focus of anthropologists has been ethnographic accounts of "forms of illegal predation," including banditry, rustling, racketeering, and trafficking, "entangled with the destabilizing effects of state-legitimated political economies" (2008:352).

20. Journalists in Puerto Iguazú, Ciudad del Este, and Foz do Iguaçu often say that the Guaraní Aquifer is the reason behind the U.S. interests in the area. See Ferradás (2004) for a discussion of how the U.S. constructs the region as a site for dormant terrorist cells in order to gain control of the water resources.

21. "¿Osama en las cataratas?" *BBC Mundo,* April 16, 2004.

22. Here and following, the brackets around the ellipsis points indicate omitted text; ellipsis points without brackets indicate a pause.

23. Javier Villegas, interview, November 2, 2010.

24. *International Narcotics Control Strategy Report* is annually published by the U.S. Department of State and can be found online at http://www.state .gov/j/inl/rls/nrcrpt/index.htm.

25. Carlos Ángel Villalba, interview, September 28, 2010.

26. Mario Antonowicz, interview, June 9, 2010.

27. Ibid.

28. After Argentina's new media law was passed in 2009, some Iguazú radio stations registered with the new institution responsible for governmental oversight, Autoridad Federal de Servicios de Comunicación Audiovisual (AFSCA, the Federal Authority of Audiovisual Communication Services), which replaced the Comité Federal de Radiodifusión (CONFER, the Federal Broadcasting Committee). Others, for various reasons, continued to operate without licenses.

CHAPTER 1: BREAKING THE CODE OF SILENCE

1. Bourdieu (2006:82–83) defines *"habitus"* as "a system of lasting, transposable dispositions which, integrating past experiences, functions at every moment as a matrix of perceptions, appreciations, and actions and makes possible the achievement of infinitely diversified tasks." I use this term to refer to bodily manifestation of social structures that function as norms guiding thinking and action.

2. Conover spoke at the panel "Ethnography and Journalism" during the American Anthropological Association Annual Meeting in Chicago in November 2013.

3. *Proximidad* was a Spanish-language program.

4. Iguazú Jungle Explorer and Iguazú Jungle Lodge, owned by the charismatic and socially engaged entrepreneur Eduardo Arrabal, paid for advertising in all local media, thereby supporting these small, private news outlets. After Eduardo's death, his son Alejandro, who took over the leadership of the company, contributed toward the cost of producing *Proximidad* by agreeing to pay for TV commercials during the program. Pablo Longo, the director of the digital daily *Iguazú Noticias,* offered to cover the remainder of our airtime costs by placing an ad for his paper.

5. The list of anthropologists who do activism-oriented research and advocate for engagement with the communities they study is extensive. Low and Merry (2010) sketch out a typology of engagement practices, distinguishing between sharing and support, teaching and public education, social critique, collaboration, advocacy, and activism.

CHAPTER 2: DISPATCHES FROM THE WILD

1. Thomas Hobbes's *Leviathan* is available online through Project Gutenberg at http://www.gutenberg.org/files/3207/3207-h/3207-h.htm.

2. Ibid.

3. Nicolas Shumway (1991) notes that not all nineteenth-century thinkers agreed with Sarmiento. For example, Juan Bautista Alberdi refuted the duality of civilization over barbarism in favor of dividing Argentine society between the "man of the coast" and the "man of the interior (Loc 1741 of 4203).

4. The concept of power as radiant from the center is elaborated in historical and anthropological studies on Southeast Asia; see Anderson (1990), Geertz (1980), and Winichakul (1994).

5. In the early accounts of the region, the Guaraní are often described as warlike (Peyret 1881; Alvear 2000; Suaiter Martínez 1928); however, authors also note their rather docile character relative to other indigenous groups in the region, particularly the Tupi and the Guayakí.

6. Daniel Crosta, interview, June 9, 2009.

7. *II Jornadas sobre poblamiento, colonización e inmigración en Misiones: 24–25 de agosto de 2001*, ed. V. Lagier et al. (Posadas, Misiones: Instituto Superior "Antonio Ruiz de Montoya," 2001:91); also in Suaiter Martínez (1928:10).

8. Censo Nacional de Población, Hogares y Viviendas 2010, conducted by the National Institute of Statistics and Census of Argentina (INDEC, Instituto Nacional de Estadística y Censos de la Republica Argentina).

9. In 2011 the per-ticket entry fees for Iguazú National Park were as follows: 100 pesos for foreign visitors, 70 pesos for citizens of other MERCOSUR countries, 40 pesos for Argentines, and 15 pesos for Misioneros. Iguazú and Andresito residents were admitted for free. Profits from admissions to the park were divided into four parts: the National Park Administration pooled its share of 27.5 percent into the institution's central budget and redistributed the funds to meet management needs across all the parks in the country; the government of Misiones and the Iguazú municipal tourism authority each took 3.5 percent; and the rest, 62.5 percent, went to the concessionary company "Iguazú Argen-

tina S.A.," which used it to reimburse costly investments in infrastructure and to maintain the park on a daily basis, including paying salaries to its employees. One peso from every ticket was reserved for the Iguazú Hospital Cooperative, which kept an ambulance staffed with a doctor and two nurses on duty, attending to emergencies in the park.

10. Oscar Fenocchio, interview, June 5, 2009.

11. "Día de Gendarmería," *La Voz de Cataratas,* July 28, 2011.

12. Oscar Fenocchio, interview, June 5, 2009.

13. Germán de los Santos, "El río Paraná, otra de las fronteras permeables," *La Nación,* November 17, 2013.

14. Gustavo Sierra, "La Argentina blanca: Cómo penetran por Salta los grandes carteles del narco," *Clarín,* November 24, 2013.

15. Using data from the Argentine Ministry of the Interior, *La Nación* published an overview of drug trafficking routes from the Argentine northern border: "La frágil frontera norte," *La Nación,* November 17, 2013.

16. The 2012 *International Narcotics Control Strategy Report* (http://www .state.gov/j/inl/rls/nrcrpt/2012/), published by the U.S. Department of State, claims that cocaine seizures during the ten months of 2011 covered in the report represent a sharp decrease from the previous years. INCSR estimated that, absent the availability of official figures, in the first nine months of 2010 Argentine authorities seized 12.7 MT of cocaine. The UNODC, using data provided by the Argentine government, estimated that Argentina seized 12.1 MT of cocaine in 2008 and 12.6 MT of cocaine in 2009. The report raised concerns that the reduction in cocaine seizures was a result of the government's suspension of DEA operations within Argentina for much of 2011. It has been suggested that the suspension could be related to a February 2011 scandal in which the Argentine government accused the United States of smuggling guns and surveillance equipment into Argentina under the guise of supplying a police training course.

17. The 2013 *International Narcotics Control Strategy Report* is available online at http://www.state.gov/j/inl/rls/nrcrpt/2013/.

18. Ernesto Azarkevich, interview, February 10, 2011.

19. The percentages of articles on violence and nature in Misiones as shown in table 1 would be even higher if not for the inclusion of a political phone-tapping scandal that shook Buenos Aires in 2009. The affair was only vaguely connected to the region (two judges from the province were among those accused of participating in spying), but the large number of publications dedicated to the issue inflated the percentage of political themes to one-fifth of the content published about Misiones, which is unusual.

20. Mariquita Torres, personal conversation, November 3, 2010.

21. In the tradition of the "Fourth Estate," journalists are civic intellectuals who criticize the government from an at least partially autonomous public sphere, thereby contributing to the quality of democracy and the level of governmental accountability throughout Latin America (e.g., Hughes 2006; Lawson 2002; Porto 2012). However, more often news media create, legitimate, and circulate national imaginaries and state ideologies. Governments in the region have been successful in using the media as a tool of power, manipulating

their complacency through state advertising, clientelism, and corruption, as well as violent repression (see Rockwell and Janus 2003; Waisbord 2000).

22. Lila Luchessi, interview, August 16, 2008.

23. *Tierra colorada* means "the colored land," a name given to Misiones due to the high concentration of iron oxide in its soil, which makes it red.

24. Herman and Chomsky define the "propaganda model" as "an analytical framework that attempts to explain the performance of the U.S. media in terms of the basic institutional structures and relationships within which they operate" (1988:xi). It shows how the mainstream media's behavior is influenced by its corporate character and integration into the political economy of the dominant economic system. Although the propaganda model was originally developed to analyze the U.S. corporate media, its insights can be applied to understanding mainstream media in other countries, including Argentina.

25. Brian Byrnes, interview, June 15, 2009.

26. Ernesto Azarkevich, interview, February 10, 2011.

27. Sandra Lion, "La eterna canción de las Cataratas," *Clarín,* August 17, 2008.

28. Leonardo Najle, "La cocina misionera es rica en sabor, pero también en leyendas," *Clarín,* July 22, 2009.

29. See Analía H. Testa, "Una aproximación al monte misionero, su misterio y sus sonidos," *La Nación,* June 28, 2008; Martín Wain, "Gotas que caen sobre tierra caliente," *La Nación,* August 24, 2008; Esteban Eliaszevich, "En el reino de las Aguas Grandes," *Clarín,* March 29, 2009; Ernesto Azarkevich, "Sorpresas en la selva, *Clarín,* December 20, 2009; Sandra Bonetto, "En el corazón de la selva," *Clarín,* June 5, 2010.

30. César Sánchez Bonifato, "Las Cataratas están casi secas, *La Nación,* May 8, 2009.

31. Ernesto Azarkevich, "Confirman en Misiones el primer caso de fiebre amarilla en humanos, *Clarín,* March 4, 2008.

32. "Misiones: Confirman que hay un segundo muerto por fiebre amarilla," *Clarín,* January 2, 2009; Valeria Roman, "Alerta por fiebre amarilla: El brote podría expandirse a más provincias," *Clarín,* January 4, 2009.

33. Daniel Gallo, "Otro riesgo de epidemia por mosquitos," *La Nación,* February 9, 2009; César Sánchez Bonifato, "Proponen eliminar perros en Misiones," *La Nación,* April 6, 2009.

34. "Alerta amarilla por el dengue en Misiones," *Clarín,* December 15, 2009; Ernesto Azarkevich, "Confirman el primer caso de dengue de la temporada," *Clarín,* December 17, 2009; Ernesto Azarkevich, "Reconocen que es difícil evitar que el dengue cruce la frontera," *Clarín,* December 18, 2009.

35. Ernesto Azarkevich, "Alerta por dengue: Atienden 60 casos diarios en Iguazú," *Clarín,* February 17, 2010.

36. Ernesto Azarkevich, "Misiones asegura que la situación por el dengue 'es complicada, pero controlada,'" *Clarín,* February 17, 2010.

37. Ernesto Azarkevich, "El gobierno de Misiones admite que hay 1,300 chicos desnutridos," *Clarín,* October 26, 2010.

38. Ernesto Azarkevich, interview, February 10, 2011.

39. Ibid.

40. Ibid.

41. "Denuncian a una pareja acusada de vender a cuatro hijos," *La Nación*, July 9, 2008; "Un niño baleó a su primo de 9 años," *La Nación,* July 21, 2008; Ernesto Azarkevich, "Un ex intendente acuchilló a dos vendedores porque no le hicieron una rebaja," *Clarín,* July 28, 2008; Georgina Elustondo, "Rescatan a una adolescente que había sido vendida por 100 pesos," *Clarín,* November 11, 2008; "Condenan a un pastor evangelista que violó durante años a sus tres hijas," *Clarín,* May 14, 2009; Ernesto Azarkevich, "Detuvieron a una mujer por la compra de un bebé," *Clarín,* October 2, 2009; "Brutal crimen de un chico aborigen en Misiones," *Clarín,* March 12, 2010.

CHAPTER 3: GLOBAL VILLAGE OF OUTLAWS

1. "Estudio revela que sobre el Puente circulan unas 15 mil personas por día," *Última Hora,* July 7, 2011.

2. Sebastian Rotella, "Jungle Hub for World's Outlaws," *Los Angeles Times,* August 24, 1998.

3. "A Place Where Crime Does Pay," CBS News, February 11, 2009. Video available at http://www.cbsnews.com/8301-18563_162-1375945.html.

4. Jeffrey Goldberg, "In The Party of God: Hezbollah Sets up Operations in South America and the United States," *New Yorker,* October 28, 2002.

5. The meeting was organized by Foro de Periodismo Argentino (FOPEA, the Argentine Journalism Forum), Foro de Periodistas Paraguayos (FOPEP, the Paraguayan Journalists Forum), Associação Brasileira de Jornalismo Investigativo (ABRAJI, the Brazilian Association for Investigative Journalism), and Foro de Trabajadores de Prensa y Comunicación Social de Misiones (FOPREMI, the Media Workers and Communicators Forum of Misiones), with sponsorship from the Open Society Institute, the World Bank, and the Knight Center for Journalism in the Americas.

6. "Para el Gobierno 'es de interés estratégico mostrar la verdad de la Triple Frontera,'" *MisionesOnline,* November 27, 2010.

7. The interest the U.S. government had in the region was further strengthened in 1996 after the discovery of an alleged plan to bomb the U.S. embassy in Paraguay.

8. Larry Rother, "Terrorists Are Sought in Latin Smugglers' Haven," *New York Times,* September 27, 2001.

9. April Howard and Benjamin Dangl, "City of Terror: Painting Paraguay's 'Casbah' as Terror Central," *FAIR,* September-October 2007.

10. Philip K. Abbott, "Terrorist Threat in the Tri-Border Area: Myth or Reality?" *Military Review,* September-October 2004.

11. "Brazil's Foreign Ministry Disses and Dismisses Three Plus One Mechanism," Embassy Brasilia, August 31 2007. Wikileaks ID #120678. Electronic document, http://www.cablegatesearch.net/cable.php?id = 07BRASILIA 1664.

12. "Counterterrorism in Brazil: Making the 3 Plus 1 Work," Embassy Brasilia, February 6, 2009. Electronic document, http://cablegatesearch.net/cable .php?id = 09BRASILIA156&q = 09brasilia156.

13. "Brazil: Police Publicly Admit Al Qaeda's Presence: GOB Denies Terrorism a Threat," Embassy Brasilia, October 1, 2009. Wikileaks ID #227899. Electronic document: http://www.wikileaks.org/plusd/cables/09BRASILIA1206_a.html.

14. Seri defines "zoning" as "a multi-layered process that results from the over-lapping and confluence of different kinds of narratives, genres, and practices" (2004:80). The "process of zoning turns any narrative able to reinforce a process of othering into a tool of sovereign exclusion" (2004:81).

15. Irina Hauser, "Corach pasó de canillita a campeón," *Página/12*, August 4, 1998.

16. "Argentina: Ambassador's Visit to the Triborder Area," Embassy Buenos Aires, September 13, 2007. Wikileaks ID #122144. Electronic document, http://www.wikileaks.org/plusd/cables/07BUENOSAIRES1833_a.html.

17. Hernán López Echagüe, "Re: Añado . . .," e-mail to the author, April 17, 2011.

18. "Lanzan hoy un mega operativo de control en la triple frontera," *El Territorio*, December 17, 1997. According to the article, Argentina, Brazil, and Paraguay were convinced that the Triple Frontier was the center of money laundering, drug trafficking, and terrorism, where annual illegal transactions were estimated to reach millions of U.S. dollars. The joint operation by the armed forces included inspections of customs and migrations offices, as well as banks. Corach also emphasized the need to take aerial photographs of the border zone to verify the presence of clandestine landing strips in the Paraguayan territory.

19. Hernán López Echagüe, "Re: Añado . . .," e-mail to the author, April 17, 2011.

20. Andrés Colmán Gutiérrez, interview, March 16, 2011.

21. *Operación Cóndor,* or *Plan Cóndor* (Operation Condor), was the name given to a secret union of the intelligence services of six U.S.-supported South American military governments (Argentina, Bolivia, Brazil, Chile, Paraguay, and Uruguay) that operated during the 1970s and into the early 1980s. Thousands of people who were suspected of involvement with leftist groups were tortured, interrogated, and then executed and secretly buried, becoming known as "the disappeared." Those that escaped their own dictatorship's security services were often captured and tortured in other Operation Condor countries and eventually returned from where they had fled to be executed. Operation Condor agents also located and killed dissidents in operations outside Latin America, in several European nations and the U.S. The clandestine nature of Operation Condor means that its full extent may never be known, but researchers estimate that 50,000 people were killed, 30,000 were "disappeared" and presumed killed, and 400,000 were jailed. See Mariano Castillo, "Trial over Terrifying 'Operation Condor' Under Way," CNN, March 5, 2013. Available online at http://edition.cnn.com/2013/03/05/world/americas/argentina-operation-condor-trial/.

22. The Vladimir Herzog Award for Human Rights (Portuguese: Prêmio Jornalistico Vladimir Herzog de Anistia e Direitos Humanos) was established in honor of Vladimir Herzog, a Brazilian journalist who was killed by the dictatorship. Since the late 1970s it has been awarded to journalists who excel in the coverage of human rights issues. The National Santiago Leguizamón Journalism

Award is given in honor of Paraguayan journalist Santiago Leguizamón, who on April 26, 1991, was killed by hired assassins in Pedro Juan Caballero, on the border between Paraguay and Brazil.

23. The town was founded in 1957 as Puerto Flor de Lis, but it was soon renamed Ciudad Puerto Stroessner. Its current name dates back to 1989, when, following a coup d'etat that toppled Stroessner's regime, local residents voted to call their city "Ciudad del Este."

24. The growth of Ciudad del Este is also linked to the hydroelectric dam project in other ways. When Paraguay and Brazil agreed to build the Itaipù Dam, which was going to submerge part of Paraguay's territory, Brazil had to give its neighbor something in exchange for their lost land. The countries settled on two infrastructural projects: a highway to connect Asunción to the Brazilian seaport of Paranaguá and a bridge across the Paraná between Ciudad del Este and Foz do Iguaçu, positioning Ciudad del Este on the lifeline of Paraguay's economy.

25. *Paraguay: Selected Issues,* IMF Country Report No. 10/170, International Monetary Fund (2010). Document available online at http://www.imf.org/external/pubs/ft/scr/2010/cr10170.pdf.

26. Tax rates are available on the KPMG website, http://www.kpmg.com/global/en/services/tax/tax-tools-and-resources/pages/tax-rates-online.aspx. Also see *Latin America Indirect Tax Country Guide,* published by KPMG International (2011).

27. "March to the East," which began in the 1960s, was the popular name of the Paraguayan government's plan to populate the country's eastern border region along the Paraná.

28. Andrés Colmán Gutiérrez, interview, March 16, 2011.

29. Guillermo Adrián D'Angelo, "March to the East: The Rise and Fall of Ciudad del Este," *Argentina Independent,* January 24, 2013.

30. *Trafficking in Persons Report* (2013), published by the U.S. Department of State, is available online at http://www.state.gov/j/tip/rls/tiprpt/2013/index.htm.

31. *International Narcotics Control Strategy Report* (2013), published by the U.S. Department of State, is available online at http://www.state.gov/j/inl/rls/nrcrpt/2013/.

32. Larry Rother, "Terrorists Are Sought in Latin Smugglers' Haven," *New York Times,* September 27, 2001.

33. *Traffic* is a 2000 American crime drama on illegal drug trade directed by Steven Soderbergh.

34. "Avanza el film de la 'Triple,'" *La Voz de Cataratas,* September 15, 2010.

35. "No queremos película," *La Voz de Cataratas,* December 7, 2010.

36. "¿Una ficción de la realidad?" Radio Cataratas, January 23, 2011.

37. "Triple Frontera, lugar satanizado por gobiernos y periodistas que desconocen la región," *ABC Digital,* November 26, 2010; "Terrorismo y crimen, aspectos de una realidad contradictoria," *Primera Edición,* December 5, 2010.

38. "No solo en la triple frontera hay un nicho de pobreza inaguantable y obsceno," *Vanguardia,* November 27, 2010.

39. *Vivir al límite* is the Spanish title of Kathryn Bigelow's 2008 thriller *The Hurt Locker*, which depicts bomb squad technicians working in Iraq.

40. Martín Granovsky, "La otra Triple Frontera," *Página/12*, March 31, 2011.

41. Jorgelina Bonetto, "Triple Frontera: No hay organizaciones terroristas," *Iguazú Noticias,* December 24, 2010; "En Iguazú no hay comunidad libanesa," *La Voz de Cataratas,* July 10, 2009.

42. "Esperanza en la frontera," *La Voz de Cataratas,* May 4, 2011; "El reflejo de la muerte de Osama en Foz," *La Voz de Cataratas,* May 6, 2011.

43. "Para el gobierno 'es de interés estratégico mostrar la verdad de la Triple Frontera,'" *MisionesOnline,* November 27, 2010.

CHAPTER 4: SMALL TOWN, BIG HELL

1. Fieldnotes, September 2, 2010.

2. Horacio Valdés, interview, September 9, 2010.

3. Committee to Protect Journalists: http://www.cpj.org/americas/argentina.

4. "Rising Violence against Journalists: A Cause for Concern as Climate Polarizes," *Reporters without Borders,* November 30, 2012.

5. Data are available through the National Institute of Statistics and Census of Argentina (INDEC, Instituto Nacional de Estadística y Censos de la Republica Argentina). Electronic document, http://www.indec.mecon.ar/principal.asp?id_tema = 358. In 2010 President Cristina Fernández de Kirchner divided the Ministry of Justice, Security and Human Rights (Ministerio de Justicia, Seguridad y Derechos Humanos) into two: the Ministry of Security and the Ministry of Justice and Human Rights.

6. UNODC homicide statistics are available online from http://www.unodc.org/unodc/en/data-and-analysis/homicide.html. Data include intentional homicide counts and rates (per 100,000 population) for the years 1995–2011.

7. Laura Reina, "El 61% de la gente teme andar de noche," *La Nación,* November 1, 2010.

8. Founded in preparation for the 1978 World Cup, when the Argentine government wanted to relocate some of the poorest residents from the center of Buenos Aires, the neighborhood was first called "Padre Mujica," in honor of a priest who protected its inhabitants while they still lived in Villa 31 in Retiro, and was later renamed "Ejército de los Andes" by the military dictatorship. The nickname "Fuerte Apache," or "Fort Apache," was given to the area in reference to the American film *Fort Apache, The Bronx* (1981) when in the 1980s it became notorious for intense gunfights between the police and the thieves in the complex. It is the hometown of Argentine soccer star Carlos Tevez.

9. "Robo a mano armada," *La Voz de Cataratas,* March 16, 2011.

10. "Homicidio familiar," Radio Cataratas, January 14, 2011.

11. "¿Inseguridad en Iguazú?" *La Voz de Cataratas,* March 17, 2011.

12. "Robo calificado a una anciana," Radio Cataratas, January 14, 2011.

13. "Abuso consentido," *La Voz de Cataratas,* December 7, 2010.

14. "Menores asaltadas," *La Voz de Cataratas,* November 29, 2010.

15. "Lo machetearon por no pagar peaje," *La Voz de Cataratas,* June 3, 2010.

16. "Delincuentes de afuera," *La Voz de Cataratas,* March 29, 2011.

17. Comments to "¿Inseguridad en Iguazú?" *La Voz de Cataratas,* March 17, 2011.

18. Comments to "Robo a mano armada," *La Voz de Cataratas,* March 16, 2011.

19. Ibid.

20. Comments to "¿Inseguridad en Iguazú?" *La Voz de Cataratas,* March 17, 2011.

21. Comments to "Robo a mano armada," *La Voz de Cataratas,* March 16, 2011.

22. Ibid.

23. Comments to "Delincuentes de afuera," *La Voz de Cataratas,* March 29, 2011.

24. Comments to "Robo a mano armada," *La Voz de Cataratas,* March 16, 2011.

25. Comments to "¿Inseguridad en Iguazú?" *La Voz de Cataratas,* March 17, 2011.

26. Héctor Vera, interview, June 1, 2009.

27. Mario Antonowicz, interview, June 9, 2010.

28. Jorgelina Bonetto, interview, May 5, 2010.

29. See *Nunca más* (Argentine National Commission on the Disappeared, 1986), p. 177.

30. Fieldnotes, May 31, 2009.

31. In the terminology of the military regime, *trasladar* (to move, to transfer) referred to taking prisoners away to be killed (see Feitlowitz 1998).

32. Fieldnotes, March 24, 2011.

33. Fieldnotes, May 31, 2009.

34. Carlos Ángel Villalba, interview, September 28, 2010.

35. Mariquita Torres, interview, November 18, 2010.

36. "Servicio militar obligatorio," *Proximidad: Periodismo de investigación,* TV program, production by Ieva Jusionyte and Javier Rotela, 2010.

37. Jorgelina Bonetto, interview, May 5, 2010.

38. On November 30, 2011, the senate of neighboring Brazil approved a bill to amend the constitution to require practicing journalists to have an advanced degree in journalism, thereby questioning the legitimacy of those without formal training. Journalism groups like the Inter American Press Association and the Brazilian Association of Journalists reacted by expressing concerns that the return of degree requirements was an attack on freedom of the press and the constitutional guarantee to free thought. In Argentina, a new media law that came into effect in 2010 obliges all media directors to have a professional degree, but does not affect reporters' credentials.

39. Michel de Certeau defined tactics as "the space of the other" because it involves using "cracks that particular conjunctions open in the surveillance of the proprietary powers," poaching on them (1984:37).

40. "Incautan pasta base y detienen a una persona," *La Voz de Cataratas,* February 22, 2013.

41. "Golpe al narcotráfico," *La Voz de Cataratas,* October 4, 2008; "Incautaron 7 toneladas de marihuana," *La Voz de Cataratas,* October 24, 2008; "Lucha contra el narcotráfico: Prefectura secuestró crack y detuvo dos personas," Radio Cataratas, January 29, 2011; "Golpe al narcotráfico," *La Voz de Cataratas,* March 7, 2011; "Secuestro de cocaína," *La Voz de Cataratas,* May 13, 2011.

42. "Vamos a rescatar misioneras estén donde estén," *La Voz de Cataratas,* October 17, 2008; "Unidos contra la trata," *La Voz de Cataratas,* June 10, 2009; "Inscripción en Gendarmería," *La Voz de Cataratas,* July 24, 2009.

43. Fieldnotes, November 26, 2010.

44. Fieldnotes, June 5, 2009.

45. Fieldnotes, June 10, 2010.

46. Fieldnotes, October 21, 2010.

47. "151 mujeres asesinadas," *La Voz de Cataratas,* July 28, 2011.

48. Quoted from Article 3 of the Protocol to Prevent, Suppress and Punish Trafficking in Persons Especially Women and Children, supplementing the United Nations Convention against Transnational Organized Crime, which was signed in 2000 in Italy. The protocol is available online at http://www.osce.org/odihr/19223.

49. Fieldnotes, June 1, 2010.

50. See p. 15 of the 2005 *Guía para periodistas* (Guide for journalists), published by the Programa de Prevención y Eliminación de la Explotación Sexual Comercial de Niños, Niñas y Adolescentes en la Triple Frontera, Ciudad del Este.

51. "Denuncie la Trata de Personas," *La Voz de Cataratas,* October 18, 2008; "Denunciá, no te calles," *La Voz de Cataratas,* April 12, 2010.

52. "Atención: El abusador puede estar en casa," *La Voz de Cataratas,* November 11, 2010.

53. "Un policía mató a su ex mujer mientras ella lo denunciaba por maltrato," *La Nación,* November 6, 2012; "Policía asesinó a su mujer cuando realizaba denuncia por maltrato," *La Voz de Cataratas,* November 6, 2012.

54. During my fieldwork in Iguazú, between 2008 and 2011, the only incident that raised safety concerns for the region's journalists was the assassination of Héctor Carballo in October 2010. In his show on the local radio, Carballo, who was an ex-mayor of San Vicente, talked about drug trafficking and contraband of cigarettes, naming the people involved. The assassination, initially attributed to the local mafia, which Carballo exposed in his program, raised a red flag for journalists. To assuage fears, in March 2011 the Media Workers and Communicators Forum of Misiones (FOPREMI, Foro de Trabajadores de Prensa y Comunicación Social de Misiones) organized a workshop called "Alerta Periodistas" (Alert to journalists) in the nearby town of El Soberbio, on the border between Argentina and Brazil. The workshop taught journalists about the measures of protection they must take when working on dangerous assignments.

CHAPTER 5: ON AND OFF THE RECORD

This chapter is an updated and expanded version of the article "On and off the Record: The Production of Legitimacy in an Argentine Border Town," which first appeared in 2013 in *PoLAR: Political and Legal Anthropology Review* 36(2):231–248.

1. Fieldnotes, May 7, 2010.

2. Once a year residents of Iguazú and its surroundings were also allowed to make purchases of up to US$300 in the duty free shop. It is located past the Argentine border checkpoint, so goods bought there must be brought into the country through customs.

3. Fieldnotes, June 1, 2009.

4. "Prefectura y su lucha contra el pique," *La Voz de Cataratas,* June 2, 2009.

5. Fieldnotes, May 10, 2010.

6. "Desde Argentina a Paraguay," *La Voz de Cataratas,* March 10, 2011.

7. According to my 2010 fieldnotes, in Ciudad del Este, a Panasonic MiniDV cassette cost US$1.65, while Fotografías Rolando, a photo center in Iguazú, sold a TDK MiniDV cassette for 26.50 pesos (US$6.37), and a small store on central Gustavo Eppens Street sold Sony MiniDV cassettes for 25 pesos each (US$6.01).

8. Fieldnotes, September 16, 2010.

9. "Sin teléfono," *La Voz de Cataratas,* March 1, 2011.

10. "Menos contrabando," *La Voz de Cataratas,* March 3, 2011.

11. "Equipaje: Sin ropas," *La Voz de Cataratas,* March 4, 2011.

12. Fieldnotes, March 4, 2011.

13. 25 de Mayo (May 25th) is the commemoration of the May Revolution of 1810, with which the Argentine War of Independence from the Spanish Crown began. On 9 de Julio (July 9th) of 1816 Argentina declared independence. The Buenos Aires Cabildo was the seat of colonial government and later housed the first local government of the Viceroyalty of the Río de la Plata.

14. Javier Villegas, interview, November 2, 2010.

15. See Roitman (2004, 2006) for a comparative discussion of the "ethics of illegality" and common sense on the borders in the Chad Basin of Africa.

16. Javier Villegas, interview, November 2, 2010.

17. Silvia Martínez, interview, September 26, 2010.

18. "Al concejo por el cupo," Radio Cataratas, December 1, 2010.

19. Communiqué on Record No. 121/10 "P", issued by the Iguazú town council, Honorable Concejo Deliberante, Ciudad del Puerto Iguazú, December 16, 2010.

20. Silvia Martínez, interview, September 26, 2010.

CHAPTER 6: BLURRED BOUNDARIES

1. Jorgelina Bonetto, interview, May 5, 2010.

2. The Grandmothers have been trying to find an estimated five hundred children of the *Desaparecidos* (the disappeared), sons and daughters who were

kidnapped and presumed murdered by the military junta ruling the country between 1976 and 1983. These young children, including babies delivered while their mothers were being held in detention centers, were illegally "appropriated" by families with close ties to the military (see Gandsman 2009). The Grand-mothers' campaign has played an important role in the trials of the former military leaders (charges for kidnapping babies were not included in the amnesty laws), and they also led to reforms of the country's adoption laws.

3. UNICEF, *Child Protection from Violence, Exploitation and Abuse.* Electronic document, http://www.unicef.org/protection/57929_58005.html.

4. Optional Protocol to the Convention on the Rights of the Child on the sale of children, child prostitution, and child pornography, adopted by U.N. General Assembly resolution A/RES/54/263 and entered into force on January 18,2002. Electronic document, http://www.ohchr.org/EN/ProfessionalInterest/Pages/OPSCCRC.aspx.

5. The Inter-American Convention on International Traffic in Minors, available at http://www.oas.org/dil/treaties_B-57_Inter-American_Convention_on_International_Traffic_in_Minors.htm.

6. "Editorial II: Transparencia en las adopciones," *La Nación,* October 7, 2008.

7. Sibila Camps, "El sistema de adopciones en Misiones, bajo sospecha," *Clarín,* October 5, 2008.

8. Camps, October 5, 2008. The high concentration of iron oxide in local soil makes it look red, distinguishing it from other parts of the country. Because of its red soil, Misiones is often called "la tierra colorada" (the colored land).

9. "Adopciones ilegales en Misiones: Una mujer vendió a cuatro de sus hijos," *Clarín,* December 18, 2008.

10. Camps, October 5, 2008.

11. Ibid.

12. Ibid.

13. Ernesto Azarkevich, "Misiones no entregaría niños en adopción a gente de otra provincia," *Clarín,* October 6, 2008.

14. Camps, October 5, 2008.

15. Azarkevich, October 6, 2008.

16. Ibid.

17. "Se derrumbó la cantidad de pedidos para adoptar legalmente a los bebés," *El Territorio,* January 10, 2010.

18. National Institute of Statistics and Censuses (INDEC), "Incidencia de la pobreza y la indigencia en el total de aglomerados urbanos y regiones estadísticas: Primer semestre 2013" (Incidence of poverty rates in all urban areas and statistical regions: First half of 2013). Data available at http://www.indec.mecon.ar/principal.asp?id_tema = 76.

19. Paula Urlen, "Hay más de 10 millones de argentinos pobres y aumentó la desigualdad," *La Nación,* December 26, 2013.

20. Azarkevich, October 6, 2008.

21. To protect privacy, some of the names in this account have been changed, while others have been left out. Only those individuals who hold public posi-

tions and who appeared as public figures in the television program are identified by their real names.

22. This and other direct quotes are transcribed from the video archives of *Proximidad: Periodismo de investigación,* production by Ieva Jusionyte and Javier Rotela, 2010.

23. "Misioneras cambian domicilio a Corrientes para dar en adopción," *El Territorio,* September 17, 2010.

24. See pp. 61–67 of the 2012 *Global Report on Trafficking in Persons,* published by the United Nations Office of Drugs and Crime. Available at http://www.unodc.org/documents/data-and-analysis/glotip/Trafficking_in_Persons_2012_web.pdf.

CONCLUSION: ETHNOGRAPHY OF IN/VISIBILITY

1. "Charla sobre periodismo de investigación en la UNaM," Facebook, April 14, 2011.

References

Abu-Lughod, Lila
  2005   *Dramas of Nationhood: The Politics of Television in Egypt.* Chicago: University of Chicago Press.
Agamben, Giorgio
  2005   *State of Exception.* Chicago: University of Chicago Press.
Althusser, Louis
  1972   Ideology and Ideological State Apparatuses. In *Lenin and Philosophy and Other Essays.* Pp. 85–126. New York: Monthly Review Press.
Alvear, Diego de
  2000   *Relación histórica y geográfica de la provincia de Misiones.* Resistencia, Chaco, Argentina: Instituto de Investigaciones Geohistóricas, CONICET.
Amable, María Angélica, Karina Dohmann, and Liliana Mirta Rojas
  2008   *Historia de la provincia de Misiones (siglo XX).* Posadas: Ediciones Montoya.
Anderson, Benedict R. O'G.
  1990   *Language and Power: Exploring Political Cultures in Indonesia.* Ithaca, NY: Cornell University Press.
  1991   *Imagined Communities: Reflections on the Origin and Spread of*
  [1983]   *Nationalism.* London: Verso.
Andreas, Peter
  2000   *Border Games: Policing the U.S.-Mexico Divide.* Ithaca, NY: Cornell University Press.
  2013   *Smuggler Nation: How Illicit Trade Made America.* New York: Oxford University Press.

Andreas, Peter, and Kelly M. Greenhill
    2010   *Sex, Drugs, and Body Counts: The Politics of Numbers in Global Crime and Conflict.* Ithaca, NY: Cornell University Press.

Aretxaga, Begoña
    1997   *Shattering Silence: Women, Nationalism, and Political Subjectivity in Northern Ireland.* Princeton, NJ: Princeton University Press.

Argentine National Commission on the Disappeared
    1986   *Nunca más: The Report of the Argentine National Commission on the Disappeared.* New York: Farrar, Straus, Giroux.

Argueta, Otto
    2012   Private Security in Guatemala: Pathway to Its Proliferation. *Bulletin of Latin American Research* 31(3):320–335.

Austin, J. L.
    1975   *How to Do Things with Words.* Oxford: Clarendon Press.

Auyero, Javier
    2003   *Contentious Lives: Two Argentine Women, Two Protests, and the Quest for Recognition.* Durham, NC: Duke University Press.
    2007   *Routine Politics and Violence in Argentina: The Gray Zone of State Power.* Cambridge: Cambridge University Press.

Benjamin, Walter
    2009   *On The Concept of History.* New York: Classic Books America.
    [1940]

Biehl, João Guilherme
    2005   *Vita: Life in a Zone of Social Abandonment.* Berkeley: University of California Press.

Bigo, Didier
    2002   Security and Immigration: Toward a Critique of the Governmentality of Unease. *Alternatives: Global, Local, Political* 27(S1):S63–S92.

Bird, S. Elizabeth, ed.
    2005   The Journalist as Ethnographer? How Anthropology Can Enrich Journalistic Practice. In *Media Anthropology.* E. Rothenbuhler and M. Coman, eds. Pp. 301–308. Thousand Oaks, CA: Sage.
    2010   *The Anthropology of News and Journalism: Global Perspectives.* Bloomington: Indiana University Press.

Bishara, Amahl
    2013   *Back Stories: U.S. News Production and Palestinian Politics.* Stanford, CA: Stanford University Press.

Bourbeau, Philippe
    2011   *The Securitization of Migration: A Study of Movement and Order.* London: Routledge.
    2014   Moving Forward Together: Logics of the Securitisation Process. *Millennium: Journal of International Studies* (43):187–206.

Bourdieu, Pierre
    2005   The Political Field, the Social Science Field, and the Journalistic Field. In *Bourdieu and the Journalistic Field.* R. D. Benson and E. Neveu, eds. Pp. 29–47. Cambridge, UK: Polity.

2006   *Outline of a Theory of Practice.* New York: Cambridge University
[1977]   Press.
Bourgois, Philippe I.
2003   *In Search of Respect: Selling Crack in El Barrio.* Cambridge: Cambridge University Press.
Bourgois, Philippe I., and Jeffrey Schonberg
2009   *Righteous Dopefiend.* Berkeley: University of California Press.
Boyer, Dominic
2005   *Spirit and System: Media, Intellectuals, and the Dialectic in Modern German Culture.* Chicago: University of Chicago Press.
2006   Turner's Anthropology of Media and Its Legacies. *Critique of Anthropology* 26(1):47–60.
2010   Divergent Temporalities: On the Division of Labor between Journalism and Anthropology. *Anthropology News* 51(4):6–9.
Boyer, Dominic, and Ulf Hannerz
2006   Introduction: Worlds of Journalism. *Ethnography* 7(1):5–17.
Briggs, Charles L.
2003   Why Nation-States and Journalists Can't Teach People to Be Healthy: Power and Pragmatic Miscalculation in Public Discourses on Health. *Medical Anthropology Quarterly* 17(3):287–321.
2004   Theorizing Modernity Conspiratorially: Science, Scale, and the Political Economy of Public Discourse in Explanations of a Cholera Epidemic. *American Ethnologist* 31(2):164–187.
2007   Mediating Infanticide: Theorizing Relations between Narrative and Violence. *Cultural Anthropology* 22(3):315–356.
Briggs, Charles L., and Clara Mantini-Briggs
2003   *Stories in the Time of Cholera: Racial Profiling during a Medical Nightmare.* Berkeley: University of California Press.
Bubandt, Nils
2005   Vernacular Security: The Politics of Feeling Safe in Global, National and Local Worlds. *Security Dialogue* 36(3):275–296.
Butler, Judith
1988   Performative Acts and Gender Constitution: An Essay in Phenomenology and Feminist Theory. *Theatre Journal* 40(4):519–531.
Buzan, Barry, Ole Waever, and Jaap de Wilde
1998   *Security: A New Framework for Analysis.* Boulder, CO: Lynne Rienner.
Caduff, Carlo
2012   The Semiotics of Security: Infectious Disease Research and the Biopolitics of Informational Bodies in the United States. *Cultural Anthropology* 27(2):333–357.
2014   On the Verge of Death: Visions of Biological Vulnerability. *Annual Review of Anthropology* 43:105–121.
Caldeira, Teresa Pires do Rio
2001   *City of Walls: Crime, Segregation, and Citizenship in São Paulo.* Berkeley: University of California Press.

Cardarello, Andréa

2009 The Movement of the Mothers of the Courthouse Square: "Legal Child Trafficking," Adoption and Poverty in Brazil. *Journal of Latin American and Caribbean Anthropology* 14(1):140–161.

Chacón, Jennifer M.

2008 The Security Myth: Punishing Immigrants in the Name of National Security. In *Immigration, Integration, and Security: America and Europe in Comparative Perspective*. A.C. d'Appollonia and S. Reich, eds. Pittsburgh: University of Pittsburgh Press.

Chavez, Leo R.

2013 *The Latino Threat: Constructing Immigrants, Citizens, and the Nation*. Stanford, CA: Stanford University Press.

Cohen, Stanley

1972 *Folk Devils and Moral Panics: The Creation of the Mods and Rockers*. London: MacGibbon and Kee.

Coleman, Mathew

2012 The "Local" Migration State: The Site-Specific Devolution of Immigration Enforcement in the U.S. South. *Law and Policy* 34(2):159–190.

Comaroff, Jean, and John L. Comaroff, eds.

2006 *Law and Disorder in the Postcolony*. Chicago: University of Chicago Press.Coronil, Fernando, and Julie Skurski

Dammert, Lucia, and Mary Fran T. Malone

2006 Does It Take a Village? Policing Strategies and Fear of Crime in Latin America. *Latin American Politics and Society* 48(4):27–51.

Das, Veena, and Deborah Poole, eds.

2004 *Anthropology in the Margins of the State*. Santa Fe: School of American Research Press.

de Certeau, Michel

1984 *The Practice of Everyday Life*. Berkeley: University of California Press.

de Genova, Nicholas

2002 Migrant "Illegality" and Deportability in Everyday Life. *Annual Review of Anthropology* 31:419–447.

2004 The Legal Production of Mexican Migrant "Illegality." *Latino Studies* 2(2):160–185.

Donnan, Hastings, and Thomas M. Wilson

1999 *Borders: Frontiers of Identity, Nation and State*. Oxford: Berg.

Doty, Roxanne Lynn

2009 *The Law into Their Own Hands: Immigration and the Politics of Exceptionalism*. Tucson: University of Arizona Press.

Douglas, Mary

1966 *Purity and Danger: An Analysis of Concepts of Pollution and Taboo*. New York: Praeger.

Dowling, Julie, and Jonathan Xavier Inda, eds.

2013 *Governing Immigration through Crime: A Reader*. Stanford: Stanford University Press.

Farmer, Paul

1992 *AIDS and Accusation: Haiti and the Geography of Blame.* Berkeley: University of California Press.

2003 On Suffering and Structural Violence: Social and Economic Rights in the Global Era. In *Pathologies of Power: Health, Human Rights, and the New War on the Poor.* P. Farmer, ed. Pp. 29–50. Berkeley: University of California Press.

2004 An Anthropology of Structural Violence. *Current Anthropology* 45(3):305–326.

Fassin, Didier

2007 *When Bodies Remember: Experiences and Politics of AIDS in South Africa.* Berkeley: University of California Press.

2013a *Enforcing Order: An Ethnography of Urban Policing.* Cambridge, UK: Polity.

2013b Why Ethnography Matters: On Anthropology and Its Publics. *Cultural Anthropology* 28(4):621–646.

Feitlowitz, Marguerite

1998 *A Lexicon of Terror: Argentina and the Legacies of Torture.* New York: Oxford University Press.

Ferradás, Carmen A.

1998 *Power in the Southern Cone Borderlands: An Anthropology of Development Practice.* Westport, CT: Bergin & Garvey.

2004 Environment, Security, and Terrorism in the Trinational Frontier of the Southern Cone. *Identities: Global Studies in Culture and Power* 11(3):417–442.

2013 The Nature of Illegality under Neoliberalism and Post-Neoliberalism. *PoLAR: Political and Legal Anthropology Review* 36(2):266–273.

Ferrario, Caterina

2006 *Tax Systems and Tax Reforms in Latin America: Paraguay.* Società italiana di economia pubblica. Pavia: University of Pavia.

Ferreira, Marcos Alan Fagner dos Santos

2010 *Terrorism in the Southern Cone? Interests and U.S. Government Perceptions about the Tri-Border (Argentina, Brazil and Paraguay).* Paper presented at the International Studies Association Convention, New Orleans. https://www.academia.edu/489091/Terrorism_in_the_Southern_Cone_Interests_and_U.S._Government_Perceptions_about_the_Tri-Border_Argentina_Brazil_and_Paraguay.

Flynn, Donna K.

1997 "We Are the Border": Identity, Exchange, and the State along the Benin-Nigeria Border. *American Ethnologist* 24(2):311–330.

Folch, Christine

2013 Surveillance and State Violence in Stroessner's Paraguay: Itaipú Hydroelectric Dam, Archive of Terror. *American Anthropologist* 115(1):44–57.

Fosher, Kerry B.

2009 *Under Construction: Making Homeland Security at the Local Level.* Chicago: University of Chicago Press.

Foucault, Michel

1991 Governmentality. In *The Foucault Effect: Studies in Governmentality.* G. G. C. Burchell and P. Miller, eds. Pp. 87–104. Chicago: University of Chicago Press.

2007 *Security, Territory, Population: Lectures at the College de France, 1977–1978.* New York: Palgrave Macmillan.

Frois, Catarina

2013 *Peripheral Vision: Politics, Technology, and Surveillance.* New York: Berghahn Books.

Galemba, Rebecca B.

2012 "Corn Is Food, not Contraband": The Right to "Free Trade" at the Mexico-Guatemala Border. *American Ethnologist* 39(4):716–734.

2013 Illegality and Invisibility at Margins and Borders. *PoLAR: Political and Legal Anthropology Review* 36(2):274–285.

Galtung, Johan

1969 Violence, Peace, and Peace Research. *Journal of Peace Research* 6(3):167–191.

Gandsman, Ari

2009 "A Prick of a Needle Can Do No Harm": Compulsory Extraction of Blood in the Search for the Children of Argentina's Disappeared. *Journal of Latin American and Caribbean Anthropology* 14(1):162–184.

Geertz, Clifford

1980 *Negara: The Theatre State in Nineteenth-Century Bali.* Princeton, NJ: Princeton University Press.

Ginsburg, Faye D., Lila Abu-Lughod, and Brian Larkin

2002 Introduction. In *Media Worlds: Anthropology on New Terrain.* F. D. Ginsburg, L. Abu-Lughod, and B. Larkin, eds. Pp. 1–38. Berkeley: University of California Press.

Goldstein, Daniel M.

2004 *The Spectacular City: Violence and Performance in Urban Bolivia.* Durham, NC: Duke University Press.

2010 Toward a Critical Anthropology of Security. *Current Anthropology* 51(4):487–517.

2012 *Outlawed: Between Security and Rights in a Bolivian City.* Durham, NC: Duke University Press.

Goldstein, Daniel M., and Fatimah Williams Castro

2006 Creative Violence: How Marginal People Make News in Bolivia. *Journal of Latin American Anthropology* 11(2):380–407.

Gordillo, Gastón, and Juan Martín Leguizamón

2002 *El río y la frontera: Movilizaciones aborígenes, obras públicas y MERCOSUR en el Pilcomayo.* Buenos Aires: Editorial Biblos.

Greenberg, Nathaniel

2010 War in Pieces: AMIA and the Triple Frontier in Argentine and American Discourse on Terrorism. *A Contra Corriente* 8(1):61–93.

Grimson, Alejandro

2002a *El otro lado del río: Periodistas, nación y Mercosur en la frontera.* Buenos Aires: EUDEBA.

2002b Hygiene Wars on the Mercosur Border: Local and National Agency in Uruguaiana (Brazil) and Paso de Los Libres (Argentina). *Identities: Global Studies in Culture and Power* 9(2):151–172.

Gusterson, Hugh
1996 *Nuclear Rites: A Weapons Laboratory at the End of the Cold War.* Berkeley: University of California Press.
2004 *People of the Bomb: Portraits of America's Nuclear Complex.* Minneapolis: University of Minnesota Press.

Gusterson, Hugh, and Catherine Besteman, eds.
2009 *The Insecure American: How We Got Here and What We Should Do about It.* Berkeley: University of California Press.

Hale, Charles R.
2006 Activist Research v. Cultural Critique: Indigenous Land Rights and the Contradictions of Politically Engaged Anthropology. *Cultural Anthropology* 21(1):96–120.

Hall, Stuart
1980 Encoding/Decoding. In *Culture, Media, Language.* S. Hall, D. Hobson, A. Lowe, and P. Willis, eds. Pp. 128–138. London: Hutchinson.

Hannerz, Ulf
1997 Borders. *International Social Science Journal* 49(4):537–548.
2004 *Foreign News: Exploring the World of Foreign Correspondents.* Chicago: University of Chicago Press.

Hasty, Jennifer
2005 *The Press and Political Culture in Ghana.* Bloomington: Indiana University Press.
2006 Performing Power, Composing Culture: The State Press in Ghana. *Ethnography* 7(1):69–98.
2010 Journalism as Fieldwork: Propaganda, Complicity, and the Ethics of Anthropology. In *The Anthropology of News and Journalism: Global Perspectives.* E. Bird, ed. Pp. 132–148. Bloomington: Indiana University Press.

Herman, Edward, and Noam Chomsky
1988 *Manufacturing Consent: The Political Economy of the Mass Media.* New York: Pantheon.

Hernández, Rafael
1973 Cartas misioneras: Reseña histórica, científica y descriptiva de las
[1887] Misiones argentinas. Buenos Aires: Estab. Tip. de Luz del Alma.

Herzfeld, Michael
1997 *Cultural Intimacy: Social Poetics in the Nation-State.* New York: Routledge.

Hetherington, Kregg
2011 *Guerrilla Auditors: The Politics of Transparency in Neoliberal Paraguay.* Durham, NC: Duke University Press.

Heyman, Josiah McC.
2013 The Study of Illegality and Legality: Which Way Forward? *PoLAR: Political and Legal Anthropology Review* 36(2):304–307.

Heyman, Josiah McC., and Alan Smart
  1999   States and Illegal Practices: An Overview. In *States and Illegal Practices*. J. Heyman, ed. Pp. 1–24. Oxford: Berg.
Himpele, Jeffrey D.
  2008   *Circuits of Culture: Media, Politics, and Indigenous Identity in the Andes*. Minneapolis: University of Minnesota Press.
Hobbes, Thomas
  2002   *Leviathan, or The Matter, Forme and Power of a Common Wealth*
  [1651] *Ecclesiasticall and Civil*. Project Gutenberg online book. http://www.gutenberg.org/files/3207/3207-h/3207-h.htm.
Holbraad, Martin, and Morten Axel Pedersen
  2012   Revolutionary Securitization: An Anthropological Extension of Securitization Theory. *International Theory* 4(02):165–197.
Holbraad, Martin, and Morten Axel Pedersen, eds.
  2013   *Times of Security: Ethnographies of Fear, Protest, and the Future*. New York: Routledge.
Holston, James
  2009   *Insurgent Citizenship: Disjunctions of Democracy and Modernity in Brazil*. Princeton, NJ: Princeton University Press.
Hudson, Rex A.
  2003   *Terrorist and Organized Crime Groups in the Tri-Border Area (TBA) of South America: A Report*. Washington, DC: Federal Research Division, Library of Congress. Electronic document, http://www.loc.gov/rr/frd/pdf-files/TerrOrgCrime_TBA.pdf.
Hughes, Sallie
  2006   *Newsrooms in Conflict: Journalism and the Democratization of Mexico*. Pittsburgh, PA: University of Pittsburgh Press.
Jaffe, Rivke
  2013   The Hybrid State: Crime and Citizenship in Urban Jamaica. *American Ethnologist* 40(4):734–748.
Jusionyte, Ieva
  2013   On and off the Record: The Production of Legitimacy in an Argentine Border Town. *PoLAR: Political and Legal Anthropology Review* 36(2):231–248.
  2014   For Social Emergencies "We Are 9-1-1": How Journalists Perform the State in an Argentine Border Town. *Anthropological Quarterly* 87(1):151–182.
  2015   States of Camouflage. *Cultural Anthropology* 30(1):113–138.
Karam, John Tofik
  2011   Crossing the Americas: The U.S. War on Terror and Arab Cross-Border Mobilizations in a South American Frontier Region. *Comparative Studies of South Asia, Africa and the Middle East* 31(2):251–266.
Kernaghan, Richard
  2009   *Coca's Gone: Of Might and Right in the Huallaga Post-Boom*. Stanford, CA: Stanford University Press.

Kim, Eleana J.
  2010   *Adopted Territory: Transnational Korean Adoptees and the Politics of Belonging.* Durham, NC: Duke University Press.
Klipphan, Andrés, and Daniel Enz
  2006   *Tierras S.A.: Crónicas de un país rematado.* Buenos Aires: Aguilar.
Kopytoff, Igor
  1987   *The African Frontier: The Reproduction of Traditional African Societies.* Bloomington: Indiana University Press.
Lakoff, Andrew
  2007   Preparing for the Next Emergency. *Public Culture* 19(2):247–271.
  2008   The Generic Biothreat, or, How We Became Unprepared. *Cultural Anthropology* 23(3):399–428.
Lakoff, Andrew, and Stephen J. Collier
  2012   *Biosecurity Interventions: Global Health and Security in Question.* New York: Columbia University Press.
Larkin, Brian
  2008   *Signal and Noise: Media, Infrastructure, and Urban Culture in Nigeria.* Durham, NC: Duke University Press.
Lawson, Joseph Chappell H.
  2002   *Building the Fourth Estate: Democratization and the Rise of a Free Press in Mexico.* Berkeley: University of California Press.
Lee, Benjamin, and Edward LiPuma
  2002   Cultures of Circulation: The Imaginations of Modernity. *Public Culture* 14(1):191–213.
Lefebvre, Henri
  1992   *The Production of Space.* Oxford: Wiley-Blackwell.
  [1974]
Leinaweaver, Jessaca B.
  2013   *Adoptive Migration: Raising Latinos in Spain.* Durham, NC: Duke University Press.
Leinaweaver, Jessaca B., and Linda J. Seligmann
  2009   Introduction: Cultural and Political Economies of Adoption in Latin America. *Journal of Latin American and Caribbean Anthropology* 14(1):1–19.
Lewis, Daniel K.
  2006   *A South American Frontier: The Tri-Border Region.* New York: Chelsea House.
López Echagüe, Hernán
  1997   *La Frontera: Viaje al misterioso triángulo de Brasil, Argentina y Paraguay.* Buenos Aires: Planeta.
Low, Setha M., and Sally Engle Merry
  2010   Engaged Anthropology: Diversity and Dilemmas: An Introduction to Supplement 2. *Current Anthropology* 51(S2):S203–S226.
Lutz, Catherine
  2001   *Homefront: A Military City and the American Twentieth Century.* Boston: Beacon Press.

2009   *The Bases of Empire: The Global Struggle against U.S. Military Posts.* New York: New York University Press.

Maguire, Mark
2012   Biopower, Racialization and New Security Technology. *Social Identities* 18(5):593–607.

Mankekar, Purnima
1999   *Screening Culture, Viewing Politics: An Ethnography of Television, Womanhood, and Nation in Postcolonial India.* Durham, NC: Duke University Press.

Markoff, John, and Silvio R. Duncan Baretta
2006   Civilization and Barbarism: Cattle Frontiers in Latin America. In *States of Violence.* Fernando Coronil and Julie Skurski, eds. pp. 33–82. Ann Arbor: University of Michigan Press.

Masco, Joseph
2006   *The Nuclear Borderlands: The Manhattan Project in Post-Cold War New Mexico.* Princeton, NJ: Princeton University Press.
2010   "Sensitive but Unclassified": Secrecy and the Counterterrorist State. *Public Culture* 22(3):433–463.
2014   *The Theater of Operations: National Security Affect from the Cold War to the War on Terror.* Durham, NC: Duke University Press.

McMurray, David A.
2003   Recognition of State Authority as a Cost of Involvement in Moroccan Border Crime. In *Crime's Power: Anthropologists and the Ethnography of Crime.* P.C. Parnell and Stephanie C. Kane, eds. Pp. 125–144. New York: Palgrave Macmillan.

Merry, Sally Engle, and Susan Bibler Coutin
2014   Technologies of Truth in the Anthropology of Conflict: AES/APLA Presidential Address, 2013. *American Ethnologist* 41(1):1–16.

Nader, Laura
1972   Up the Anthropologist: Perspectives Gained from Studying Up. In *Reinventing Anthropology.* D.H. Hymes, ed. Pp. 284–311. New York: Pantheon.

Ngai, Mae M.
2004   *Impossible Subjects: Illegal Aliens and the Making of Modern America.* Princeton, NJ: Princeton University Press.

Nordstrom, Carolyn
2007   *Global Outlaws: Crime, Money, and Power in the Contemporary World.* Berkeley: University of California Press.

Nugent, Daniel, and Ana Maria Alonso
1994   Multiple Selective Traditions in Agrarian Reform and Agrarian Struggle: Popular Culture and State Formation in the Ejido of Namiquipa, Chihuahua. In *Everyday Forms of State Formation: Revolution and the Negotiation of Rule in Modern Mexico.* G.M. Joseph and D. Nugent, eds. Pp. 209–246. Durham, NC: Duke University Press.

Núñez Cabeza de Vaca, Álvar
1902   *Commentarios de Álvar Núñez Cabeza de Vaca.* Asunción: Talleres
[1555]   Nacionales de H. Kraus.

Pedelty, Mark
  1995 *War Stories: The Culture of Foreign Correspondents.* New York: Routledge.
Penglase, Ben
  2007 Barbarians on the Beach: Media Narratives of Violence in Rio de Janeiro, Brazil. *Crime, Media, Culture* 3(3):305–325.
  2009 States of Insecurity: Everyday Emergencies, Public Secrets, and Drug Trafficker Power in a Brazilian Favela. *PoLAR: Political and Legal Anthropology Review* 32(1):47–63.
  2014 *Living with Insecurity in a Brazilian Favela: Urban Violence and Daily Life.* New Brunswick, NJ: Rutgers University Press.
Peyret, Alejo
  1881 *Cartas sobre Misiones.* Buenos Aires: Imprenta de la Tribuna Nacional.
Poole, Deborah
  2004 Between Threat and Guarantee: Justice and Community in the Margins of the Peruvian State. In *Anthropology in the Margins of the State.* Veena Das and Deborah Poole, eds. Pp. 35–65. Santa Fe, NM: School of American Research Press.
Porto, Mauro
  2012 *Media Power and Democratization in Brazil: TV Globo and the Dilemmas of Political Accountability.* New York: Routledge.
Prescott, J. R. V.
  1987 *Political frontiers and boundaries.* London: Allen & Unwin.
Reeves, Madeleine
  2013 Clean Fake: Authenticating Documents and Persons in Migrant Moscow. *American Ethnologist* 40(3):508–524.
  2014 *Border Work: Spatial Lives of the State in Rural Central Asia.* Ithaca, NY: Cornell University Press.
Reyes-Foster, Beatriz
  2013 He Followed the Funereal Steps of Ixtab: The Pleasurable Aesthetics of Suicide in Newspaper Journalism in Yucatán, Mexico. *Journal of Latin American and Caribbean Anthropology* 18(2):251–273.
Risør, Helene
  2010 "Twenty Hanging Dolls and a Lynching": Defacing Dangerousness and Enacting Citizenship in El Alto, Bolivia. *Public Culture* 22 (3):465–485.
Robben, Antonius C. G. M.
  2000 State Terror in the Netherworld: Disappearance and Reburial in Argentina. In *Death Squad: The Anthropology of State Terror.* J. A. Sluka, ed. Pp. 91–113. Philadelphia: University of Pennsylvania Press.
  2005 *Political Violence and Trauma in Argentina.* Philadelphia: University of Pennsylvania Press.
Rockwell, Rick, and Noreene Janus
  2003 *Media Power in Central America.* Chicago: University of Illinois Press.
Rodríguez, Clemencia
  2011 *Citizens' Media against Armed Conflict: Disrupting Violence in Colombia.* Minneapolis: University of Minnesota Press.

Roitman, Janet L.

2004   *Fiscal Disobedience: An Anthropology of Economic Regulation in Central Africa.* Princeton, NJ: Princeton University Press.

2006   The Ethics of Illegality in the Chad Basin. In *Law and Disorder in the Postcolony.* Jean Comaroff and John L. Comaroff, eds. Pp. 247–272: Chicago: University of Chicago Press.

Romero, Luis Alberto

2002   *A History of Argentina in the Twentieth Century.* University Park: Pennsylvania State University Press.

Sarmiento, Domingo Faustino

2003   *Facundo: Civilization and Barbarism.* K. Ross, transl. Berkeley: Uni
[1845]   versity of California Press.

Scheper-Hughes, Nancy

1992   *Death without Weeping: The Violence of Everyday Life in Brazil.* Berkeley: University of California Press.

Scheper-Hughes, Nancy, and Philippe I. Bourgois

2004   Introduction: Making Sense of Violence. In *Violence in War and Peace.* Vol. 5. N. Scheper-Hughes and P. Bourgois, eds. Pp. 1–32. Malden, MA: Blackwell.

Schmitt, Carl

1985   *Political Theology: Four Chapters on the Concept of Sovereignty.*
[1922]   Cambridge, MA: MIT Press.

Schneider, Jane, and Peter Schneider

2003   *Reversible Destiny: Mafia, Antimafia, and the Struggle for Palermo.* Berkeley: University of California Press.

2008   The Anthropology of Crime and Criminalization. *Annual Review of Anthropology* 37:351–373.

Scott, James C.

1998   *Seeing like a State: How Certain Schemes to Improve the Human Condition Have Failed.* New Haven, CT: Yale University Press.

Seligmann, Linda J.

2013   *Broken Links, Enduring Ties: American Adoption across Race, Class, and Nation.* Stanford, CA: Stanford University Press.

Seri, Guillermina

2003   *On Borders and Zoning: The Vilification of the "Triple Frontier."* Paper presented at LASA International Congress. Electronic document, http://lasa.international.pitt.edu/Lasa2003/SeriGuillermina.pdf.

2004   On the "Triple Frontier" and the "Borderization" of Argentina: A Tale of Zones. In *Sovereign Lives: Power in Global Politics.* J. Edkins, V. Pin Fat, and M. J. Shapiro, eds. Pp. 79–100. New York: Routledge.

2012   *Seguridad: Crime, Police Power, and Democracy in Argentina.* New York: Continuum.

Shelley, Louise, and John Picarelli

2005   Methods and Motives: Exploring Links between Transnational Organized Crime and International Terrorism. *Trends in Organized Crime* 9(2):52–67.

Shumway, Nicolas
1991 *The Invention of Argentina.* Berkeley: University of California Press.
Sieder, Rachel
2011 Contested Sovereignties: Indigenous Law, Violence and State Effects in Postwar Guatemala. *Critique of Anthropology* 31(3):161–184.
Skurski, Julie, and Fernando Coronil
2006 Introduction: States of Violence and the Violence of States. In *States of Violence.* Fernando Coronil and Julie Skurski, eds. Pp. 1–31. Ann Arbor: University of Michigan Press.
Sluka, Jeffrey
2013 Virtual War in the Tribal Zone: Air Strikes, Drones, Civilian Casualties, and Losing Hearts and Minds in Afghanistan and Pakistan. In *Virtual War and Magical Death: Technologies and Imaginaries for Terror and Killing.* N. Whitehead and S. Finnstrom, eds. Pp. 171–193. Durham, NC: Duke University Press.
Spitulnik, Debra
1998 Mediating Unity and Diversity: The Production of Language Ideologies in Zambian Broadcasting. In *Language Ideologies: Practice and Theory.* B. Schieffelin et al., eds. Pp. 163–188. New York: Oxford University Press.
Stuesse, Angela, and Mathew Coleman
2014 Automobility, Immobility, Altermobility: Surviving and Resisting the Intensification of Immigrant Policing. *City and Society* 26:51–72.
Suaiter Martínez, Francisco
1928 *Problemas sociales y económicos de Misiones.* Buenos Aires: Instituto Cultural "Joaquin V. Gonzalez."
Tarducci, Mónica
2006 "Tráficos fronterizos": Introducción a la problemática de la adopción de niños en Misiones, Argentina. *Cadernos Pagu* 26:45–57. http://www.scielo.br/scielo.php?script=sci_arttext&pid=S0104-83332006000100003&lng=en&tlng=es. 10.1590/S0104-83332006000100003.
Tate, Winifred
2007 *Counting the Dead: The Culture and Politics of Human Rights Activism in Colombia.* Berkeley: University of California Press.
2013 Proxy Citizenship and Transnational Advocacy: Colombian Activists from Putumayo to Washington, DC. *American Ethnologist* 40(1):55–70.
Taussig, Michael T.
1987 *Shamanism, Colonialism, and the Wild Man: A Study in Terror and Healing.* Chicago: University of Chicago Press.
1992 *The Nervous System.* New York: Routledge.
1999 *Defacement: Public Secrecy and the Labor of the Negative.* Stanford, CA: Stanford University Press.
2003 *Law in a Lawless Land: Diary of a "Limpieza" in Colombia.* New York: New Press.

Taylor, Diana
  1997   *Disappearing Acts: Spectacles of Gender and Nationalism in Argen-
         tina's "Dirty War."* Durham, NC: Duke University Press.
Thomas, Kedron
  2012   Intellectual Property Law and the Ethics of Imitation in Guatemala.
         Anthropological Quarterly 85(3):785–815.
Thompson, E. P.
  1971   The Moral Economy of the English Crowd in the Eighteenth Century.
         Past and Present (50):76–136.
  1975   *Whigs and Hunters: The Origin of the Black Act.* London: Penguin.
Tilly, Charles
  1985   War Making and State Making as Organized Crime. In *Bringing the
         State Back In.* P. B. Evans and D. T. Skocpol, eds. Pp. 169–191. Cam-
         bridge: Cambridge University Press.
Torres, M. Gabriela
  2014   Art and Labor in the Framing of Guatemala's Dead. *Anthropology of
         Work Review* 35(1):14–24.
Tsing, Anna Lowenhaupt
  2005   *Friction: An Ethnography of Global Connection.* Princeton, NJ:
         Princeton University Press.
Turner, Frederick Jackson
  1962   *The Frontier in American history.* New York: Holt, Rinehart &
  [1893] Winston.
Turner, Terence
  1992   Defiant Images: The Kayapo Appropriation of Video. *Anthropology
         Today* 8(6):5–16.
van Schendel, Willem, and Abraham Itty, eds.
  2005   *Illicit Flows and Criminal Things: States, Borders, and the Other Side
         of Globalization.* Bloomington: Indiana University Press.
Vásquez-León, Marcela
  1999   Neoliberalism, Environmentalism, and Scientific Knowledge: Rede-
         fining Use Rights in the Gulf of California Fisheries. In *States and
         Illegal Practices.* Josiah Heyman, ed. Pp. 233–260. Oxford: Berg.
Vesperi, Maria D.
  2010   Attend to the Differences First: Conflict and Collaboration in Anthro-
         pology and Journalism. *Anthropology News* 51(4):7–9.
Villalba, Carlos Angel
  2010   *Apuntes históricos de Puerto Iguazú.* Puerto Iguazú.
Villalta, Carla
  2010   De los derechos de los adoptantes al derecho a la identidad: Los pro-
         cedimientos de adopción y la apropiación criminal de niños en la
         Argentina. *Journal of Latin American and Caribbean Anthropology*
         15(2):338–362.
Wacquant, Loïc
  2008   The Militarization of Urban Marginality: Lessons from the Brazilian
         Metropolis. *International Political Sociology* 2(1):56–74.

Waisbord, Silvio R.
    2000   *Watchdog Journalism in South America: News, Accountability, and Democracy.* New York: Columbia University Press.

Warner, Michael
    2002   Publics and Counterpublics. *Public Culture* 14(1):49–90.

Warren, Kay B.
    2007   The 2000 UN Human Trafficking Protocol: Rights, Enforcement, Vulnerabilities. In *The Practice of Human Rights: Tracking Law between the Global and the Local.* M. Goodale and S. E. Merry, eds. Pp. 242–271: Cambridge: Cambridge University Press.

    2012   Troubling the Victim/Trafficker Dichotomy in Efforts to Combat Human Trafficking: The Unintended Consequences of Moralizing Labor Migration. *Indiana Journal of Global Legal Studies* 19(1):105–120.

Weber, Max
    2004   Politics as Vocation. In *The Vocation Lectures.* Pp. 32–94. Indianapolis:
    [1919] Hackett.

Wiley, Andrea, and John S. Allen
    2009   *Medical Anthropology: A Biocultural Approach.* New York: Oxford University Press.

Winichakul, Thongchai
    1994   *Siam Mapped: A History of the Geo-Body of a Nation.* Honolulu: University of Hawaii Press.

Index

Abbott, Philip K., 107
Abuelas de la Plaza de Mayo, 207, 261–62n2
adoption: code of silence about irregular, 202, 231, 233; difficulties in investigating, 204, 213–14, 218–21, 222, 225–26, 230–31; divergences in legal categories regarding, 232; government actions to reduce actually increase, 232–33; illegal, 211, 216, 227–29, 232–33; informal fostering (criadazgo), 205, 207; irregular may fall into the category of trafficking, 208, 232; Misiones attractive to prospective parents, 207, 209–11; Misiones compensates low-income pregnant women to reduce, 211; plenary, 206; preference for light-skinned, blue-eyed children in, 207; relationship to poverty of, 206, 211, 213, 216, 217, 220, 222, 224; simple, 206; traditional fostering, 205
Agamben, Giorgio, 16
Aguirre, Victoria, 71
Al Qaeda, 105
Alvarez, Claudio, 221–22
AMIA (Mutual Israeli-Argentine Association) attack, 14, 104–5
Andreas, Peter, 80
anthropology/ethnography: based upon creating long-term relationships of accountability, 235; boundary between

journalism can be thin, 234; cannot escape politics of representation, 235–36; collaborative fieldwork in, 56, 241; compared with journalism, 40–43, 46, 47, 203–4, 244; done off the record, 203; engaged, 54; ethics of, 42, 44, 246; faces risk of being misinterpreted and misappropriated, 246–47; interest in journalism is new in, 33; issues of privacy important to, 42; of media as cultural activism, 57; politics of representation in, 42–43, 52; public work of, 55
Antonowicz, Mario, 31, 32, 167
Antúnez, Marcelina, 171, 214–17
Aranda, Luis, 196–97, 219–20
Argentina: "civilization" and "barbarism" as theme in nineteenth century in, 62–64; import regulations criminalize informal economy, 28–29; insecurity in, 17–18; media market in, 82–84; neoliberal reforms in, 17; no freedom of information law in, 47, 189, 250–51n16
Argentine Naval Prefecture, 76–77
Arias, Ronnie, 2
Arrúa, Ricardo, 103
Azarkevich, Ernesto, 81, 85; coverage of crime by, 82, 95; criticism of local media by, 86–87; on dengue fever, 90; as gatekeeper between locals and nationwide public, 97; on malnutrition, 94